Praise for the First Edition of *The CyberSecurity Leadership Handbook*

This book is a must for any executive concerned with increasing an organization's cyber defenses. *The CyberSecurity Leadership Handbook for the CISO and the CEO* by JC Gaillard details the security and organizational flaws—often resulting from decade-old issues—that trip up many organizations and leave them vulnerable to being hacked. Highly recommended for CEOs, CISOs, and any other executives concerned with staying on top of the latest and greatest methods for defending their data from cyber threats.

Martin de Vries | CISO, Eindhoven University of Technology (TU/e)

With digital transformations sweeping the corporate landscape, all too many businesses fail to do what is needed to adequately secure their data. In *The CyberSecurity Leadership Handbook for the CISO and the CEO*, industry expert and advisor JC Gaillard demonstrates why this occurs and explains how you can protect your organization from data breaches by more effectively responding to threats—many stemming from unaddressed legacy issues.

Jason Tooley | VP, North EMEA, Informatica

In today's business world, digital transformation has made optimizing your cybersecurity defenses more important than ever. Yet, as information security expert JC Gaillard details in *The CyberSecurity Leadership Handbook for the CISO and the CEO*, many companies still fall short of the mark. If you are interested in finding out how best to combine your organizational and technological resources in order to secure your vital data in today's threat rich environment, this is the book for you.

Glenn Hopper | CFO, Sandline Global, and bestselling author of Deep Finance

As business models, products and technology continue to change, security must evolve too. There is no one-size-fits-all solution. It is vital to equip your organization with the resources to develop processes and controls with security in mind. In his book, a must for CIOs and CEOs alike, JC Gaillard channels his experience to show you how to take control using changes in approach and mindset to prevent cyber incidents as you grow your business.

Christine Ashton | Global CIO, SUSE

If you want to learn how legacy cybersecurity issues can lead to data breaches at even the most security-aware organizations—and more importantly, how you can prevent this from happening to you—*The CyberSecurity Leadership Handbook for the CISO and the CEO* is the book to get. Information security expert JC Gaillard provides a detailed description of how decade-old issues can wreak havoc on an organization's cybersecurity defenses and what you can do to protect your organization against legacy and current threats.

Neil Cordell | Head of cyber and information security, Swansea University

With ever larger and more damaging hacks hitting the headlines on a regular basis, failing to take action to secure your organization's data is not an option. The collection of articles in *The CyberSecurity Leadership Handbook for the CISO and the CEO* provides keen insight into what it takes to secure an organization's valuable data in today's threat-rich data online landscape. An essential tool for anyone interested in minimizing an organization's exposure to security breaches.

Robert Davies | CEO, Stealth ISS Group

With information and misinformation proliferating about the threat landscape and cyber risk, genuine insight can be difficult to find. In *The CyberSecurity Leadership Handbook for the CISO and the CEO*, JC has done the sorely needed task of cutting through the jargon that permeates our industry to deliver practical, actionable advice for senior leaders.

Ryan Kalember |
EVP of cybersecurity strategy, Proofpoint

To protect your organization's data in today's forbidding threat environment, you need the know-how to organize a robust layer of defenses. Luckily for anyone concerned about these threats, information security expert JC Gaillard has pooled his extensive writings on the topic into a single book: *The CyberSecurity Leadership Handbook for the CISO and the CEO*. Packed with helpful information about the steps you can take to avoid threats stemming from legacy issues while positioning your organization to repel new threats as they arise, this book is a must for security conscious executives.

Greg White | Director of enterprise
security and risk, EMEA ServiceNow

Have you ever wondered why the best technology money can buy hasn't put an end to damaging data breaches? Wonder no more. In *The CyberSecurity Leadership Handbook for the CISO and the CEO,* JC Gaillard uses his decades of experience as a security expert to explain why security lapses happen and the proactive steps you can take to shield your organization from them.

Ray Stanton | Executive partner, IBM

The CyberSecurity Leadership Handbook for the CISO and the CEO

How to fix decade-old issues and protect your organization from cyber threats

Selection of Key Articles 2015 – 2024

Jean-Christophe Gaillard

Leaders Press

Leaders Press

Published in the United States by Leaders Press.
www.leaderspress.com
Updated Edition

ISBN (pbk) **978-1-63735-319-6**
ISBN (ebook) **978-1-63735-318-9**

Library of Congress Control Number: 2024910593

Contents

1

Preface
Cybersecurity: The Lost Decade

I have been involved with information security matters for over twenty years and started writing regularly on the topic since 2015.

Talking to CISOs, CIOs, CEOs, and their teams as part of my day-to-day field work as a consultant, I was horrified by what I was seeing in too many large corporates in terms of security maturity levels and the actual problems some were still struggling with—something that went way beyond anecdotal evidence and were at the heart of survey after survey every year.

After all, good information security practices have been well established for over twenty years, and many industry bodies have been promoting them and evolving them throughout that period.

Why is it that large firms that have had fully functioning information security teams in place all that time, and have spent collectively hundreds of millions—if not more—on the topic of cybersecurity are still struggling today with issues such as patch management that should have been on their radar for over twenty years?

There is truly a cybersecurity lost decade for many between the Code Red, Slammer, and Blaster outbreaks of 2001–2003 and the Wannacry and Not Petya attacks of 2017.

By failing to get the basics right in terms of security during that time, while continuing to engage in massive cloud-driven business transformation programmes that have turned the enterprise into a truly borderless hybrid, many large firms have dramatically increased their level of exposure to cyber threats. And now the acceleration of the digital transformation emboldened by the COVID crisis and its aftermath, and the emergence of disruptive artificial intelligence products, is making things even more complex.

Politicians and regulators are now involved as the GDPR and other similar legislations across the world have shown us over the past few years, now with an even increased regulatory burden building up across the United States and worldwide.

At board level, the "when-not-if" paradigm around cyber-attacks has taken root, but it creates fundamentally different dynamics for CISOs and CIOs as the focus shifts radically from risk and compliance towards execution and delivery, often in exchange for massive investments around security.

To embed those different dynamics around cybersecurity and make true progress, large organisations must stop thinking of the topic in purely technological terms, look back, and address urgently the underlying cultural and governance issues that have been the true roadblocks of those "lost decades."

This is the theme I have been developing over the past nine years through my contribution to the Corix Partners blog.

The second edition of this "Handbook" offers a selection of over 100 articles published between 2015 and 2024, some in collaboration with Neil Cordell, Natasha McCabe, and Vincent Viers: They frame my reflexion on those matters over the period and offer—I think—elements of solutions to start changing the narrative around cybersecurity.

Most articles would have been reposted on LinkedIn and syndicated on Medium and other blogs or websites, such as CIO WaterCooler or London Tech Leaders; in addition, some would have appeared on *Forbes*—in an edited format—as part of my membership of the Forbes Business Council. I would like to take the opportunity here to thank them for their support.

Overall, many thanks to all—clients, partners, friends—who have been at the heart of this body of work.

I hope that the readers will find what follows to be thought-provoking and that it can help some moving forward.

JC Gaillard
May 2024

2

Cybersecurity Is Not a Risk

(24 April–13 August 2015, for the original articles; 10 August 2017, for the combined article)[1]

Boards Must Now Focus on Reality and Take Genuine Action

Describing cybersecurity as a risk is a language oddity that keeps appearing at an alarming rate.

It is a dangerous and simplistic shortcut, typical of the shallow nature of some debates taking place around these issues on social media.

Cybersecurity is not a "risk." Cybersecurity results from the proper application of proportionate controls to protect an organisation from the cyber threats it faces. Cyber risk results from the absence or inefficiency of such controls.

With survey after survey highlighting that large organisations struggle to demonstrate any kind of cybersecurity maturity, the time has come for the boards to approach the problem from the right management angle and take real action.

Cybersecurity can no longer be treated as a balancing act between costs, risks, and the need to ensure regulatory compliance.

The boards of large organisations must focus on ensuring that the necessary controls are properly implemented across the true geographic perimeter of the enterprise, taking into account without complacency the role of external partners and suppliers.

Technology alone will not help large organisations get out of such a dead end. They have focused for too long on merely technical and tactical solutions to their cybersecurity challenges in search of silver bullets that simply don't exist.

Organisations need to reflect on where the roadblocks are that have prevented them from reaching a satisfactory level of maturity in the face of current threats, in spite of decades' worth of spending in the IT and information security space.

They need to rethink and rewire their approach in a way that will enable them to demonstrate a degree of genuine resilience instead of merely throwing money at the latest technology product. Boards must focus on ensuring that accountabilities and responsibilities are properly in place to make sure the enterprise remains adequately protected from cyber threats.

Cybersecurity cannot be the responsibility of "everybody." In most cases, it should fall on the portfolio of the CIO or the COO and be cascaded down to a CISO, who has the management experience, personal gravitas, and political acumen to drive change.

Lasting change in that space will be complex and take time. Boards must ensure that a long-term cybersecurity road map is in place and stick to it. Changing approaches every time an incident happens elsewhere—or every time a new CISO comes in—will simply kill any change momentum. This long-term road map must be supported by a governance framework that distributes accountabilities and responsibilities from the board down across the entire enterprise—including IT, HR, business units, and geographies.

The time has come for boards to stop treating cybersecurity as a "risk" (i.e., something that may or may not happen). This is now a matter of *when*, not *if*. Boards must focus on reality and take genuine management action to drive the implementation of protective controls against the genuine cyber threats their business is facing. This is not a matter of budget or resources anymore but a very simple matter of priorities—and possibly a matter of survival for some firms.

Technology Alone Will Not Help

3

Information Security Governance: Building Lasting Protection against Cyber Threats

(19 February 2015)

Defining Governance within the Context of Information Security

Governance will always mean different things to different people.

In small organisations, governance tends to be seen as a mere piece of a consultant's jargon. Relationships, politics, and decision-making processes are simpler, and it is easier to make sure that everyone pulls in the same direction.

But as organisations grow in size and become operationally more complex (often through acquisitions), those aspects become more complex as well. Coherent action becomes less of a natural concept, and making things happen in a coherent manner requires concerted management action.

This is particularly true in the information security space because of the inherent cross-silo nature of the actions involved to protect the business. For example, a coherent identity and access management platform requires concerted action across HR, business units, and IT—and each of them may have their own agenda and understanding of the problems.

Information security governance needs to encompass all the management mechanisms that ensure coherent action across all stakeholders with the view of delivering effective and efficient information protection to the business. It can only stem from a clear information security strategic vision and requires all stakeholders to agree on a clear definition of their respective roles and responsibilities.

The term *governance* has long suffered from a serious lack of comprehension surrounding its meaning, and poor governance around information security has led to many organisations putting themselves at unnecessary levels of cyber risk.

Effective information security governance must involve the proper management of all the activities that an organisation needs to carry out in order to maximise the protection of the information it processes. It should ensure the protection of key information assets from relevant threats through the layered application of the right controls at people, process, and technology levels—while managing any element of risk that may result from the absence or inefficiencies of these controls.

The Problems with the Reactive Approach to Information Security

Unfortunately, many large organisations have historically seen and continue to approach information security mostly from a compliance angle—essentially managing information security issues on an adhoc basis, in a reactive manner, in order to satisfy the audit and compliance needs. Throwing money at the problem, through vast audit or compliance-driven programmes of work, is often frightfully expensive (for larger firms in particular) and rarely delivers in full across all geographies. While this approach may provide a degree of temporary protection in some areas, it is often financially inefficient to tend to focus on arbitrary controls and, as a result, leave organisations exposed.

To break this cycle and protect themselves against those threats, large organisations need to build a true understanding of the real nature of the threats they face—and the real controls they have in place at people, process, and technology levels. By doing so, many of them will realise that the potential damage that may result from those threats (in their operations, finances, and reputation) is primarily the result of the absence of (known and implementable) controls at a number of levels. They will realise that effective long-term information protection cannot stem only from reactive or technical one-off solutions.

They will also realise that it is key to bringing all the relevant stakeholders on board and driving concerted actions among them to fix those problems. To achieve that, large organisations need to build a strategic vision and the right governance framework around information security.

It's often the responsibility of the CIO to ensure that the whole organisation, including board-level management, understands the importance and complexity of information security challenges. It is also the CIO's responsibility to architect coherent action through the implementation of a medium- to long-term information security strategy to engineer lasting protection.

In order to thoroughly address the issue of information security on an ongoing basis, information security must become part of a mindset embedded into the broader governance and culture of an organisation. For many organisations, this is a true quantum leap in terms of change.

Creating Lasting Organisational Change within the Context of Information Security

For large organisations, where the information security focus has been for a long time on tactical projects, real change is always a challenging medium- to long-term journey. Effective change has its roots firmly planted in corporate governance and culture and can take years to achieve.

From directors who may be unconcerned about the information security risk the business faces to IT teams who may view strict information security governance as a barrier to their flexibility and ability to innovate, it's important to break down organisational silos and get all stakeholders working towards a common goal.

An effective information security governance framework is one essential piece of that jigsaw. It should distribute roles and responsibilities clearly among all stakeholders and act as a dampener—keeping things smoothly in motion (aligned with business objectives across the entire organisation) while reducing the risk of rapid and potentially damaging negative tactical reactions to information security issues.

It is only by getting key employees on board with a medium- to long-term information security vision and giving them clear roles and responsibilities as part of a clear information security governance framework that you can create a sense of direction and purpose—and it's only through sustaining this over the medium- to long-term period that true organisational change can occur.

4

Technology Alone Cannot Transform Failing Cybersecurity Practices

(16 July 2015)

The first RSA Cybersecurity Poverty Index,[2] published in June **2015**, measures a number of large organisations against a sample of controls taken out of the US NIST Cybersecurity Framework—collecting data from four hundred security professionals across sixty-one countries. The results highlight that **75%** of participants show significant cybersecurity risk exposure. This recent survey is likely to drive discussions at the upcoming **2015** RSA Asia, Pacific, and Japan conference due to be held on July **22–24** July in Singapore.

The road map proposed by RSA to move out of "cyber poverty" involves endorsing the NIST Cybersecurity Framework, balancing controls against prevention, monitoring, and resilience (claiming **80%** of resources are currently focused on prevention)—and finally fixing the disconnect between cyber policies and operational execution.

RSA qualifies the results of their survey as reflecting an "unacceptable status quo" and concludes by saying that it is time to "start thinking about security differently and start doing security differently."

None of this is really new, and in fact, the results strongly echo those of an earlier survey conducted by McKinsey & Company for the 2014 World Economic Forum. We commented on those in an article published on Computing.co.uk in February 2015.[3]

There is little to argue in principle about the road map suggested by RSA, but large organisations that want to transform their cybersecurity practice and build maturity must look at their current cybersecurity situation—without complacency and before jumping into action.

Endorsing the NIST Cybersecurity Framework and better balancing resources between prevention, monitoring, and resilience is a good thing to do, but again, it's nothing new. Large organisations must look back and confront the reasons why they have not acted before on matters of information or cybersecurity.

The NIST Cybersecurity Framework in particular follows in a long series of similar approaches that spans the best part of the last ten to fifteen years: "Identify, Protect, Detect, Respond, Recover" sounds a lot like an update to the "Plan, Do, Check, Act" of ISO 27001:2005, itself replicating a concept introduced in BS 7799-2 back in 2002.

Of course, threats continue to evolve and are now more virulent than ever, but basic controls (in particular around monitoring and resilience) have been well mapped out for a long time. Large organisations that have been spending large sums on information security over the past decade—with fully staffed, fully functioning information security functions during this time—should not be in a position of such low maturity today.

Those large organisations (including those in the public sector, where maturity levels seem to be even lower) have to examine where the roadblocks are that have prevented them from making progress in the past and ensure these are neutralised or removed. In our opinion, this is a problem deeply rooted in governance, organisational and cultural matters underpinning the disconnect between policy and execution that RSA has rightly diagnosed.

With maturity levels at rock bottom, in spite of decades of information security spending, it is indeed time to start thinking about cybersecurity differently. However, it is not a technical revolution that is required, and there is no software, hardware, or technical service alone that can make change happen in that space.

Security technology can support the right security organisation and enable the right security processes, but a genuine and lasting transformation of cybersecurity approaches can only come from a full rewiring of existing information security practices. This must come from the top and will require a long-term, transformative vision articulated into a strategic security road map and a sound security governance model reaching across all corporate silos and geographies.

5

The Misleading Message of the Technology Industry

(26 April–23 June 2016)

True Independence Is a Rare Commodity in the Cybersecurity World

There is an incredible amount of material online and on social media around cybersecurity. But the vast majority of it is either sponsored by technology vendors or directly associated with them. They range from start-ups or specialised software houses (large and small) all the way up to industry heavyweights. They sponsor industry events, conferences, and publications of all sorts, including the specialised supplements of many broadsheets and magazines. They produce white papers, reports, surveys, and the like in numbers sufficient to fill several bookcases every year.

Broadly speaking, those reports have been saying the same thing for the past few years:

- Cyber threats are evolving faster than people can react.
- Investments in cybersecurity are insufficient to keep up.
- Maturity stays at low levels in large corporations and across the public sector.
- It must now become a "board-level priority" for things to change.

Some of those aspects match what we observe in the field every day, but the overall message coming from technology vendors is simplistic and has two major flaws:

1. It tricks large corporations and the general public into believing that cybersecurity is something new.

   This is not the case. Cyber threats have not appeared overnight. In fact, they have been evolving for the best part of the last fifteen years, and therefore there is a vast body of good practice that will go a long way to protect any business.

   Those good practices have to be in place but often are not. Cutting corners around those on grounds of costs or convenience simply creates opportunities that cyber threats can target. And indeed, many recent breaches seem to relate to the absence of security controls that have been regarded as good practice for years and should have been in place. The sad reality is that, in spite of decades of spending in the information security space, many large organisations are still struggling today with problems going back to an era where security measures were seen as a necessary evil imposed by regulations—at odds with functionality and preventing innovation and agility.

2. It perpetuates the false idea that the problem is technical in nature.

   In fact, it is increasingly becoming a matter of mindset, culture, and governance.

   Many problems are rooted in decades of neglect, badly targeted investments, adverse prioritisation, or complacency. And there can be no miracle solution—technical or otherwise—in such situations. Avoiding cybersecurity breaches, or dealing with them, requires coherent action over time across the whole organisation.

   Only by identifying and removing the roadblocks that have prevented progress in the past can large organisations establish a genuine and lasting transformation dynamic. This is often a complex change process that could take years and require a relentless drive to succeed. It is not about deploying yet another piece of security software.

   Of course, technology can and does enable some aspects of the cybersecurity transformation, but it needs to be rooted in a transformative vision that puts people and process first. And it needs to be embedded within a target operating model that allocates clear roles and responsibilities across the whole enterprise, not just the IT department.

   These messages are rarely heard in the media, which is often dominated by the short-term agenda of tech vendors. Even when they do get mentioned, they are often lost in the midst of a vast amount of technology noise and are hardly audible or credible.

True independence is a rare commodity in the cybersecurity world, but it is essential for large organisations to navigate those waters and develop a genuinely protective practice instead of simply listening to the latest technology buzz.

6

Understanding Historic Roadblocks Is Key to Unlocking the Dynamics of Digital Resilience

(23 July 2015)

McKinsey & Company, together with most leaders in strategy consulting, have involved themselves more and more in cybersecurity over the past few years. Their latest article, "Repelling the Cyberattackers,"[4] offers an excellent analysis and set of actions towards digital resilience. Congratulations to James Kaplan, Allen Weinberg, and their teams.

In fact, the article echoes many themes we have mentioned here repeatedly, in particular throughout our series *The CIO Guide to a Successful Information Security Practice* (see "The Fabric to a Successful Practice" section for the summary).

Cybersecurity is too often seen as a mere technical discipline, while in fact, it is a complex cross-silo activity that has to reach beyond

IT into the business and other corporate practices—such as HR, legal, and procurement. Cybersecurity must be approached as a structured practice, not just a collection of IT projects, and sound governance is paramount.

It is essential to think of cybersecurity from a business process perspective, supported by technology, not the other way round. The business will always understand controls when spoken to in its own language.

In such a context, reporting lines, organisational structures, and the personal profile of the cybersecurity transformation agents (the CISO and their team in most large organisations) are key to success.

The article rightly focuses on driving tangible action instead of "highly abstract (and therefore largely meaningless)" risk discussions, which is a view we totally endorse.

It puts the road to digital resilience into some historical perspective, which was one of our criticisms of the 2014 report "Cybersecurity in a Hyperconnected World,"[5] published ahead of the World Economic Forum meeting in Davos last year.[6] But it must be acknowledged that the journey to digital resilience will be specific to each large organisation and that most are still at fairly low levels of cybersecurity maturity.

In spite of decades of spending in the IT and information security space, many large organisations are still struggling with "pre-2007" problems (in reference to exhibit 1 from the McKinsey article), where cybersecurity is seen as a necessary evil imposed by regulations—at odds with functionality and preventing innovation and agility—instead of a necessary barrier to protect the business from real and active threats.

On their road to digital resilience, organisations have to accept first that controls are essential, but getting to that realisation after ten to fifteen years of complacency, neglect, or short-termist "tick-in-the-box" practices will not be simple. Only by identifying and removing the roadblocks that have prevented progress in the past can they establish a genuine and lasting transformation dynamic.

In our opinion, this is a problem deeply rooted in governance, organisational and cultural matters, that requires a fundamental rethinking and rewiring of information security practices. This must come from the top, and in that context, board involvement and "senior cross-functional oversight" is essential—as the article rightly states—to avoid a "mere patchwork of compromises." The board must be prepared (and able) to look at the problem over the long term and stick to it.

Of course, real change in that space will require a long-term, transformative vision (supported and funded by the board), articulated into a strategic security road map and a sound security governance model—reaching across all corporate silos and geographies.

But fundamental to success will be the personal gravitas, political acumen, and management skills of the key transformation agent (the CISO in most large organisations). The CISO should have the seniority and experience required and remain in charge over the necessary period to oversee real change—meaning, they may have to consider their tenure over a five- to seven-year horizon in many cases.

In such a sensitive area, changing approaches every two to three years, every time a new CISO comes in, or every time something happens at board level is simply a recipe for failure. And when coupled with an excessive technical focus and short-termist compliance obsession, this could be the main reason why so many large organisations still show such low levels of cybersecurity maturity today.

7

Cybersecurity Skills Gap: What Skills Gap?

(2 March 2017)

The Cybersecurity Industry Needs More Talent, but at Which Level and to Do What?

Here is a theme that has cybersecurity experts gripped. There is an enormous problem of skills across the cybersecurity industry: not enough professionals. Hundreds of thousands of jobs remaining unfilled. It's a massive challenge and a key to the evolution of the industry. A fundamental factor preventing progress.

But frankly, what is all this about? What are those jobs? What would be their purpose?

You don't have to read much between the lines to see that most of the skills gap message emanates from the incestuous ecosystem formed by large consultancies; their clients in large, established security teams in large organisations; and the recruitment firms servicing both.

Most of the language used when describing the missing skills is heavily technical in nature and points towards the same IT security space (pen testers, SOC engineers, threat analysts, etc.), as many jobs supporting large tech platforms are built on tech products, and behind that is the same misleading message from the tech industry that all this is a just technical problem that can be fixed by buying more tech.

So it becomes apparent pretty quickly that the "cyber skills gap" story dominating the headlines is just another aspect to an old theme: the cybersecurity industry's obsession with finding technical and tactical silver bullets to solve a problem that is, in too many cases, rooted in decades of adverse prioritisation, complacency, a "tick-in-the-box" culture around compliance, and fundamentally poor corporate governance.

I am not in denial about the threats, and I fully appreciate the challenges faced by large global firms and government agencies in dealing with cyber defence, but when talking to CISOs and senior executives in smaller firms (and those truly trying to create a long-term transformational dynamic around cybersecurity), it is a very different skills gap we hear about.

What they crave is management experience, personal gravitas, political acumen, and internal business focus—coupled with strong control-mindedness and a degree of cyber knowledge of course—because this is the true combination that drives change.

These are attributes that you develop through real field experience. You are not likely to find them in junior consultants or ex-auditors, and few successful IT executives are likely to follow that path because the whole IT industry is measuring success in terms of delivery, functionality, and performance—not in terms of controls or security. Therefore, IT security has never been—and will not be for the short term—a rewarding path to the top for most IT executives.

So there is, indeed, a skills gap in the security management space—and a pretty serious one. This is the real big story around missing cyber skills. To fix this, you have to make the control functions attractive to increase the pool of younger professionals who want to get involved in, learn about, and build a career out of them, both within and outside IT.

It requires reliable board-level support and engagement; a credible regime of tangible incentives, both in terms of financial rewards and training; and sound role models and career success stories. There may also be a role to play for business schools to start shifting the narrative around cybersecurity leadership.

It can be done in firms—large and small—but it becomes a true matter of corporate culture and, in many cases, a matter of real transformation.

8
Rethinking and Rewiring Information Security

(30 June 2015)

Information security is still broadly perceived as an IT discipline built around technical products and projects; you just have to open any industry magazine or publication to see it. The InfoSec Europe exhibition in London in June **2015** would have attracted around **350** vendors and tens of thousands of technologists, and there are several similar shows around the world every year.

The "three lines of defence" models promoted in some form or another by various standards, such as COSO or ISO **31000**, are poorly understood and poorly applied. Information security is often arbitrarily kept in a technical first line, in spite of its complex nature, requiring a true implementation across the three lines of defence and across many corporate silos.

In practice, this excessive technical focus, which spans the entire industry history, is failing for most large organisations. In fact, many of these organisations claim to spend in excess of **3%**

of their total IT spending on cybersecurity, but in spite of the amounts invested over the years, **79%** have not yet achieved an acceptable level of cybersecurity maturity.[7]

In our opinion, this failing situation is rooted in the lack of cultural fit between security and IT mindsets. Technologists are trained and incentivised to deliver functionality, not controls, and this fundamental mismatch has two critical consequences:

Firstly, it deprives information security of the raw talents it deserves. Information security is rarely seen as a career path to the top, and high-potential IT executives look elsewhere for development. As a result, information security leaders are often good technologists but lack the management experience, personal gravitas, or political acumen they would need to be truly successful in such a complex role.

Secondly, it drives adverse prioritisation and focuses information security towards ad hoc tactical point solutions. At best, the CISO becomes a "firefighter"; at worst, an IT program manager, among many others. Or the CISO becomes a hobbyist, playing around with "pet projects" and changing jobs every couple of years as soon as the going gets tough.

This tactical and technical focus rarely delivers true results in large organisations. They have become increasingly dependent on a larger and larger number of third parties; their information security problems are often global and complex in nature; and the threats they face continue to evolve at a faster and faster pace. The geographical, operational, and technical complexity of large organisations requires a proper governance framework—which is rarely in place—to enable the true delivery of information security solutions on a global scale.

This lack of results can drive middle management's frustration and budgetary tensions around information security internally, which in turn brews demotivation and further talent alienation away from InfoSec functions. It is often also the lack of results (or insufficient or slow progress) that attracts the attention of auditors and regulators on these matters. Those are often "low-hanging fruits" in the absence of any strategic vision around information security.

This, in turn, is effective at drawing the attention of executive management towards the topic, but for all the wrong reasons. And when coupled with the increasing media and political attention around cybersecurity, it simply aggravates the tactical dynamics around InfoSec. Driven by endemic fears of negligence claims and short-termist compliance obsessions, money that wasn't there yesterday suddenly appears out of nowhere just to fix audit or compliance issues. Senior executives can go to the media or claim between themselves that "cyber is on our agenda and money is there," but in practice, the lines haven't really moved at all—and the same old mistakes are being perpetuated.

Over time, information security becomes an overhead and a problem instead of a necessary barrier against real and active threats to the business. In practice, money is often simply wasted to tick off boxes. A large number of technology companies make a good living in that space, but this ecosystem is inherently unhealthy. This results in stagnating protection levels and low cybersecurity maturity, which is what the World Economic Forum report highlighted last year.

Organisations that find themselves in such a situation—and want to break these dynamics of failure—must rethink their approach and rewire their information security practice by acting at three levels:

1. The profile of the CISO needs to be right in order to drive change. Look without complacency at the information security history across the firm and at the barriers that

have prevented progress. The CISO needs to have the right amount of management experience, personal gravitas, and political acumen to be credible with all stakeholders across corporate silos (not just technologists); these are attributes of seniority. Information security is not just a technical discipline. Information exists in physical as well as digital forms, and it is constantly manipulated by people as part of business processes. It needs to be protected at the digital, physical, and functional levels. Only with the right attitude and experience will the CISO be able to reach out of IT to all stakeholders and drive success. Of course, the reporting line of the CISO is of paramount importance in that context, and we have commented several times about that in earlier articles. It should be to the CIO or the COO in most cases, and delegating down must be avoided at all costs as it would simply confuse objectives, create opportunities for political tensions with stakeholders, and destroy any credibility around the real desire of executive management to drive change.

2. The CISO needs to structure their relationship with all stakeholders as part of an information security governance framework—positioning roles, responsibilities, and accountabilities across the information security space and across the whole organisation from the top down. The CISO must also define a proper target operating model for the information security team itself, which would give it a strong backbone, a clear structure, and an unambiguous sense of purpose internally. All this is key to driving success. For example, you cannot imagine delivering a successful identity and access management programme of work without the involvement of HR (and the business units, if they are allowed to hire and fire directly) and without clear demarcation lines around what gets done within the InfoSec team and what remains outside of it.

The whole governance model should also address, without complacency, the full geographical spectrum of the business and its true nature in terms of dependencies on third parties.

3. The CISO needs to build a long-term information security strategic road map and be prepared to stay in charge for the time it will take to deliver it. Real and long-lasting change in the information security space for most large organisations will involve a cultural shift, the embedding of a structured practice, and a controls mindset in the way the organisation works. It will not happen quickly. It could typically involve an initial transformation cycle of several years, followed by a consolidation cycle of several years. The CISO and key team members may have to consider their tenure over a five- to seven-year horizon to genuinely drive change through. During the period, all actions (technical or not) must be pinned against a consistent long-term backdrop, including any unavoidable short-term tactical initiatives (typically driven by incidents, audit observations, or compliance requirements). Inconsistencies and a constant reshuffling of priorities would simply kill the change momentum, and so would the untimely removal of key personnel.

Raising the profile of the CISO (and their reporting line where necessary) will break the dynamics of talent alienation around information security. Sound governance, coupled with better management and political acumen at senior level, within InfoSec will break the dynamics of failure around delivery. Pinning success against a long-term backdrop and ensuring that the CISO and key personnel remain in place throughout will help executive management develop a true sense of purpose around information security, beyond short-termism or audit and compliance obsessions.

Over time, information security should become a valuable protective function at the heart of the organisation—not just an IT department that deals with audit issues.

9

Why Are We Still Facing So Many Security Products and Vendors?

(23 May 2019)

A Symptom of the Unhealthy Relationship between Cybersecurity and Large Firms

As we reach one of the high points of each year's conference season, one has to reflect once more on the staggering number of products and vendors active across the cybersecurity space.

Once again, they will line up in their hundreds at InfoSec in London and elsewhere. Of course, not all of them are making money; many are still burning the cash of their generous VCs. But the fact that such a crowded market still attracts large amounts of investment is still, in itself, bewildering.

In addition, many of those products still aim to address security requirements that are as old as good security practices themselves (e.g., across segments such as incident and event management or identity and access management).

To see those segments so fragmented across so many players after fifteen or twenty years of evolution is not a sign of a healthy marketplace. They should have been consolidated years ago, and each should have been dominated by a few players, in addition to the usual big names, all bound by healthy competition.

The fact that it's not the case simply tells us that the buyers are not serious. They do not buy those products because they address a real business need. They only buy those products to put ticks in compliance boxes; close down some audit points; support somebody's pet project; or, very often, in reactive mode and under pressure to show responsiveness after an incident—without any attempt or time to analyse the market, compare offerings, and structure a defensive strategy.

Even if the "tick-in-the-box" market is huge (and GDPR has just made it bigger), in the long term, nobody wins at that game. Product development ends up being driven by regressive compliance-led dynamics instead of positive dynamics aimed at countering ever-evolving threats. Poorly protected buyers get breached, and the industry at large stagnates.

In many large organisations, the situation has reached astounding levels. The **2019** Cisco CISO benchmark study highlights that **37%** of respondents have more than ten security vendors to manage (**3%** have more than fifty!).

"Best of breed" may be an interesting concept in the security space, but as we pointed out above, it is rarely the real reason behind product proliferation, and in practice, it presents operational teams with considerable challenges:

- How to orchestrate an efficient incident response when the data you need is scattered across so many platforms
- How to build an effective and meaningful reporting capability

The situation is often compounded by the fact that many security tools only end up being partially deployed or simply covering a fraction of the estate—functionally or geographically.

Firms that find themselves in that mess must stop buying more tech, look back at their genuine security requirements in relation to the threats they face, and start building a consolidation strategy.

They should also look beyond the products' marketplace and consider the ever-growing service offerings in that space. MSSPs have been active for over fifteen years, but the cloud has also facilitated the emergence of a number of new players in recent years.

Consolidation and integration become key factors as the "*when,* not, *if*" paradigm around cyber-attacks takes centre stage with senior executives and their focus shifts away from risk and compliance towards execution and delivery.

All those who have been riding the compliance wave should bear that in mind.

10

Cybersecurity: The Operational Illusion

(21 January 2021)

Security Culture and Governance Eat Tech for Breakfast

Looking back at what happened at ground level throughout the COVID crisis, it is clear that the focus has been entirely on operational matters: from moving into remote working at scale for the services industry, to keeping supply chains working for the manufacturing sector, or to many retail firms having to reinvent themselves as digital businesses literally within weeks. It has all been about keeping the lights on, understandably.

Tech and cybersecurity have been—and still are—at the heart of all this, and as we wrote back in April **2020**, it is hard not to see those sectors coming out as winners once the dust has settled over the pandemic.

But for now, the focus has been entirely tactical; nobody can see beyond the short term, and it is likely to remain the case for the best part of **2021**. This is hard to criticise as a business approach, given the scale and depth of the crisis; but in many firms, when it comes to cybersecurity, it is simply perpetuating and aggravating an endemic tendency—which, over the past ten years, has kept CISOs trapped in endless firefighting, prevented them from developing in terms of leadership and management skills, and not brought forward the necessary maturity changes around security in terms of governance, organisation, and culture.

This will be a serious problem in many firms that would have been locked for years in slow-moving and expensive security programmes, and they now need to transform their security practices at pace as cybersecurity has become a pillar of their "new normal."

It is an illusion to think that all the tactical and operational focus that has been prevailing around cybersecurity since the start of the pandemic is transformative. It may be counterintuitive, but moving past this operational obsession with cybersecurity is key, as we look ahead, to unlock long-term transformational dynamics.

The idea that the consistent protection of the business from cyber threats can result entirely and purely from the implementation of technical tools—or ad hoc pen tests, for that matter—is fundamentally flawed in the absence of a coherent overarching vision.

Tactical knee-jerk reactions simply add layer upon layer of technical legacy. Over time, the subpar delivery of poorly selected tools breeds distrust with senior management, who can't help but see that breaches continue to happen in spite of the millions spent. The inefficient reverse engineering of security processes around the capabilities of the tools leads to escalating operational costs, staff shortages, and apparent skill gaps. CISOs feel alienated and leave. All this builds a narrative in which security becomes a cost and a problem, and over time, nobody wins.

Throwing money at the problem—for the industries where that is still an option in the midst of the COVID crisis—is not the answer for firms where security maturity has stagnated as a result of decades of underinvestment and adverse prioritisation by the business.

More than ever, now is the time to think in terms of people first, then process, *then* technology, if the objective is to build a lasting transformational dynamic around cybersecurity.

It is a vision that has to come from the top and be relayed across all the silos of the enterprise. Cybersecurity cannot be seen as the responsibility of the CIO or the CISO. It needs to be visible and credible as part of a coherent business purpose, communicated coherently to the staff by senior management and relayed—and enforced—by a proper governance framework.

It is the embedding of security values in corporate culture and corporate governance that should drive the transformative efforts around cybersecurity and lead ultimately to effective cyber resilience.

This is certainly harder to put in place than buying more tech or doing one more pen test, but it is the key to long-term, transformative success around cybersecurity—in particular as younger generations become more and more sensitive to the clarity of purpose and positive business values.

11

Time to Bring the Cybersecurity Technical Debt under Control

(10 February 2022)

Stop Buying More Tech for the Sake of It, and Start Focusing on Decluttering Your Cybersecurity Landscape

For the past two decades, most large organisations have kept addressing cybersecurity as a purely technical problem. And let's face it. Many are failing to protect themselves, not just because the threats morph constantly and faster than they can adapt, but primarily because of endemic execution problems around the deployment of technical solutions and the disconnect between primarily short-termist business cycles and the longer time frames required to develop cybersecurity maturity levels in large firms.

In short, cybersecurity strategies are invariably architected around technical projects and tools, but deployment rarely goes beyond alleged quick wins. This is because business priorities shift constantly and rarely look over the medium to long term—as would be required in many firms to deliver real and lasting change around cybersecurity.

CISOs leave after a few years out of frustration over slow progress (and for more money), and the technical debt keeps piling up—all tendencies that have been greatly aggravated by the COVID pandemic.

After two decades of playing that game, some cybersecurity practices are now operating around up to twenty or thirty different tools in large organisations.

Nothing is ever joined up because it is simply the result of decades of organic short-termism; "strategic" plans that were never strategic or never rolled out; and knee-jerk reactions in response to incidents, audit observations, or panic buying ahead of regulatory inspections.

It results in complex security operational processes: poorly integrated, excessively manual, repetitive and boring for the analysts in charge of delivering them, and tremendously expensive to scale up—if you can find the skills, that is.

Because most industry sectors have woken up to the criticalness of cybersecurity following the avalanche of cyber-attacks we have been seeing over the past decade, they are now competing for a resource pool that has not grown sufficiently over the period.

People asking themselves why it has not grown sufficiently need to look beyond educational and training issues. It is not only the talent acquisition rate that is too low across the cybersecurity industry. It is also the retention rate, and that is essentially linked to those dysfunctional operational processes and the "boring" entry-level jobs of many analysts, who undoubtedly didn't get into cybersecurity to end up cutting and pasting data into Excel sheets or producing useless reports simply designed to put ticks in compliance boxes. At the first available opportunity, they leave to do something more exciting, and they don't come back.

At the heart of this, conveniently fuelled by the tech industry, lies the excessive focus on tech products to solve cybersecurity challenges, the reverse engineering of processes around the capabilities of tools, and the colossal accumulation of technical debt in that space over the past two decades, which is the result of execution failures and lack of priority focus by business leaders.

Senior executives who want to break out of that spiral need to stop buying more tech for the sake of it and start focusing on decluttering their cybersecurity landscape.

"For every one new solution, remove two legacy solutions," suggests Greg Day (VP and CSO, EMEA, Palo Alto Networks).

It sounds like a good start. But to achieve that, cybersecurity leaders will have to look back at the structure of their operational processes and streamline those.

They will also have to look differently at automation and focus it on improving analysts' efficiency, allowing them to dedicate more time to the challenging tasks for which they have been trained and hired.

Ultimately, cybersecurity leaders will have to go back where all this should have started: people, process, then technology—technology not for technology's sake but in support of security processes that are designed to protect the firm and its people from the cyber threats they face.

It is more difficult to execute and sell internally than buying the next shiny tool to put a tick in some compliance box, but stopping the creation of technical debt and bringing the existing one under control have become vital to the future of the cybersecurity industry.

12

Time to Deal With Cybersecurity Strategically and from the Top Down

(17 March 2022)

This Is No Longer Just about Tech—If It Ever Was

Surveys focused on the concerns and priorities of the CISO community have been quite consistent over the last few years, and collectively, they paint a slightly uncomfortable picture. The picture of CISO roles and security practices still operating bottom-up, disconnected from the dynamics of the business and the broader culture of their organisation.

In spite of the non-stop avalanche of cyber-attacks we have seen over the past decade, many CISOs still complain about a lack of board-level engagement and difficulties in getting sufficient budgets.

The overall sentiment is one of frustration, leading to (well-documented) shorter tenures and burnout problems. But another aspect that is often overlooked in the background is the lack of operating structure many cybersecurity practices seem to have.

Instead of being built around some form of operating model that would detail processes, tasks, roles, and responsibilities for all stakeholders, they seem to be driven by projects (in proactive or reactive mode) and operational tasks aggregated over time (exception management for some, privileged access management for others, etc.)

In fact, in the absence of a structured framework to work against, this is often the only way those cybersecurity practices can operate, evolving "as they go along," in project mode or in firefighting mode.

Security awareness ends up being a perennial low-hanging fruit and an easy sell for CISOs when they cannot find other levers, but the emphasis on developing a stronger security culture cannot be the only axis of action for the CISO.

But how can you justify budgets and attract or retain talent without a structured referential to work against—and in the absence of a clear governance model, roles, responsibilities, and to a degree (with regard to staff retention), clear career paths?

And again, how can you claim you do not have enough staff in the absence of a target operating model detailing tasks and the resources required to deliver those tasks? It can only be a finger-in-the-air exercise, the very kind any half-decent CFO would smell miles away.

This kind of empirical, bottom-up, and organically developed cybersecurity function does not work. It has failed to protect large organisations over the past two decades and needs to evolve. What is required is structure, business acumen, and top-down engagement.

The culture of frustration many CISOs have developed is probably comfortable for some; there is always someone to blame ("the business") and another juicy job to move into afterwards. But it does not help organisations and society at large. To break this spiral of failure, the profile of the CISO needs to evolve, and the board needs to take ownership.

This is no longer just about tech—if it ever was. This is about protecting the business against cyber-attacks that have now become a matter of "*when,* not *if.*" This is no longer something you can push down in the organisation.

If the board does not see the need—or does not feel qualified—to step in, nothing will ever change for good around cybersecurity because it has simply become too complex and too transversal in large organisations. Bottom-up approaches will continue to pour cash down the drain, CISOs will continue to leave every other year out of frustration, and breaches will continue to happen.

If the board wants to set directions, they should drive. They should appoint someone they trust and can talk to (it does not have to be a technologist) and empower that person to build or rebuild cybersecurity practices across the firm, in light of what the board wants and expects.

The COVID crisis has presented most organisations with unprecedented situations, but it has not made cybersecurity less of a priority. On the contrary, cybersecurity—whether it is in support of remote working, e-commerce, or digitalised supply chains—has become a pillar of the "new normal."

Now is the time to deal with it strategically, and from the top down.

13
The Cybersecurity Parallel Universe

(22 September 2022)

It's about Time We Go Back to Basics with Most of Our Cybersecurity Commentaries

Re-reading some articles I wrote years ago, it worries me that I would hardly change a word in this 2016 piece.[8]

Sometimes I wonder if some cybersecurity experts, journalists or tech vendors live in a parallel universe.

They would have you believe that quantum computing and its impact on current cryptography, or cybersecurity in the metaverse should be on the agenda of any CISO, and that zero-trust (or whatever tech they sell) will solve all the problems of the industry; that all problems come invariably from a lack of "user awareness," and that all solutions can only involve buying new technical tools (the ones the sell or represent, obviously).

Meanwhile, CISOs and other field practitioners struggle with a different reality:

HR departments unwilling to accept a role in joiners and leavers processes, or pretending they do not handle sensitive personal data; IT departments still failing at patch deployment or at building a unified CMDB across their estate in spite of fifteen years of investments in those areas; Legal departments treating compliance around data privacy as a matter of regulatory risk.

It's about time we go back to basics with most of our cybersecurity commentaries and refocus attention on a few key points:

Ownership of the matter is key: This is no longer about "wheeling in" the CISO in front of the board every year, or every time something happens somewhere. This is about the board owning cybersecurity as a board-level topic, and handling it as a board-level topic, not as something you delegate down because it is "too technical."

Cybersecurity is not the responsibility of the security team. Key stakeholders have to be identified across business units, geographies and support functions and made accountable for the adequate handling of cybersecurity matters at their level, as part of a structured operating model, under the supervision of a board member.

This is no longer just a matter of throwing money at the problems: Buying more tech and focusing only on operational matters is not likely to help with those, where cybersecurity maturity has remained low over the past decades in spite of all investments in that space.

Two aspects are key to acknowledge:

Cybersecurity didn't appear with the COVID crisis or the ransomware epidemic, and doing the basics right still provide a good degree of protection against most threats and a good degree of compliance against most regulations.

Large organisations have been spending billions collectively with security vendors and consultants over the years, and without identifying where the roadblocks have been in the past which have prevented those investments to come to fruition, nothing will change.

Looking at the topic through that prism will invariably take senior executives towards governance and cultural matters: Endemic short-termism leading to adverse prioritisation of security matters, incapacity of the organisation to look beyond alleged "quick wins," endless merry-go-round of cybersecurity leaders.

Real and lasting change takes time and relentless drive, and many large organisations struggle with long-term focus, in particular with complex and transversal matters such as cybersecurity.

Nevertheless, this spiral of failure can only be broken top-down, by pragmatic senior executives willing to confront the field reality of their problems in that space, without listening to the hype and the sirens of the tech world.

Cybersecurity problems can only be resolved in the real world, not in the parallel universe of tech vendors.

14

There Are Just Too Many Security Tools and Products

(9 February 2023)

The Focus Needs to Shift from Point-Solutions towards a Structured Approach to Security Automation and the Decluttering of the Toolkit Landscape

Most large organisations are suffering from a security solutions proliferation problem which complexifies their operations beyond what is currently manageable and requires levels of resources to scale up which are simply not available in the current skills market.

This is the result of decades of organic development of cybersecurity practices, without any significant architectural effort over the mid to long-term, compounded by panic buying in response to incidents and knee-jerk reactions to put ticks in boxes after audit or regulatory observations.

This purely reactive approach to cybersecurity has had a perverse effect on the marketplace, because, in fact, it is often coupled with poor procurement and selection practices.

CISOs, under pressure on a number of fronts, often follow the path of least resistance: They go back to tools and vendors they know, or solutions they have used elsewhere.

Procurement practices, also under pressure in large firms, tend to focus on large contract values and major suppliers, allowing security vendors to stay off their radar.

Because many of those tools are purchased in urgency, from known vendors, without procurement scrutiny, there is often little pressure on prices.

Vendors can appear to be successful—to their investors—with relatively limited features because their tools are simply purchased as point-solutions and are rarely evaluated thoroughly against their competitors.

This is the engine that has led to the proliferation of tools and solutions we can see today, and has allowed countless cyber vendors to parade every year at all the tech shows.

But in addition, many of those tools are rarely deployed or used extensively, either because priorities shift, budget runs out, the CISO leaves, or the project stops after addressing low-hanging fruits.

So not only can vendors appear to be successful with relatively limited features, but they can also appear to be successful if those features don't work very well, because they are rarely tested at scale.

This is why CISOs often need more tools to fix what the existing tools cannot do, compounding the "solutions" proliferation problem large firms are facing, and leading to the over-engineering of security operational processes, excessively manual investigation and response procedures, and SOC analysts burnouts.

Meanwhile breaches keep happening and business leaders wonder whether the millions invested in cyber over the years were really worthwhile.

CISOs and the security industry at large need to reflect on the resulting situation.

The skills gap is real across the industry and the piling-up of tools is just aggravating it.

The focus needs to shift from point-solutions towards a structured approach to security automation and the decluttering of the toolkit landscape.

Organising for Success

15
The Reporting Line of the CISO Is Key to Success

(16 April 2015)

Why Is the Reporting Line of the CISO Still a Hot Topic among Security Communities?

The actual role of the CISO varies greatly from one organisation to another—even if, on paper, job descriptions often look similar.

Of course, the best reporting line for the CISO is the one that positions the role in the best way within the organisation, in relation to the real challenges that the CISO is expected to resolve. But in practice, corporate governance across large organisations also varies greatly, depending on industry sectors and geographical dispersion. Many large organisations operate (efficiently or not) matrix organisations. In those cases, it's unlikely that the CISO will have a single reporting line, leading to a large number of variations where formal and informal authority have to be combined. This is well analysed by Peter Berlich in a recent post.[9]

Annual surveys published by the Big **4** consultancy firms over the past ten years have been highlighting such diversity. They show that the reporting lines now span almost the entire spectrum of board members (including the CEO, COO, CAO, CFO, CRO, and legal counsel). The results indicate that a reporting line to the CIO seems to be the most common in the field. However, this still only accounts for approximately one-third of the responses to the surveys on average (with all caveats due to the fact that the methodologies vary from one firm to another and respondents could be different from one year to the next).

Reporting lines into IT departments (at levels below the CIO) remain common in many industries (e.g., accounting for up to **26**% of respondents in the life sciences sector according to the EY **2014**).[10] Reporting lines into audit and compliance departments are still commonplace today.

In addition, many of these job titles—in particular, the COO, CAO, CRO, and CIO—could hide a variety of actual roles and individual profiles. This is particularly true in larger firms, where multiple reporting and "dotted lines" can also lead to situations where accountability is seen as a vague and relative concept.

In short, the current situation seems to reflect the confusion that has been surrounding information security strategy and governance for the past ten to fifteen years. Beyond the natural diversity of the CISO roles in terms of content, it seems that many large organisations have treated the CISO reporting line in a casual and ambiguous manner instead of positioning it in the best way to protect themselves against the genuine threats they're facing.

How Important Is the Reporting Line of the CISO?

The reporting line of the CISO is the most essential channel of authority as it presents to all stakeholders—in an unequivocal manner—the real level of importance placed on information security by the organisation.

Because information security is a matter that cuts across too many corporate silos (HR, legal, business units, IT, etc.), matrix reporting and "dotted lines" should be avoided. These multiple reporting lines are rarely efficient, rarely understood fully, and generally add to the confusion. This can hinder the leadership of the CISO and their ability to deliver.

It is key to go back to basic organisational principles. Ideally, the CISO should have a single reporting line—positioned at a level in the organisation that will maximise the impact of the role. The profile of the CISO should be adequate and suited to a board-level reporting line, and the CISO should have the gravitas, credibility, and management experience to influence their peers (as discussed in our February **2015** feature on the C-suite blog). If the board feels that's not the case, the board should start by addressing this issue.

If the CISO is expected to get things done across the organisation, the reporting line should be to the CIO or the COO—as these executives are most likely to be the closest to information security matters within an organisation.

Ultimately, the actual reporting line decision should be made at the board level based on the high-level assessment results of the security controls maturity across the organisation. From that point, the board should be able to focus on inspiring the right spirit for the role.

There are, broadly speaking, three different types of profiles the CISO can fall under:

The CISO as a Figurehead

The board may feel that the business is well protected against information threats and that the CISO needs to be a "figurehead"—a well-networked senior executive, credible with business leaders and capable of representing the firm at conferences and global events. A reporting line to the CEO or another board member (possibly the COO) may be suitable, particularly for industry sectors or smaller firms where controls are already a mindset.

The CISO as a Firefighter

If the board is primarily driven by short-termist views and concerned only with the resolution of recurring audit or compliance matters, its priorities will almost always drive a tactical agenda. The CISO will end up in a complex programme manager role, constantly having to influence stakeholders and acting as a "firefighter" to keep projects on track, ensuring priorities remain set as they should be across IT and the business.

A reporting line to the CIO or the COO is essential in such a context, given the complexity of the CISO role and the cross-silo nature of information security challenges. Delegating down must be avoided at all costs, simply because it sends a highly dangerous message across the organisation. Irrespective of the personal profile of the CISO, downward delegation implies that information security is not that important and can only fuel internal politics and confuse prioritisation among stakeholders.

But this alone is not sufficient enough to ensure success. The actual success of the CISO will rely entirely on having a proper information security governance framework in place to ensure that all stakeholders have a clear understanding of their respective roles and responsibilities in the programme delivery and the way C-level management will be involved.

Most tactical approaches in the information security space fail simply because they compromise too much on the last two points.

The CISO as a Change Agent

If the board is concerned about the maturity level of controls and wants to drive lasting improvements across the organisation, the CISO needs to be a "change agent." It's in this situation that the positioning of the reporting line is most critical.

The reporting line must be given, without exception, to a control-minded senior executive that the board trusts to supervise change in the information security space. Again, this should ideally be the CIO or the COO, and delegating down must still be avoided at all costs as this is one of the most common failure factors.

Where controls maturity issues are serious enough—particularly in large organisations with a high internet footprint facing serious cybersecurity challenges that can bring the whole business down—the CEO must consider whether the situation has reached a critical point. Here, a direct involvement in the resolution of these issues is required, and as a result, the CEO must consider taking the CISO role as a direct report.

In other situations, where controls maturity is low, it's the need to drive improvement that should be a key factor in the reporting-line decision, not arbitrary separation-of-duties considerations. Separation-of-duties considerations are often negative organisational devices aimed at dealing with conflicts of priorities generated by non-control-minded executives. In large organisations, these considerations can create more problems than they solve, by engineering arbitrary political barriers with the potential to damage the CISO's leadership ability and hinder change delivery. Internal politics often make it extremely hard to influence change "across the fence" (i.e., in parts of the organisations where you don't belong). It is key to look at the problem from a positive angle and only give the CISO reporting line to a control-minded senior executive who can be trusted by the board on their prioritisation, because the key issues are in their area of accountability.

How to Determine the Best Reporting Line for the CISO?

The prime focus should be on delivering results based on a thorough examination of the prime operational focus of the organisation (people, process, technology) and its dependency on information attributes (confidentiality, integrity, availability). The CISO reporting line should be positioned in the area where the most change is required and where most of the efforts will be targeted.

Fig. 1. The CISO Reporting Line: Decision Matrix

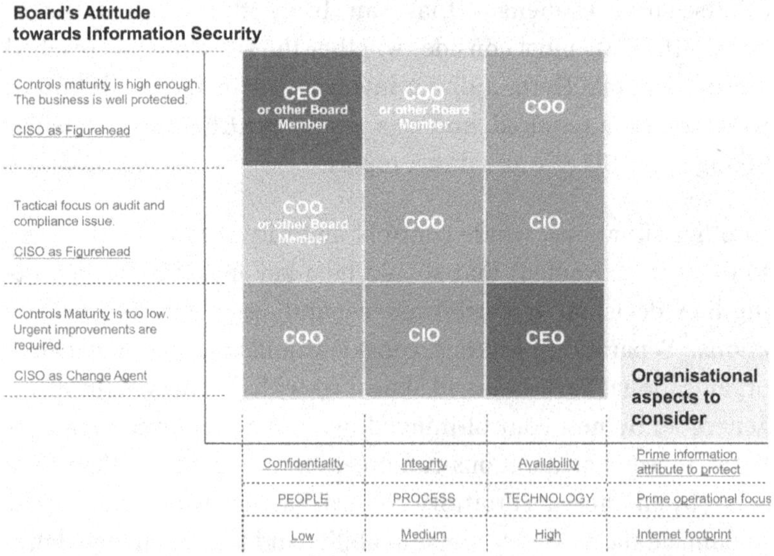

If most of the problems are in IT, the reporting line of the CISO should be to the CIO. If most of the problems are outside IT, the reporting line of the CISO should be to the COO.

Multiple lines of defence and separation-of-duties considerations must come second to, or be wrapped around, the need to drive results—in particular where information security maturity levels are low. Those can be left for the CIO or the COO to drive, as mentioned in our February **2015** feature on the C-suite blog.[11]

If these individuals are not control-minded or the board feels they cannot be trusted with a security change programme (or if these individuals simply think they're too busy to take on the role), the board should ask itself whether it is the attitude that the CIO or COO shows towards security and controls that is the root cause of the low maturity situation the board is aiming to resolve.

16
The Role of the CISO, the CIO, and the Board

(22–29 October 2015)

Digital Transformation versus Organisational Legacy: The Hybrid Role of the CISO

The lines are shifting for the CISO and the CIO.

Beyond the functional distinctions we analysed in our reporting line article ("CISO as a Figurehead," "CISO as a Firefighter, "CISO as a Change Agent"), we need to consider the positioning of the role in the "three lines of defence" model in more depth.

Our analysis of the best reporting lines for the CISO can be read and would function well in a first- or second-line positioning for the role. We have expanded upon this in a separate article, focused on GRC and making it work for InfoSec, in which we highlighted a functional model for information security to be effective and efficient in a proper second-line position.

However, these reflexions assumed a reasonably pure application of the concepts and a clear, traditional demarcation between first and second lines. In practice, this is rarely the case. The "three lines of defence" model is often poorly understood and poorly applied, leading to a variety of (more or less dysfunctional) hybrid models.

Judging by social media and broader online engagements, most people holding a CISO job title seem to be in a first-line position, in charge of delivering technical protective measures across the IT estate. They have a strong interest in technical security matters, breaches, and products. But the reality is that the role of the CISO has been evolving organically and tactically for many years.

Many CISOs have been forced to develop risk-management and compliance-reporting capabilities, which should normally sit in second line. This is often driven by the immaturity, irrelevance, or lack of interest of the corporate risk-and-compliance functions around them. In a number of cases, this move was prompted or encouraged by auditors or regulators. This is common in many financial firms where risk and compliance have been well-established corporate practices for decades but have only just woken up to information and cyber risk fairly recently—and often struggling to articulate a meaningful message in that space.

In a different type of hybrid scenario, some of the few CISOs who seem to be positioned in the second line might have been forced to take on board "first-line" operational duties because they were seen as the most able to deliver those successfully.

At the same time, the CISO is almost always a technologist by background—but not always a successful one. We have highlighted many times in previous articles that IT professionals are trained and incentivised to deliver functionality, not controls, and as a result, IT security is rarely a path to the top.

Information risk-and-compliance practices developed by first-line CISOs in a "bottom-up" manner are rarely comprehensive and often poorly connected to other risk-and-compliance activities taking place across the organisation. Operational activities delivered by second-line CISOs are often seen as inefficient and expensive, as many service management activities and technology platforms are often duplicated. This is generally a symptom of broader governance problems, and it is not rare to encounter large organisations where various overlapping functions—such as information security, data management, and data protection—coexist under different reporting lines with little coherent coordination between them.

This is an environment where many CISOs struggle, burdened with a legacy position and legacy organisational arrangements that do not suit the needs of today's enterprise.

The Changing Role of the CIO

Most surveys indicate that a majority of CISOs report to the CIO. We have stated repeatedly that it is not necessarily a problem and that the reporting line should be determined on the basis of functional objectives instead of being driven by arbitrary separation-of-duties considerations. Those often create unnecessary barriers, fuel internal politics, and prevent progress.

At the same time, the role of the CIO has changed and will continue to evolve over the short- to medium-term period. This is simply driven by the fast-paced evolution of technology over the past ten years.

Cloud computing has dramatically changed the way IT is structured, delivered, and supported. At the coalface, a CTO (chief technology officer) is often in charge of all IT infrastructure aspects, working closely with a large array of external vendors while still dealing with all the legacy systems and their problems.

Many CIOs must respond to digital transformation challenges and data monetisation opportunities, but they may have to compete with two different types of CDO (chief digital officer / data officer) in translating business needs into IT requirements and delivering them. The chief digital officer typically helps the business embrace digital innovation and stay ahead of the competition, and often, the chief data officer is charged with helping the business make the most of the data it uses, monetising it where possible using big data technology.

Parallel to these changes, IT commoditisation at large has introduced layers of "shadow IT" across the enterprise that have to be managed. All these factors considerably alter the background against which technology solutions have to be conceived and delivered.

The CIO has to learn to deal with new stakeholders internally and externally. He needs to become more of an influencer and less of a technologist. The CIO also has to learn to be less "in control" of IT and needs to develop a more structured attitude towards risk, in particular with regard to third parties.

Large organisations are not all in the same degree of maturity in relation to these concepts, but failure to grasp the depth of such transformational challenges may confine the CIO to the management of legacy IT while the CDO role takes centre stage.

New Directions

A structured InfoSec practice can be a key ally for the CIO, but the board must reward protection to attract and retain talent.

Organising Information Security for a Changing IT World

In such a context, a strong information security practice can be a key asset for the CIO. However, a strong practice must have a clear sense of purpose and a visible backbone upon which the CIO can rely to keep a grip in a changing IT world.

In practice, the CIO must not allow separation to be blurred between the first and second lines, and he should structure the organisation accordingly.

Enforcing a degree of separation between risk management and controls enforcement within the CIO's organisation could lead to the emergence of three distinct functional activities:

- An "information risk management" function, aggregating all traditional second-line activities across that space.
- An "IT security" function, focused on the architecture of functional and technical controls (essentially designing IT security measures and working with all IT stakeholders in that respect, both internally and externally).
- A "security operations" function, focused on driving the implementation of controls through the application of technical standards and procedures (these should be designed jointly with the "IT security" function, based on policies set out by the "information risk management" function and under their validation). The "security operations" function (externalised or not) could take a direct role in the delivery of some of these—in particular in the security monitoring or identity management spaces—and should deal with associated events and incidents.

The "information risk management" function should report to the CIO and interface with all non-IT stakeholders, internally and externally, as necessary (risk, compliance, internal and external audit, regulators, etc.). The other two functions could be structured at a CIO-**1** level (possibly under the CTO or the head of IT infrastructure, where such roles exist) and would interface with all IT stakeholders as required.

Fig. 2. Distribution of Information Security Roles against a PDCA Cycle

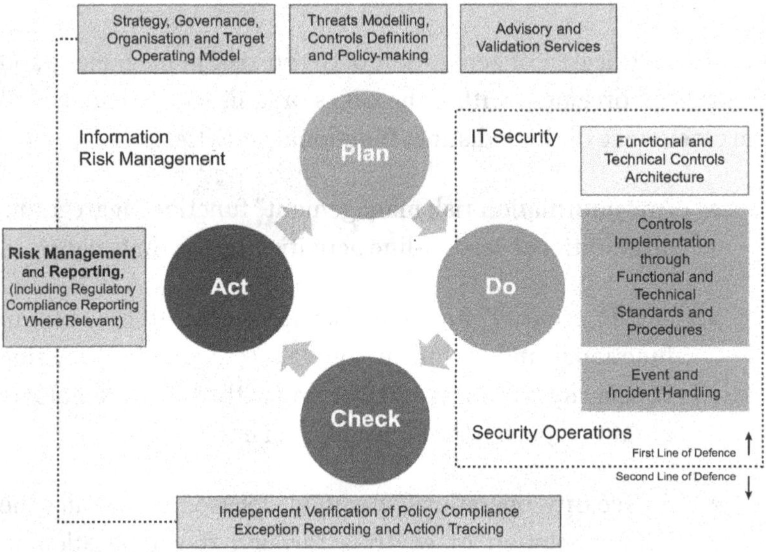

What happens to the CISO tag in such a context? It continues to imply a degree of seniority in the role and, if kept in this type of model, should be applied to the "information risk management" function—which is the most complex from a corporate perspective and has the broader managerial remit.

This is leading us to suggest an alternative organisational model for large corporates to structure InfoSec in the portfolio of the CIO—updating the previous model published in April **2015** (itself the result of an earlier research work dating back to **2012**).

Fig. 3. Organisational Model for Large Firms

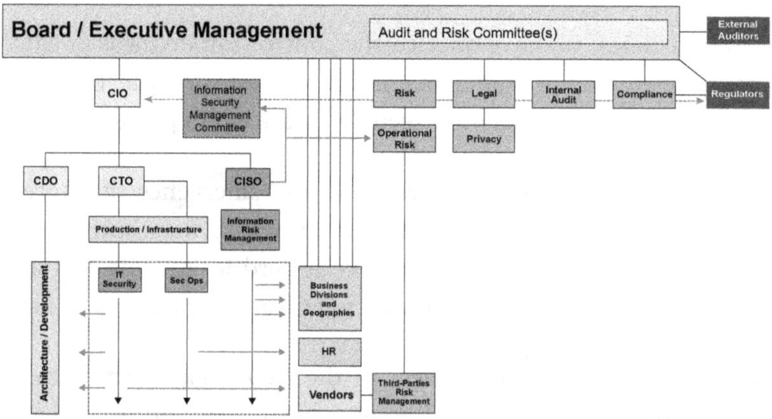

It would, invariably, involve some form of redistribution of personnel, and skill sets may have to be reviewed and adjusted. In some cases, it may highlight a critical need to invest more in resources to cover areas where little had been done up to now.

The CIO and the board should consider this as a major step towards building a resilient IT practice in the face of virulent cyber threats—rather than continuing to pour resources, on an ad hoc basis, into arbitrary technical projects.

The argument that this type of model could lead to a "conflict of interests" for the CIO needs to be handled with common sense (in particular in large organisations), and it is key to look beyond simplistic positions. A sound and comprehensive operating model is key to driving change, if that's what is required around information security. Arbitrary separations often fuel internal politics and can create unnecessary conflicts.

Boards Must Incentivise CIOs on Cybersecurity

In past articles, we have queried the control-mindedness of CIOs and implied that it was a major prerequisite for the board to consider placing information security in the CIO's portfolio.

The events of the past few years and the emergence of unprecedented media and political interest around cybersecurity, as a result of major cyber breaches, make it hard to imagine that any CIO in any large organisation would not take such threats seriously.

Beyond the control-mindedness of the CIO, what matters most today is the way the CIO addresses cybersecurity priorities—and this is something on which the board can have a direct influence.

The board should take an active interest in cybersecurity matters and drive real action in that space, but it can only work in real life if it translates into real incentives for real people.

CIOs have always been incentivised on cost control and the timely delivery of functionality. It is time for the board to incentivise CIOs also on the delivery of security controls and the actual protection of the organisation from cyber threats.

These incentives should cascade down to attract and retain talent. Only attracting talent, retaining it over the right time frames, and applying it at the right level across a structured InfoSec organisation will drive more comprehensive and structured protective operating models and disrupt the mediocrity dynamics around information security to create the conditions of a true security transformation.

17
The CISO and the Business

(15 June 2017)

Keep Appointing Pure Technologists in CISO Roles, and You'll Never Win

The WannaCry ransomware attack that affected so many large firms in May **2017** led to a number of animated discussions among InfoSec communities. The corrective patch (fixing the vulnerability targeted by the malware) was out in March for supported systems, and many firms were badly hit because of their reliance on the unsupported Windows XP (which reached the end of life in **2014**).

The timely deployment of security patches has been regarded as a good fundamental security practice since the Code Red, Slammer, and Blaster virus outbreaks over ten years ago, so how can it be that so many large firms are still struggling with this today?

It cannot be just a matter of security investment. Many of the firms reportedly affected by the outbreak would have had fully functioning security practices all that time and would have been spending millions every year on security products.

It has to be a plain matter of adverse prioritisation of security issues by IT and business leaders—which brings under the spotlight the role and profile of the CISO in those firms. Surely, it would have been the CISO's job to ensure that those matters remain on the agenda of the right leaders: to communicate their urgency, to drive remedial programmes, and to keep hammering at it until it gets fixed.

What is the security community doing wrong if it is collectively unable to address a technical issue such as the timely deployment of security patches over a period spanning more than a decade?

One reason often put forward by security technologists refers to a language disconnect between the CISO and the business. Somehow, CISOs are not being heard by business leaders and need to learn to "speak the language of the business." Such an assertion in itself raises concerns about the actual profile of the CISO if there are question marks over their ability to rise above mere technological arguments and present them in a language a nonspecialist would understand.

Of course, many CISOs are technologists by background, and frankly, security has rarely been seen as a pathway to the top in IT circles, so very often, the CISO is either in that job because of a personal interest in the technical aspects of the the topic—or because there was little else for them to do.

To break the spiral that has led to the past "lost decade" on cyber-security matters, you urgently need to inject talent into the security industry. It is primarily managerial excellence that is missing, and it will have to be attracted by rewarding the right skills at the right level. It is also a matter of cultural transformation for many firms because it is about changing the value scale on which security is being judged.

To attract the best leaders, security (i.e., the protection of a firm's assets) has to be seen from the board down as something fundamental that the firm values and rewards, not something you can compromise on to maximise profits or imposed upon you arbitrarily by regulators.

And if you want your CISO to "talk the language of the business," you could start by appointing someone from the business—or at least an IT leader who is not a mere technology hobbyist and has a true transversal view of your business.

A lot of this is about context. If you present the patch deployment issue as an IT issue, you will be heard by your business in an IT context and prioritised against other IT topics. If you present it as a matter of fundamental protection against real and active threats, you will be engaging at a different level. But as a CISO, you will need the right voice, the right gravitas, and the right profile in the firm to be heard.

This is not only a rational argument. You'll have to use every fact you can find and always focus your communication with other business leaders on those facts and the reality of the threats. You'll have to pick your battles and strike at the right time to convince the right people. You'll have to break the "bias of imaginability" (theorised by Kahneman),[12] and it will take time. This is a very serious management role that requires a truly senior profile, a considerable amount of experience, and a willingness to stay on for the right course—and that could be considerably more than a mere couple of years.

Keep appointing pure technologists in CISO roles, and you'll never win. The level of information protection the firm needs to function is not a mere technology matter, contrary to what many tech vendors would like you to believe. It has a profound cultural dimension that is at the heart of the relationship between the firm and its employees. You naturally protect what you care about. If your CISO embodies that relation, everything they do will carry that weight, and you'll move forward.

18

What Role for the Group CISO?

(27 July 2017)

The role of the CISO and their reporting line seems to be a continuing topic of discussion among cybersecurity professionals.

The same title often hides a large diversity of roles, positioned differently across their respective organisations. It often reflects the maturity of each firm towards the appreciation of the threats it faces, the need for business protection, and its appetite for controls.

For large groups in particular—where business units or geographies manage their own bottom line and have a significant degree of autonomy in real terms—it can result in a large population of security practitioners across the group with very diverse approaches, objectives, and priorities.

This is becoming increasingly a major source of concern in a world that is more and more "hyperconnected" and where data is the real "fuel" the business needs to burn on its journey towards digital transformation.

Often at the top is a group CISO, but what could be their role in such a context? And how do they make it work?

Of course, security governance at group level cannot exist on its own, and somehow it can only work if it follows broadly (and is embedded within) the governance model of the whole group.

As a result, the group CISO will have to position their role based on two broad dimensions:

1. A sound appreciation of the real nature of the governance model at group level:

   Some large groups operate very efficiently in a centralised model, driven by "command-and-control" principles, in which business units and geographies have a limited degree of real autonomy.

   At the other end of the spectrum, and often in different industries, some large groups operate by influence in a very decentralised way, where business units and geographies have a large degree of real autonomy.

   In between, a number of (more or less) dysfunctional models are quite common, many inspired by a strong distrust from the head office and fuelled by internal politics and individual interests.

2. A sound appreciation of the real need for group-wide business interaction:

   Again, large groups are very diverse in these aspects. Many would have grown by acquisition over time in a more or less structured manner, and those different acquisitions might be at different degrees of integration.

It could be that, historically, the different parts of the group have always had little in common and, therefore, little interest in exchanging information or needs to integrate IT systems to operate.

Equally, it could be that the digital transformation is introducing the need for stronger cooperation across the group, as it opens up considerable competitive opportunities for cross-selling that could bring enormous growth (or, indeed, leave the group behind forever if they are missed as competitors sail past).

Understanding these nuances is key for the group CISO when positioning their role and its key objectives. They would be instinctive to a senior executive who might have spent years or decades in the organisation, but it could be much harder for a newcomer and could take time to grasp.

It is nevertheless a key step, and it leads to three broad patterns in terms of role for the group CISO, which we have already identified and analysed in earlier articles, focused on organisation and reporting lines:

The Group CISO as a Figurehead

This is typical of large organisations, where diversity is high and leaders lead primarily by influence. The prime objective of the group CISO should be to communicate and drive a common degree of understanding and awareness among all stakeholders' communities. There may also be an element of external representation to the role, within industry bodies, academia, or similar groups.

Fig. 4. The Three Main Roles of the Group CISO

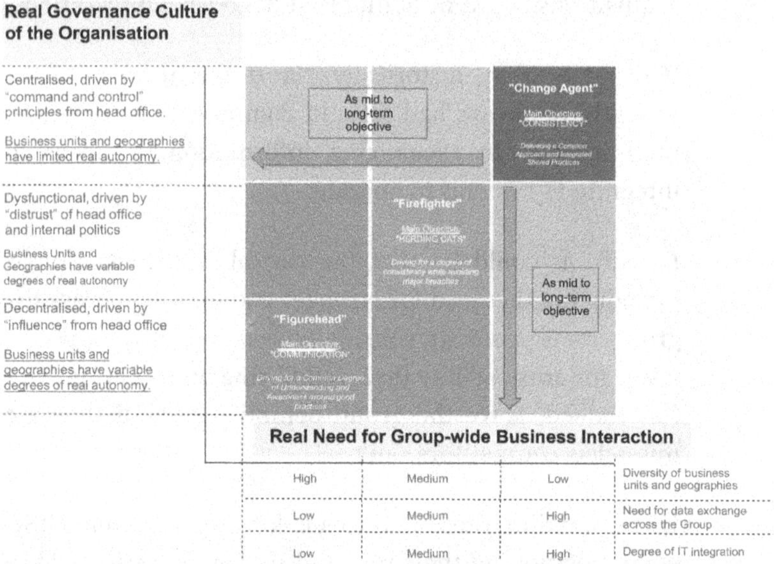

The Group CISO as a Firefighter

This is typical of dysfunctional governance situations, and the prime objective of the group CISO should be to drive, as much as possible, towards a degree of consistency in security practices across the group, while avoiding major breaches. This is by far the most complex role profile, and it will feel like "herding cats" most of the time for the group CISO.

The Group CISO as a Change Agent

This is typical of situations where diversity is low and integration is high, with a strong "command and control" culture, but where security has never had a high degree of priority. The prime objective of the group CISO should be to drive for consistency and the delivery of a common approach to security across the group, including shared integrated practices (such as a SOC, for instance) where necessary.

How to Drive Action in All Cases: Building a Sense of Community

In all cases, driving action, creating a sense of value around the group CISO role, and avoiding the "ivory tower" syndrome will involve a number of key principles:

1. *Create a clear mission statement for the group CISO role, aimed at all security and business stakeholders across the group.* The role of the group CISO cannot be vague (or difficult to read from the bottom up or from the top down). But in particular, all security stakeholders across the group must have a clear idea of who the group CISO is and what they do and why, even if the mandate coming from the top down from executive management is not always that clear at their level.

2. *Lead by listening.* The group CISO function must bring something tangible to the various security stakeholders across the group. It is key to listen to them upfront to understand their constraints and expectations. Ignoring those would kill trust and emphasise the idea of a head office "ivory tower" function. This is the most important part and often the hardest, as objectives, maturities, and priorities across the group could vary enormously.

3. *In return, build a clear plan with realistic expectations of delivery for all* (at the level in which the group governance model allows you to work with realistic expectations of delivery). It is key to have a clear security plan of action at group level, in which each and every security stakeholder across the group fits and has a role to play with something clear and achievable for them to deliver. They need to have a sense of purpose and feel that, collectively, they achieve something for the group. This sense of community is the real key to success. In

return, the group CISO should leverage their influence at group level to bring common resources and budgets to the table that can help achieve common objectives and deliver work on common projects.

4. *Bring all security stakeholders together at least once a year to keep contact, build trust, and leverage on their skills and knowledge.* It could be an annual general event, where they all come to report on progress and share achievements and issues. It could be several events per year, with stronger themes. In all cases, it is key to periodically reinforce a strong sense of community that transcends what may be happening around the security stakeholders in terms of management, governance, or politics at their level, in their region, business unit, or subsidiary. It is likely that many will find value in those exchanges—if anything, at human level, but also in terms of personal development and technical benchmarking. It can be sometimes a lonely role to be the CISO for a small division or a small region within a large group.

Across all those matters, the reporting line of the group CISO will be important. As we pointed out above, the different role types overlap those identified in earlier articles. It should be at board level and dictated by overall objectives for the role, but it's only one aspect.

The personal profile of the group CISO is essential. Many elements highlighted above call for a degree of seniority, gravitas, and political acumen, as well as human qualities to listen to potentially very diverse people and bring them together.

Time is also a key factor as it could take five to ten years to build a genuine security practice at group level in large firms where nothing existed before. The group CISO has to be prepared and rewarded to stay the course, and executive management above him has to be capable of working on medium- to long-term objectives without deviating every time something happens internally or externally. Knee-jerk reactions on these matters just kill momentum and trust.

Success for the group CISO role will come from working on all these fronts.

19

The Current Role of Most CISOs Lacks Clarity and Needs to Change

(8 March–28 April 2016)[13]

Cyber threats are a growing concern for most organisations. However, it appears that reactive, expensive, and inefficient practices are still underpinning most InfoSec strategies. As we have argued in previous articles, it is an issue that must be addressed primarily at the people and process levels through an effective cybersecurity governance framework instead of traditional approaches that have historically treated the problem as a mere IT problem and focused only on technology solutions.

The three key pieces of this model are the CISO, the CIO, and the board, whose roles in protecting the organisation against cyber threats must be clearly outlined and commonly understood. However, each of those is currently facing its own challenges in terms of maturity.

In spite of the function having been in existence for decades, the CISO's role and mission still lack clarity and consistency in many large organisations. As a result, the formal distinction between the first and second lines of defence in the traditional "three lines of defence" model is often blurred, and the whole model is generally poorly applied.

The structural pressure that the emergence of shadow IT and cloud computing are exercising on organisations' IT environment is forcing an inevitable and ongoing shift in the role of CIOs. They must aim for more cooperation and influence with both internal and external stakeholders and are forced to focus less on the purely technological aspects of the role.

The board—often scared by recent data breaches—is in the process of becoming fully aware of the cybersecurity challenges that its organisation is faced with, and its behaviour with regard to InfoSec governance must reflect that acknowledgement. The board must be consistent in its expectations and explicitly incentivise key senior executives on cyber protection and not just on product delivery, revenue generation, or cost-cutting.

The reporting line of the CISO, in particular, must unambiguously lie at board level in order to reflect the importance and the consideration that should be given to this crucial role. The reporting line should be determined on the basis of the challenges the role is facing. Arbitrary separations of duty considerations must be avoided at all costs as they simply fuel internal politics and inefficiencies, and in practice, they often hinder the implementation of much-needed changes.

In such a context, the time has come to deconstruct and reforge the former legacy role of the CISO. Three distinct functions can be identified that would allow the lines between risk-management and controls-enforcement tasks to be drawn more clearly around traditional PDCA principles.

This new operating model would benefit the CIO by providing them with a stronger and more efficient cyber governance framework. The CISO would also gain seniority and consideration in the process and could become a key ally to the CIO around digital transformation challenges.

20

The Tenure of the CISO Is Key to Driving Security Transformation

(26 April 2018)

Nothing Will Change until the Profile of the CISO Is Raised and They Start to See Their Role over the Medium to Long Term

Surveys suggest that the average tenure in a CISO position is around two years.[14]

Although it seems to vary depending on industry sectors, it is supported by vast amounts of anecdotal evidence, and it matches our field experience working with clients. The same goes for the reasons behind the early departures of many CISOs.

It often starts with the sense that the internal situation is vastly different from what they had been "sold" to throughout the recruitment process. They don't feel valued or listened to; they feel trapped in management models where many key decisions are made elsewhere without their involvement; and they feel like they haven't got adequate resources in terms of budget or staff to do what they would like to do. So they leave, having achieved very little in practice. And in a number of cases, they leave for larger organisations or a larger pay package because of tensions in the recruitment market around those roles.

Then, at best, a caretaker manager is appointed—or worse, the role is left vacant for months until a recruitment is made internally or externally. Then someone new comes in, almost always with different views compared to their predecessors, and with the risk of seeing the same scenario repeating itself.

This type of managerial discontinuity—in particular, when experienced repeatedly over a decade or so—is at the root of the maturity problems many large firms are facing around cybersecurity. Over time, as almost nothing gets achieved at each iteration, the need to drive a fundamental transformation around security practices becomes more and more crucial, but creating true change dynamics also becomes more and more complex as management gets frustrated and security becomes a problem and a failed topic.

The whole situation questions the average profile of the CISO as much as it does the appetite of their management for security. In particular where driving a fundamental transformation programme around security practices is a key objective, the CISO needs to be an executive with the right amount of management experience, personal gravitas, and political acumen. This cannot be a job for a technology hobbyist, an ex-auditor, or a lifelong consultant.

With the right level of seniority should come a sense that "Rome wasn't built in a day"—a sound and honest appreciation of the culture of the firm, the pace at which it may change, and as a result, a sound appreciation of the time it can take to turn things around. With it also comes a sense that only a shared transformative vision (shared with senior management and stakeholders) can drive and sustain change over the medium to long term.

It would not take two years for the CISO to realise that they are in the wrong job. In fact, the first six weeks are key. Over that period, the new CISO would have met with their management and their team. They would have met with key stakeholders and developed a sense of the challenges ahead, including the cultural and geographical diversity of their new organisation. They would have built a sense of what needs to be done, where they are in terms of budgetary cycle, and the resources they have or could claim to deliver.

If the points of divergence with their management are too salient, it is at this point that they should leave, and they should have the management experience and self-confidence to see it that way. Of course, it does make the first six weeks in the new job hard and challenging, but it is also about building trust, and only trust between the CISO and key stakeholders will sustain change.

Spending the first six weeks or the first six months putting off burning fires or politically pushing a technical agenda the business stakeholders don't quite understand is a recipe for building frustration, not trust. Constant firefighting downgrades the role of the CISO. Pushing an arbitrary technical agenda and focusing only on the resources to deliver it also downgrades the role of the CISO and takes the debate to the political minefield of priorities. Every senior manager in the firm has their own views on what needs to be done next, their own pet project, and their own political weight. This is something the new CISO should avoid.

Instead, they should spend their first six months building a coalition around a transformative agenda that is right for the firm, together with an execution framework and a governance model to deliver it. The whole exercise should clarify priorities, time frames, and resources for all stakeholders.

It should give the new CISO a view over their tenure that should be commensurate to the task at hand. In most cases, it will spread well over the average two years and could point towards a five-year horizon, or maybe a six- to nine-year horizon. Taking on a CISO role becomes a very significant career step in that light. Even more significant, if we take into account the seniority requirements we are placing on the role, which will make it necessarily a mid to late-career step.

As a result, the CISO will have to be incentivised to stay the course, and executive management must remain consistent with the agreed direction of travel. It will be hard for firms where short-termism prevails, but those who achieve it should start breaking the spiral of security failure in which they were entrapped.

21

GDPR and the DPO: Threats or Levers for the CISO?

(5 April 2018)

The GDPR Is Not Just about Security, but It Has Been Dominating the Life of Many CISOs Since Last Year

Notoriously, the regulation contains only a few actual references to data security. Article **32** mentions the need to have "appropriate" technical and organisational measures in place to ensure a level of security "appropriate to the risk" and quotes "inter alia" a few possible measures (pseudonymisation, encryption, etc.), but that's almost the only specific reference to security in the whole text.

The "appropriateness" of the technical and organisational measures in relation to the risk has to be understood in the context of Article **32**, (i.e., "taking into account" the elements listed in the article):

- The state of the art
- The costs of implementation
- The nature, scope, context, and purposes of processing
- The risk of varying likelihood and severity for the rights and freedoms of natural persons

Article **32** also cross-references Articles **40** and **42**, and it allows the use of approved codes of conduct and certification schemes to demonstrate compliance. But those won't be in place for a while given the way approval is described in the mentioned articles.

Beyond the lack of explicit definitions for the key terms (*appropriate, state-of-the-art*) over which the guidance from the WP**29** has shed little light so far, what does that mean in practice for the CISO?

Frankly, it should change very little to their practice. The GDPR simply seems to endorse a risk-based approach to delivering up-to-date good security practices to protect personal data. It is an approach that should be in place in many firms to protect any type of sensitive data (personal or not).

Having security measures appropriate to the "nature, scope, context, and purpose of processing" should be a perfectly normal way of working (you don't secure an e-commerce website in the same way you secure a back-office in-house accounting system). The reference to the "costs of implementation" is simply a reality check and hints at something that happens all the time in real life.

Every CISO will be used to having security measures rejected by their business on grounds of costs.

Good information security practices and risk-based approaches have been well established for the best part of the last fifteen to twenty years. Most large firms would have had fully functioning security teams in place for the best part of that period and would have spent collectively billions on security products and consultants. So why would a CISO be worried?

CISO and DPO: Allies or Enemies?

Could it be that in spite of the billions spent, little demonstrable alignment to good security practices was actually achieved in real terms over the past decade in many large firms? (There is ample anecdotal evidence of that surrounding the WannaCry ransomware outbreak in May **2017**).

Outside already-regulated industries (where the role of compliance and audit departments has been better established for a long time), could it be that the CISO is now worried that they will have a DPO "breathing down their neck" and that the threat of massive fines is going to change the managerial dynamics of the game in favour of the DPO—who, in addition, benefits from a somehow protected regulatory status?

Of course, it depends on the profile of the individuals involved, and we have analysed several times since **2015** the profile of CISO roles, their reporting lines, and the types of interaction they can drive across large firms.

Where the CISO role is positioned as a "change agent" (in the language of those earlier articles), there should be little friction with the DPO, and the GDPR offers fundamental levers to the transformational CISO.

The DPO is likely to be a new player in the security governance game, and it could be that he/she brings a different outlook and a different background to the table (very often, it is likely to be somebody with some form of legal training).

The DPO will face many challenges similar to those faced by the transformational CISO around driving cultural change and engineering new dynamics around "privacy by design."

Working together, they can be strong allies if they manage to build and push from different angles a common transformative agenda and create together the structures they will need to demonstrate GDPR compliance (for the DPO) and ensure the adequate protection of information assets (for the CISO).

Where the CISO role is positioned as a "firefighter" or a "figurehead," the situation could be quite distinct. To both, the DPO could start demanding answers to difficult questions around the actual structure of their practice or its tangible output, and their relationship could become complex.

In all cases, the GDPR brings an opportunity to rethink InfoSec and, where necessary, make it work better.

The role of the CISO is often the result of organic evolutions going back a decade or more. The new role of the DPO cannot exist on its own and will require a proper governance model to function and bring value to the whole organisation, despite its imposed independence.

They need to converge into a coherent operating model that builds on positive interactions between the functions while respecting the constraints of each. It is a considerable challenge—in particular in large firms—but a necessary one, and it is absolutely key to ensuring ongoing GDPR compliance post May 25 and adherence to the "privacy by design" objectives that are at the heart of the regulation.

22

The Digital Transformation and the Role of the CISO

(9 July 2018)[15]

Cybersecurity Needs to Be at the Heart of the Digital Transformation, but Organisational Models Will Have to Evolve

Cybersecurity is in the process of becoming an essential component of any organisation's digital transformation journey. There is no way around this, especially as policymakers start dipping their toes into privacy and security issues, and societal norms are shifting on the topic.

In fact, privacy and security considerations are the key ingredients of digital trust and must be at the heart of any industry's digital transformation. Far from being solely technological issues, they encompass for many firms profound cultural and governance issues.

The necessarily transversal nature of security and privacy matters needs to be woven into the fabric of an organisation for the digital transformation to succeed over the long term, and this will force existing organisational models to evolve.

Of course, most new technology layers enabling the digital transformation need to be protected from interference, intrusion, or corruption. This is especially the case across industry sectors seeking to take advantage of the enormous opportunities offered by driverless vehicles, and the logistics sector, among others, could be unrecognizable in ten years' time.

New technologies will also generate and feed on massive amounts of data—most of it sensitive or private—that will need to be collected, processed, and safeguarded in a way that is both sensible and ethical. This is absolutely key, for example, in the retail sector where the growing trends towards the enhanced personalisation and the digitalisation of the consumer's journey are literally turning the industry on its head.

The concepts of security by design and privacy by design will inevitably become any organisation's best allies in its innovative endeavours and must be taken seriously by all digital transformation players, especially as the regulatory and social contexts become harder to navigate.

Fig. 5. Digital Transformation and the Logistics Sector

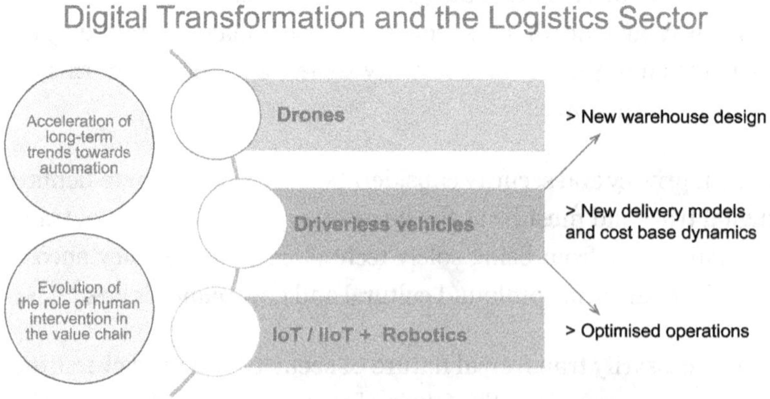
Digital Transformation and the Logistics Sector
Acceleration of long-term trends towards automation
Evolution of the role of human intervention in the value chain
Drones
Driverless vehicles
IoT / IIoT + Robotics
> New warehouse design
> New delivery models and cost base dynamics
> Optimised operations

Fig. 6. Digital Transformation and the Retail Sector

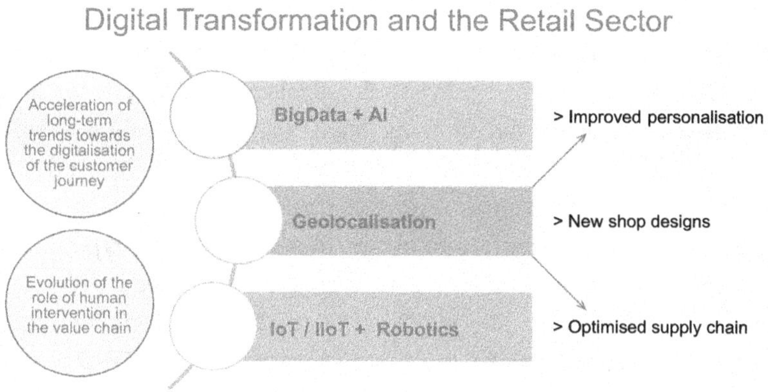

As data is increasingly becoming the fuel of the digital value chain, it needs to be understood and treated as a truly valuable asset by all firms and protected as such. But this must not be seen as a mere technical matter. It needs to be addressed across the corporate spectrum as a full managerial and cultural matter and could have deep organisational implications.

There is no doubt, in our opinion, that organisations that put information security and privacy at the heart of their digital transformation from the start could obtain a real competitive advantage in the medium to long run.

As a matter of fact, the recent launch of the General Data Protection Regulation (GDPR) in the European Union is dramatically changing the incentives landscape for all businesses active in Europe.

Make no mistakes. The GDPR is an integral part of the digital transformation paradigm and illustrates how external forces (in this case, regulation) can and will be applied by politicians to try to restore market equilibrium (in this case, in the face of ruthless data monetisation) to protect the perceived interests of consumers and citizens.

Organisations can now be fined up to **4%** of their global turnover for noncompliance but may be faced over the short term with incoherent rulings and shifting legal norms (as nobody really knows yet how the regulators will act in practice). In addition, firms are now required to report any relevant data breach to the regulator within seventy-two hours. This will require capabilities of detection, analysis, and reaction that go far beyond the scope of the security teams and will force many corporate stakeholders to work together on those matters (security, IT, legal, DPO teams, senior management, etc.). As such, the GDPR could be a painful lesson as to why cybersecurity is necessarily a transversal matter for organisations of all sizes.

Finally, and perhaps most importantly, respect for privacy and protection of personal data are likely to become true competitive advantages as our societies become increasingly wary of these issues.

This shift is well illustrated by the first complaints filed under the GDPR framework. Privacy activists such as Max Schrems or the French Quadrature du Net, for example, have already started to drag high-profile tech companies (Facebook, Google, Instagram, etc.) into what could become lengthy legal proceedings. Depending on how the regulators react, this could have deep implications on how data-driven businesses are to operate in Europe.

As consumers and other stakeholders start scrutinising more and more the corporate attitude towards data, failing to acknowledge their concerns over these privacy issues (or worse, making the headlines when the next scandal hits) could do more harm to any business than a regulator's fine.

At the heart of those matters lies a deep reliance on digital trust. Once broken, it is the entire digital value chain that collapses.

Investors themselves are starting to regard digital trust as the true "secret sauce" of the digital transformation, and security and privacy as its key ingredients are fast becoming serious components at the heart of any sound ESG framework.

Increasingly, security and privacy become intertwined, but it makes little sense from a corporate governance perspective to allow a new privacy organisation under a DPO to grow in parallel to—or in conflict with—existing security structures. Synergies are obvious and need to be leveraged, and where security practices are deemed dysfunctional or in need of improvement, this could provide an ideal opportunity.

In fact, it could be the start of a major evolution around corporate perceptions of security and privacy—from burden, annoyance, and costs towards becoming central management functions. But organisational models will have to evolve as a result to accommodate the truly transversal nature of security and privacy matters and carve out a niche for those new corporate functions.

At this junction, the traditional role of the CISO (heavily influenced by a technical bias, tactically oriented, and project-driven in many firms) could become exposed—not in its functional existence (IT security is more essential than ever), but in its corporate prominence.

Having failed to project their roles beyond the tactical and technical fields for the best part of the last decade, many CISOs could find themselves pushed down the organisation while CSO and DPO roles take centre stage at the top.

Fig. 7. A New Transversal Organisational Model

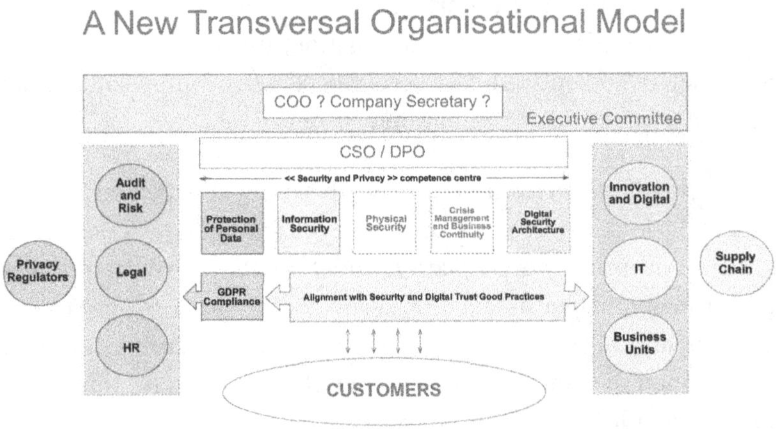

With those new roles should come new people and a new focus, and probably a different way to approach security matters and talk about them.

We could be at the start of an exciting decade for all security professionals.

23

Who Wants to Be a CISO?

(3 January 2019)

Talent Alienation Is the Biggest Issue behind the Cybersecurity Management Skills Gap, but It Shouldn't Be the Case

Who wants to be a CISO these days? And at which stage in your career should you consider the move? What balance of managerial and technical experience do you need to have? And where do you go from there? ("What's the step after next?" is always the most important question in terms of career development.)

Those would be valid questions for many executive positions, but when it comes to the role of the CISO, they seem to acquire a different meaning.

Let's evacuate the first two aspects from the start.

Cybersecurity has developed a high profile in many organisations over the past few years. Many firms are engaged in transformation programmes in that space—which will require strong leadership, transversal vision, and managerial and political acumen from the CISO. The role is no longer a role for a junior technologist, an ex-auditor, or a lifelong consultant. Of course, control-mindedness and a solid understanding of the technical aspects relevant to their industry sector are important, but they must not be seen as the only key aspects.

It's the "step after next" question that seems to be the dominant factor preventing people from moving into CISO jobs.

Security still carries an image problem, in spite of the recent high-profile cyber incidents and the undeniable interest developed by top executives around the topic over the past few years (and the additional layer of emphasis brought in by the GDPR). It is still seen by many as a highly specialised field and a dead end, plagued by underinvestment and management lip service, where you cannot really achieve anything.

This is becoming wrong on all fronts, in particular in large firms involved in fundamental transformation programmes around cybersecurity.

Security can no longer be seen as a specialised technical silo. It is a transversal discipline rooted in corporate culture and governance that will take the CISO in contact with IT, business, HR, legal, and risk and compliance functions. The digital transformation and the "security and privacy by design" principles coming with GDPR accentuate that trend even further. Only by looking at security in that way can large-scale transformation programmes be truly successful.

The underinvestment and lip-service era is behind us in many firms. Cybersecurity is on the board agenda, and "Are we spending enough on cyber?" is becoming one of the most common questions at that level. The GDPR brings business-threatening fines of unprecedented proportions that can turn cynical lip service into an expensive habit. Priorities and resources are shifting towards cybersecurity, but with those come management expectations and execution responsibilities for the CISO.

As a consequence of the two points above, large-scale cybersecurity transformation programmes can be very complex and very exposed. They are nothing but dead ends. They are exceptional training grounds and prime areas where ambitious leaders can develop and prove themselves to the board.

Of course, ambition is required, as well as realism around the time frames involved with delivering lasting change. It could take three to five years (or longer) to turn a security practice around, and that would make it a significant career step for the individual involved. But the role of the transformational CISO has all the attributes to attract the best talents, and it is now down to the board to raise its profile so that it does.

This goes beyond compensation and reporting lines. It is time for role models to emerge to illustrate that the successful transformational CISO is not condemned to hopping from one CISO job to another but can move into CIO, CRO, or CDO roles—or, indeed, any leadership position where strong turnaround skills are required.

24
The Impossible Role of the CISO

(20 June 2019)

Security Organisations Must Evolve; The CISO Cannot Be Credible on All Fronts

A recent comment I read on LinkedIn made me think. It was in response to a post on zero-day vulnerabilities and software patching. Roughly translated from French, it reads as follows:

> One day, you stand in front of the Ex-Co having to explain how the millions spent on cyber over the years have improved their level of protection; then you go back to your desk to discover that three new vulnerabilities have just turned up which need patching across the entire estate; Welcome to my world!

While I accept this reflects the life of many CISOs, it attracts comments at two levels:

First of all, if the "millions spent on cyber over the years" had been spent in the right places, none of the issues highlighted here should be a challenge for the CISO.

A cybersecurity practice needs to be a structured practice built around people and processes, supported by technology. Reporting capabilities should be embedded in it and inform any management decision up to the board. You build those over time. It requires a medium- to long-term vision and leadership from the CISO, but that's how the "millions" should have been invested over the years: people, process, *then* technology.

Of course, many cybersecurity practices have been built the other way round: jumping straight at the first technology solution every time something happens or at the first sight of an audit point, buying some tech product to address alleged quick wins, then wrapping processes around the capabilities of the product—only to discover that you can't justify the resources to operate the way the product needs to be operated (before complaining endlessly about management and budgets, at which point the CISO generally moves on to their next job).

This cannot carry on. Short-term focus on non-existent quick wins has led to a product-proliferation problem that is simply killing security operations practices, and many large organisations are nowhere near the level of security maturity they should have reached with regard to the amounts invested over the last ten to fifteen years.

Many CISOs are simply trapped in endless projects, tactical games, and firefighting. They struggle to see the bigger picture, while at the same time, many senior executives have now entered the "*when*, not *if*" era and expect real action. Meanwhile, breaches keep happening, and over time, distrust sets in between business and security leaders. This spiral of failure also breeds a talent-alienation dynamic, and security problems can rapidly become self-perpetuating.

Organisations that find themselves in such a situation must look back without complacency at the roadblocks that have prevented progress in the past around security matters. Invariably, they will be rooted in culture, governance, and managerial short-termism.

To break this deadlock, they will have to attract and inject raw management talent into the security equation, and to that effect, current security organisations will have to evolve.

This takes me to my second point, in relation to the LinkedIn comment I started from.

The CISO role that it refers to—although very real today in many organisations—is inherently flawed.

Nobody can be reasonably expected to be *genuinely* and *effectively* credible from the board down—across all managerial and technical layers of the enterprise, transversally across all its silos (from HR to legal, procurement, or compliance), and of course, across all geographies and cultures for global firms.

This profile simply does not exist (or is so rare it's not worth looking for). Yet in many organisations, it is a little bit what is expected of the CISO, partly because of the inherently transversal nature of security and partly because no one else appears to be relaying the security message.

This also cannot carry on. Security organisations in large firms have to restructure themselves in-depth to encompass and structure all relevant disciplines and allow each of them to develop, as it should, at its level.

Within a structured organisation, roles should be defined and distributed to attract the best. The person talking to the board on security matters and the person making sure the IT estate is patched should not—and cannot—be the same.

In this context, the traditional role of the CISO will have to evolve and probably leave the centre stage to a broader CSO role, which could be used to attract and develop a new generation of leaders into security roles.

This is absolutely necessary to address the transversal nature of security—and privacy—matters in large firms and break the spiral of failure that has plagued cybersecurity for the last decade.

25
The Tactical Trap

(18 July 2019)

Cybersecurity Maturity Stagnates Because Many CISOs Are Structurally Prevented from Looking Beyond Day-to-Day Firefighting

Many CISOs struggle to look beyond day-to-day firefighting and get trapped in tactical games. We highlighted this last year in the context of our *100 Days* series, and it is one of the major factors preventing organisations from developing better levels of cyber-security maturity.

In many firms, this goes beyond incidents and the natural need to address those. It is often compounded by three structural elements literally trapping the CISO in tactical games, forcing endemic short tenures and creating the conditions for a systemic spiral of failure around cybersecurity.

- First, corporate short-termism, which is still prevalent in many organisations among senior executive communities:

"In the long term, we're all dead," and anything that would not impact the next quarter's figures does not grab the interest for very long. Cybersecurity matters are being pushed towards those levels of management by non-stop media reports around data breaches and the potential level of GDPR fines. But when faced with multiyear, seven- or eight-digit transformative programmes of work around security that would genuinely force the firm to alter the way it works, those executives often revert to what they've been doing for decades around compliance: looking for quick wins and cheap boxes to tick so that they can "show progress" while minimising spend and disruption.

The problem with cybersecurity is that organisations facing that type of problem are generally in need of a structural overhaul of their security practices, and "quick wins" are often non-existent. Driving real and lasting change takes time. Simply "fixing" illusory quick wins has never been the base of any transformation.

- Second, plain old office politics between IT and security—which have always been a component of the life of many CISOs, irrespective of their reporting line (and this is undoubtedly worse where the CISO does not report to the CIO):

  Technologists are trained and incentivised to deliver functionality, not controls, and many over the past decades have developed a culture that sees security measures as constraints instead of requirements.

  Many CISOs are constantly bombarded by "urgent" requests to define security measures coming from IT people who should know better but are just "passing the buck."

  The CISOs often feel that they would fail by not responding, not realising that this is a game they cannot win and a form of political and emotional blackmail that must be avoided, especially outside large organisations where teams and resources tend to be smaller. The CISO and their team simply cannot be expected to be deep technical security experts on all technology streams and across all platforms, or to "drop everything" at any time to help projects.

Of course, they can rely on external skills (budgets permitting), but fundamentally, roles, responsibilities, and demarcation lines should be clear and resources placed where they should be. The security of IT systems should be the responsibility of the respective IT teams. The security team should assist, validate, and control while retaining a degree of independence. This is the spirit of all organisational models developed over the past twenty years around IT security. It should be clear, and the CISO and their boss should have the backbone to enforce it.

- Finally, in many cases, the greed of the tech industry, which is only aggravating the situation:

  For each of those alleged "quick wins" or "urgent" issues to fix, there are countless vendors bidding to sell their stuff to put a tick in that box, irrespective of any bigger picture.

  This is a pressure the CISO must resist. Over time, this accumulation of point solutions simply leads to a product-proliferation problem that makes everything more difficult for the CISO and their team. From incident management to compliance reporting, security operations become burdened by the need to collect data across multiple platforms, often in inconsistent formats. Resources requirements escalate, and it aggravates the perception that security is just a cost and a pain instead of a necessary barrier against real and active threats.

The CISO and IT must build the discipline to work with a small number of security vendors and service providers around which they can structure effective and efficient security operations, properly segregated and proportionate to the threats the business is facing and the resources available to fight them.

Clarity of roles and responsibilities across security and IT and a clear approach (putting *people* and *process* first ahead of ready-made *technology* solutions) are the bases on which the CISO can avoid the tactical trap. It is also the only basis on which cybersecurity maturity can grow, across any organisation, large or small.

26

Towards a New Profile for the CISO

(12 September 2019)

A Decade of Firefighting Has Taken Its Toll on the CISO Profession

The role of the CISO is changing. If that was ever the case, it can no longer be seen *just* as a technical role.

In some industries, it is being challenged by the worldwide tightening of regulations around privacy and the emergence of DPOs and other related roles.

Everywhere, it is being challenged by the non-stop avalanche of cyber-attacks and data breaches over the past decade, which have raised the visibility of cybersecurity to board level but at the same time have also prevented many CISOs from getting out of firefighting mode.

This is the crux of the matter.

Senior executives are increasingly endorsing a "*when,* not *if*" paradigm around cyber-attacks and are demanding fundamental change and action beyond day-to-day firefighting, often in exchange for very significant investments around security.

They are expecting the CISO to lead such programmes of work, but many CISOs have never been recruited or trained for such a challenge, under such level of scrutiny. Very often, it is about addressing problems rooted in a decade of lip service or underinvestment around security, and it involves a true transformation of many business practices across the firm.

You don't become a transformational leader overnight—in particular if your background, your skills, and your core interests are centred around the more technical aspects of cybersecurity. Nothing is wrong with that. While the focus was on firefighting cyber-attacks all the time, those would have been valuable qualities, but as the focus shifts towards transformation and execution, the ability to influence across silos and understand the true nature of the business and the more transversal aspects of security becomes paramount. Those are rarely attributes of a native technologist, and they are not attributes you develop through the constant firefighting of technical problems.

So parallel to the "lost decade" of cybersecurity and reflecting it, there is also a lost decade for the CISO profession. It is a lost decade during which many have hopped from job to job, collecting higher and higher salaries for their technical firefighting skills, but without encountering the terrain in which to develop true enterprise-level leadership and transformational skills.

As senior executives turn a page and we enter—possibly—an execution-dominated decade around cybersecurity, many CISOs are just not equipped to lead.

Let's say this one more time: Just throwing money at cybersecurity problems won't make them disappear overnight. Remediating issues rooted in a decade of adverse prioritisation by the business will cost money, but it will also require time and, in many cases, a relentless drive to change mindsets.

Who should do this, if the CISO can't?

There are broadly two types of options:

Organisational models may need to evolve to allow a broader CSO type of role to emerge in large firms—encompassing security at large, continuity, and privacy—with the CISO role retreating back to its technical roots. This would, by itself, attract a different calibre of individuals into each role, and such rebalancing of skills could be key to the success of large-scale cybersecurity transformation programmes.

Alternatively, the profile of the CISO needs to change to adjust to the imperatives of the "*when*, not *if*" era. It becomes essential to start prioritising leadership skills over technical skills and distributing roles across a structured function instead of looking for "unicorn" profiles. Nobody can be credible on all fronts all day long, from the board down and horizontally across all functions and geographies of the business. Those profiles don't exist, and pretending otherwise is just setting up the CISO to fail.

27

The Real Leadership Challenges around Cybersecurity

(9 January 2020)

The World Economic Forum's "The Cybersecurity Guide for Leaders in Today's Digital World"[16] makes an interesting read, but frankly, does it move the needle?

It does provide a solid and up-to-date summary on good cybersecurity practices and rightly puts a strong emphasis on the cultural aspects and the importance of trust.

It acknowledges the execution failure around cybersecurity:

> Current approaches make it difficult to implement comprehensive best practices across the full extent of the digital and operating environments in organizations.

This is at the heart of what we have been calling the "lost decade," as well as the product-proliferation problem that is plaguing the industry as a whole and the lives of many CISOs and their teams:

> Although organizations have many tools in place, the tools often cannot be used in concert.

It also acknowledges the transversal nature of security matters and the pressing need for the CISO and their teams to work across corporate silos (with support functions, business units, business partners, and suppliers) and to build trust with each of those. But in essence, it says very little about how to get things done, and that's the crux of the matter.

Many of those issues have been on the table for years. Some of the best practices pushed by the report (around inventories, patching, identity, continuity, or crisis management, for example) would have been included in similar reports ten years ago.

So the real questions are still very much, "Why are so many large organisations still struggling with those? And how do they remove the roadblocks that have prevented them from making progress over such a long period in spite of colossal investments?"

We wrote on this very matter for the first time in **2015**, echoing an article from McKinsey[17] and an earlier WEF report, also co-authored with McKinsey.[18]

The **2019** report makes the right diagnostic around execution, as we pointed out above, but overlooks significantly the real challenges involved in getting things right and their real underlying governance and human dimension.

The security industry needs to pivot away from "talking about things" and why they go wrong to "getting things done" and fixing things.

This is not a problem that has—or can have—a purely technological solution. Leadership and the profile of the leaders—*not technology*—are at the heart of the execution paradigm around cybersecurity in today's digital world.

People trust other people, and you need the right leaders to get things done around security, with the right balance of technical understanding, management acumen, personal gravitas, and emotional intelligence.

Where do you find such people in a context where there are hardly any role models around and most CISOs are technologists by background?

Getting them out of business roles seems the right approach, but to incentivise the right profiles, security roles have to be elevated to attract and retain the best. And to that effect, organisations and governance models have to evolve, as we pointed out in **2018**.

A clear and solid governance model established upfront is key to driving any type of large-scale security transformation programme, and old clichés such as "cybersecurity [being] everyone's responsibility in an organization" are totally meaningless in the absence of clear roles and responsibilities reflected in job descriptions and pegged to annual objectives and compensation schemes, at all levels up to the board.

These are the real challenges in today's digital world as the focus shifts, for senior executives, away from risk-and-compliance considerations towards the real execution and delivery of protective measures.

For too long, the security industry has been talking about what goes wrong without focusing enough on making sure that protective measures are in place. This is actually reflected directly—and quantitatively—in our **2019** semantic analysis of the seventeen annual Global Information Security Surveys from EY spanning the period of **2002** to **2019**, with keyword markers such as *risk, threat, compliance,* or *incident* **3.5** times more frequent across all surveys than words like *governance, budget, delivery, priority, culture,* or *skill.*

Threats evolve constantly, but old and well-established security basics do go a long way to ensure protection in many firms. In the face of escalating cyber-attacks and increasing regulatory pressure, the challenges around cybersecurity are no longer about knowing what to do but getting it done—and getting it done now and for good.

28

"Good Security Governance" Is Not a Piece of Useless Consultant Jargon

(12 March 2020)

It Is an Essential Protective Layer for Any Organisation

Irrespective of what many of us may say or write, the cybersecurity agenda remains dominated by products and technology.

Of course, the problem has a technical dimension and the protection of any firm against cyber threats will require the application of technical countermeasures at a number of levels. But there are countless tech vendors and service providers out there trying to sell their products as the silver bullet that will protect you from anything. And countless small firms are still holding simplistic views on cyber threats:

"We're fine, all our data is in the cloud."

For any organisation above a certain size, effective and efficient protection can only result from the layered application of protective measures at the people, process, and technology levels—in that order.

It has to start with people, and that doesn't mean rolling out a security awareness programme. Middle management has always had the tendency to jump straight into the solution space at the back of a simplistic analysis of the problem, but at the heart of the "people" aspects of any security strategy lie issues of corporate culture and corporate governance.

"Good security governance" is not a piece of useless consultant jargon. It is an essential protective layer for any organisation.

It ensures a visible endorsement of security values from the top down; it brings clarity around security roles, responsibilities, and accountabilities across the whole organisation; and more importantly, it is the cornerstone that "gets things done" around security through an effective and efficient layer of reporting.

Only the actual execution of security measures (i.e., the actual deployment of security processes and the technology required to support them) will protect the business. And that's where many organisations, large and small, have failed over the past decades in spite of colossal investments in cybersecurity. Security projects get deprioritised halfway through or focus only on non-existent low-hanging fruits. Over time, people get demotivated and leave, nothing gets finished, and half-baked "solutions" proliferate. According to a recent survey by Cisco, the average organisation now uses twenty different security technologies.

Let's get this straight. This is plain governance failure, and it has been plaguing organisations, large and small, around security for the best part of the last two decades.

To avoid those mistakes, break that spiral, and target the management and governance roadblocks that have prevented progress in the past, most organisations need to act at three levels:

First, get a good understanding of your security maturity posture to start with, and set realistic time frames around change. Change takes "the time it takes," and there may be no quick wins.

Then, be objective about the skills and resources that you have to deliver change, and set realistic improvement goals. Jumping straight at ineffective "virtual CISO" solutions in the hope of making the problem disappear will not help if nobody is there to execute them.

Finally, stay focused. Security transformation often involves a change in mindset that needs stability to develop and takes time to set in. Changing directions or priorities every time something happens in the business or elsewhere will simply kill any transformational momentum around security.

29

The CISO Must Be—First and Foremost—a Leader

(29 October 2020)

The Key Challenges of the Transformational CISO Are Not Technological but Managerial

There is still a vast amount of debate across the cybersecurity industry about the role of the CISO, their reporting line, their tenure, the levels of stress they're under, and the burnout epidemic they're suffering.

But looking into the actual profile of real people in those jobs, talking to them and listening to their problems, you'd quickly realise that there is a fair amount of creative writing involved in a lot that's being posted.

It is easy to write about "the CISO," thinking this is a fully established C-level role and one of the pillars of corporate governance. In practice, this is far from being the case, and the harsh reality is that the role itself is far from mature—in spite of having been in existence, in some shape or another, for about two decades.

To start with, the job title is far from universal (and has never been). A large number of variants are in use, and behind those are different role descriptions reflecting the perceptions and priorities of each organisation, which in turn find themselves reflected in the reporting line of the function.

Compounded by the natural differences between industry sectors and the security maturity levels of each company, it creates a myriad of roles, which, in the end, can have very little in common.

The reality of the role of a "CISO" reporting to a board member in a mining firm will have very little to do with the role of a "CISO" reporting two levels below the CIO in a retail organisation. Even if good practices are the same—and have been for a long time, and they still protect—putting them in place in each of those situations will have very different meanings.

So talking about "the CISO" is often a dangerous shortcut when trying to address the functional or operational aspects of the role.

The commonalities are to be found around the softer aspects of the role.

First of all, if an organisation is large enough to frame the role in CISO terms, it is likely the CISO will have a team below them. This is where many articles on the theme often go wrong. They talk about "the CISO" as if he or she was a one-man (one-woman) band, directly involved in the delivery of all aspects of their cybersecurity practice. That's rarely the case. In most organisations, the CISO is effectively a leader—structuring, organising, delegating, and orchestrating work across their team, the firm, and the multiple third parties involved in delivering or supporting the business.

The CISO should also be expected to be able to listen to business leaders across corporate silos, understand their priorities, and adjust security practices to their demands and expectations.

It is simply absurd to pretend that the CISO should have those managerial skills and at the same time expect them to constantly put out burning fires and be credible all the time—all the way across all technical stacks and across all silos of a large corporate. These unicorn profiles simply don't exist.

What is not absurd is to expect the CISO to structure and lead a team that can be credible on all those fronts, firefight, and bring along long-term change. That's the only way it can work in large firms.

Senior executives also need to understand the complexities involved in leading true security transformation across large corporates and accept the gaps that may exist at times between knowing what needs to be done to protect the business, saying it should be done, and making sure it gets done for good and across the real breadth and depth of the enterprise.

In bridging those gaps lie the real challenges of the role of the transformational CISO. Those are not technological challenges but managerial, political, and governance challenges.

To be successful, the transformational CISO needs to be—first and foremost—a leader with a good business brain, not just a firefighting technologist.

30

The Way Forward with Cybersecurity Target Operating Models

(14 October 2021)

"Process and People First, *Then* Technology" Will Always Be at the Heart of the Winning Formula Here

Many large organisations across all industries face the same challenges around cybersecurity and privacy: (**1**) growing regulatory demands compounded by escalating cyber threats and skills shortages and (**2**) a business landscape dominated by the COVID pandemic and its aftermath.

Very often, their cybersecurity operating model has simply grown organically over the years and needs reengineering or restructuring to bring it in line with evolving regulatory frameworks, align it with the industry's best practices in terms of three lines of defence and risk management, and fundamentally give senior executives assurance that their business remains adequately protected from cyber threats across people, process, and technology levels.

So what are the best ways to move forward with a cybersecurity operating model reengineering programme?

First of all, it is key to accept that the main challenges in delivering a new operating model will be leadership challenges. Creating an effective cybersecurity practice often stems from driving cultural and governance changes across an organisation. It requires a coherent leadership vision, long-term action, and a relentless drive to succeed.

That's why the approach to building the new operating model must be as interactive and iterative as possible. Engaging with all stakeholders and getting them on board from the start is key as, going forward, *they* will have to live the values of the TOM and make it happen in real life.

Also another key is understanding that a radical shake-up of approaches around cybersecurity (if that's what's required) cannot be driven simply bottom-up, or horizontally, across the business. It needs a top-down element to succeed. In that respect, a clear endorsement from senior stakeholders is also essential before the new operating model is taken to its actors for validation and implementation. Quite often, the involvement of HR will also be required if organisational arrangements or job descriptions have to change. (In some geographies or industries, employee representatives, trade unions, or workers' councils may also have to be informed or consulted.)

Finally, all too often, we see those projects failing on excessive complexity and internal politics. Simplicity, clarity, and transparency of objectives are always the best success factors in any new operating model implementation.

A cybersecurity TOM has to be seen as a high-level description of the operational *processes* that need to be in place across the cybersecurity team, the business, and the support functions to ensure adequate and regulatory-compliant protection of the organisation from cyber threats. The TOM is implemented through an organisational model, which documents specific roles (through role descriptions), accountabilities, and responsibilities (through an overall RACI mapping) for all the *people* involved in the delivery of the TOM.

Going forward, it is the new leadership structure defined as part of the new organisational model that needs to take ownership in building up action plans to deliver on the actual alignment of their respective practices with the process content of the TOM (each depending on the specific level of maturity of their area). It is in that context that they should drive the selection of the relevant *technology* products and service providers to help them with that.

There is no need for specific technical requirements to be an integral part of the TOM itself, which should remain a governance framework.

Regulatory frameworks (such as NIS, PCI DSS, GDPR, etc.) must inform the TOM, which in turn must contain the right process components to ensure that the relevant technical aspects coming from those regulations are embedded in technical policies, procedures, and standards and are properly implemented within critical systems.

A review of the content of technical policies, procedures, and standards may be required as part of the implementation of the new TOM to ensure all regulatory requirements are captured, and the TOM should also ensure that a process is in place to periodically review the technical compliance of critical systems against all the regulatory frameworks and internal policies they need to comply with.

"Process and people first, *then* technology" will always be at the heart of the winning formula here—technology to support a structured set of processes that enable people to protect the business from cyber threats.

31

Getting Things Done: The Secret Sauce for the CISO

(20 January 2022)

The Key around Cybersecurity Remains Execution, Execution, and Execution

The short tenure of the CISO continues to generate a vast amount of debate, aggravated by the COVID pandemic and the "great resignation" episode that it is inducing.

Looking beyond its reasons, the short tenure of the CISO raises another question:

What do you actually achieve in two or three years in a complex and transversal field such as cybersecurity and, in particular, in large firms?

One of my readers pointed out that some CISOs work precisely on those patterns because they are hired to put specific compliance-alignment programmes in place, and they leave when the job is done, which typically involves those two- to three-year time frames.

But what happens next? What guarantees can the business have that the next CISO will follow in the footsteps of the previous one? There are many ways to interpret and execute compliance requirements, and no doubt every cybersecurity professional has specific areas of expertise and particular pet subjects. It is not easy to step in and execute a programme of work designed by someone else. Because in my view, the key around cybersecurity remains execution, execution, and execution.

Knowing what to do is reasonably well established, and good cybersecurity practice at large still protects from most threats and still ensures a degree of compliance with most regulations. Putting it in place in real life, across the depth and breadth of the modern enterprise, is exactly where large firms have failed over the past twenty years in spite of the colossal investments in that space with tech vendors and large consultancies.

Large organisations morph constantly, either through mergers, organic expansion, or their digital transformation (not mentioning major disruptive global events such as the **2008–2009** financial crisis or the COVID pandemic). Business priorities and perceptions of risk shift accordingly, and they mechanically follow business cycles (long or short) and the visibility those cycles can afford business leaders at any given time. Those dynamics are unavoidable.

But cybersecurity works on different patterns—in particular where maturity is low and real change is required to face escalating threats.

Very often, past execution failure in that space has left scars on senior execs. Some would have seen several generations of CISOs coming in with a grandiose transformative plan asking for millions, before disappearing after a few years having achieved very little in practice in terms of real change.

The secret sauce for new CISOs will be in demonstrating that they can get things done over the right time frames by manoeuvring around the political maze of large organisations and understanding how they really operate.

This is rarely about buying more tech but more about understanding where the roadblocks are that have prevented progress in the past (and how they link with the business culture of the firm) and working out ways to remove or circumnavigate them.

It requires real-life managerial experience, personal gravitas, and political acumen—more than raw technical skills—because the CISO will not deliver change on their own and cannot be expected to.

They will do it by leading a team of experts, influencing change, and driving the execution of protective measures across the organisation and its supply chain.

More than ever, the key issue for the transformational CISO is time. It takes "the time it takes" to build the right team and drive the long-term dynamics of change around cybersecurity practices, across a more and more complex business environment also changing all the time, possibly on different cycles.

As well as business cycles, CISOs must be realistic around the perspective they give themselves to achieve change in order to place their role on the right trajectory over the medium to long term; they must also be allowed and incentivised by their business to do so.

This is much harder than it might have been ten or fifteen years ago, when the enterprise was more self-contained. To keep a bond of trust with senior stakeholders, they must focus all the time on getting things done, not just over the short term, as inevitably, tactical initiatives and firefighting requirements will emerge, but also strategically over the medium to long term as part of a structured and coherent vision for business protection endorsed by all from the board down.

32

Leading by Listening: The Other Secret Sauce for the CISO

(28 April 2022)

The Times Have Gone When the CISO Had to Explain What Cybersecurity Was about and the Value It Brought

In the face of non-stop cyber-attacks, and the urgency of change around cybersecurity practices in large firms, the CISO has to be, first and foremost, a leader. The role can no longer be limited to its technical content. Cybersecurity has a technical dimension, of course, and a fundamental one; but it was never just about tech.

Delivering real and lasting change around cybersecurity across the complexity of large organisations has to involve all corporate silos: business units, geographies and support functions, as well as IT and suppliers. Bringing them all on board with a common and coherent cybersecurity agenda cannot be something arbitrary or predetermined.

It can only be built on the basis of the situation and priorities of all stakeholders. They will buy into it if there is something in it for them; they will resent it and drag their feet if it comes across as something arbitrary imposed by the head office.

So understanding the firm's governance dynamics—and frankly, the internal politics—will be key for the CISO in large organisations to calibrate the change agenda to a level the fabric of the business can tolerate. That has to start by listening to key stakeholders, understanding their challenges and priorities around cybersecurity, as well as the general situation of the business.

The times have gone when the CISO had to explain what cybersecurity was about and the value it brought. All business leaders would have been exposed to the concept of cyber threats and cyber-attacks given the level of media coverage over the last decade. Many would have faced their impact in other roles. They will have a view on the matter and, quite often, a balanced business view of what to do—or not to do—about it.

Too many CISOs jump straight at technical recipes or try to apply ready-made solutions they have used or seen elsewhere.

"What can I do to help you?" should be the opening question for the CISO in their exchanges with stakeholders.

Listening to the answers, accepting them for what they are (irrespective of the CISO's personal inclinations), structuring them into a strategic change agenda, and most importantly, delivering on the expectations created are the pillars on which a successful CISO should build their practice (in particular the incoming CISO).

At this point, we start to see emerging a profile of a certain type for the CISO that will be key for the role to be successful. The profile of an individual who has sufficient management experience and political acumen to navigate the complex governance waters of large firms, the ability to listen without jumping to a predetermined agenda, and the ability to deliver on expectations in a complex and transversal field.

Where maturity is low and aggressive change is required around cybersecurity practices, those attributes are more important, in my view, than the native ability to understand the technology context in which cybersecurity is rooted.

Of course, these are attributes that some technologists can develop naturally over the course of a career in tech (in particular in senior roles). But fundamentally, they are leadership attributes that come with time and experience.

The key for me is the quality of listening and building some realistic and achievable consensus around the expectations collected from stakeholders without always dropping to the lowest common denominator (Generally, that's awareness development in the cybersecurity space—whatever that means in practice.)

It's a difficult task, but it is the essence of true leadership. Going back to the basic meaning of the word, a *leader* is someone who is followed, and people generally follow when they have the sense that they will get something in return.

These are the simple dynamics successful CISOs have to build around cybersecurity.

33

Three Keys to Understand the Cybersecurity Skills Gap (and Deal with it)

(28 July 2022)

Look at It in All Its Dimensions before Jumping to Ready-Made Solutions

You don't have to go far to find cybersecurity professionals complaining about skills shortages, but the problem has several dimensions which have to be understood and mapped out, before we can start to figure out possible solutions.

First of all, the problem is absolutely real, but it goes way beyond a lack of educational or training opportunities, and acting at those levels only will not fix it.

The cybersecurity skills gap has its roots in the avalanche of cyber-attacks we have seen over the past decade and the awakening of most industries to the reality and virulence of cyber threats.

Many firms which did not have a cybersecurity practice ten years ago now have one or are building one. This is creating an escalating demand for cyber talents, at all levels, from CISOs to developers, architects, trainers, auditors, or pen testers.

But the fact that the demand for talent outstrips the supply is not the only factor here.

In fact, the cybersecurity industry has a perennial image problem: The image of a complex technical niche; something for geeks and nerds; the negative image of "the-guy-who-says-no."

Of course, those are clichés, but the security industry and its tech vendors do little to redress them. Just look out for the padlock and hoodie imagery they constantly use.

The imagery is also massively male-dominated and coupled with the already prevalent lack of diversity in tech and in STEM, I doubt it acts as an attractive factor for women and girls.

Those are the cornerstones of a talent acquisition problem, which can only be dealt with by moving away from the purely technical positioning of cyber roles, showcasing the full spectrum of jobs and careers the industry can offer, and pushing forward role models from more diverse backgrounds.

But it is only one side of the whole skills gap landscape.

The cybersecurity industry has also a significant talent retention problem, which is rooted in a different set of factors.

Many entry-level jobs are simply too repetitive and boring. This is a direct consequence of the fact that many security operational processes have been reversely-engineered organically and tactically around the capabilities of countless tools. Without any overarching view in many cases, they have remained excessively manual and are often inefficient and disjointed.

Nobody joins cybersecurity to end up cutting and pasting data into Excel sheets or to produce useless reports simply designed to put ticks in compliance boxes. But that's the life of many young analysts; they leave as soon as they find something more attractive, and they don't come back.

At a higher level, CISOs are feeling a different type of pain.

Most have been forced into a constant firefighting mode by the non-stop cyber-attacks of the past ten years. Now that the penny is dropping in board room and the "when-not-if" paradigm is taking root, they are being pushed into an impossible role, where they are expected to be credible one day in front of the board, the next in front of pen testers, the day after, in front of regulators or auditors, and so on.

Firefighting technical problems does not lead to the development of the type of managerial experience or political acumen which is now expected of many CISOs. They struggle with a situation for which they have been poorly prepared by the last decade, and stories abound of mental health issues and burnout.

Those aspects are more difficult to deal with than the talent acquisition aspects, because here, it is cybersecurity practices that need to change.

It has to start with the decluttering of cybersecurity estates and the streamlining of operational processes around fewer tools.

Automation is key, but "clever automation," aimed at reducing the number of tools in use and optimising process efficiency.

The objective here should be to free up time for a smaller number of analysts to perform less repetitive tasks so that they can be involved in the more challenging roles for which they have been hired (maybe looking towards threat intelligence or incident forensics).

Successful action at this level would have an impact around acquisition and retention rates.

At the top, cybersecurity functions have to be reorganised and redistributed to remove excessive dependency on key profiles and other bottlenecks.

The profile of the CISO has to be raised—at least in large organizations—and the role has to be seen as a true leadership role, orchestrating work across a team of experts, as well as across the firm and its supply chain.

In many cases, it may require expanding the cybersecurity team, but it should also force to redesign it functionally in a structured way around some form of operating model, away from the legacy and project-led type of organisations still prevailing today in many firms.

Overall, the cybersecurity skills gap is not a fatality, but it is key to look at it in all its dimensions before jumping to ready-made solutions and dealing with it may involve facing a number of deep-rooted and inconvenient truths for many organizations and the security industry at large.

34

The Three Traits of Successful Cybersecurity Leaders

(8 September 2022)

The Cybersecurity Transformative Urgency in Many Firms Forces to Look Beyond Traditional Technology Profiles

Cybersecurity has risen to prominence on the agenda of many business leaders.

Large firms have been struggling with it for decades in spite of significant investments in that space, but for many across the boardroom, the realisation has taken place over the past few years that cyber-attacks were simply a matter of "*when*, not *if*."

In many organizations and industries where cybersecurity maturity has been low for decades, large scale transformative initiatives are shaping up, but in the current context of the global enterprise, with supply chains disrupted by the post-pandemic chaos, climate change and geopolitical imbalances, leading those initiatives and successfully delivering them requires a certain type of profile, which may be far from the profile of your traditional CISO.

First of all, we have reached a point in terms of urgency and complexity where successful cybersecurity leaders have to be trusted business insiders.

That goes way beyond the usual cliches by which the CISO "has to talk to the business in their own language" in order to paint security to them as an "enabler." Those ships sailed long ago. Cybersecurity is now an imperative in the face of global and virulent threats that can simply take your business down. Period.

Business leaders want to be given assurances by somebody they can trust, that their activities are adequately protected in terms of prevention, detection, reaction and recovery. So cybersecurity leaders cannot be technology outsiders anymore; they have to be—and be seen as—experienced and trusted business leaders; it means understanding the day-to-day of the business, its real dynamics and challenges, and where the real pain points are for other business leaders.

That's the basis of a common understanding on which trust will be built, and that trust platform is the only platform on which successful cybersecurity leaders can build the long-term foundations of any transformative efforts.

Second, cybersecurity leaders have to be good listeners.

That's the other key ingredient they will need to drive a successful and lasting transformation.

Going back to the most basics of leadership, you are a leader when people follow you, and most people will follow you if there is something in it for them: Listening to the expectation of all stakeholders around cybersecurity, taking into account their constraints and their own priorities, and embedding those into the transformation road map is the best recipe to build endorsement and acceptance around cybersecurity transformative objectives.

Such acceptance, coupled with—and maybe born out of—the trust of business leaders, will form the bedrock on which the execution of the cybersecurity transformative road map can succeed.

But one final ingredient is also required: time

Cybersecurity leaders have to be mid to long-term players and visionaries.

We see too many CISOs changing jobs after two to three years[19] out of frustration, having achieved very little apart from kick-starting a number of technical pet projects. This is not transformative in essence and has contributed to the long-term stagnation of many organizations around cybersecurity matters.

Even on the bedrock of trust from business leaders and their acceptance of long-term objectives, real and lasting transformation across a field as complex and transversal as cybersecurity can only take time, in particular where initial maturity levels are low.

In large organizations, this could mean navigating across multiple business cycles while keeping priorities set on the same long term transformative goals.

Those are capabilities which come with experience and require significant political acumen, as well as the personal commitment and willingness of the cybersecurity leaders to stay the course (and the commitment from senior executives that they will be incentivised to do so).

Readers may notice that I have hardly mentioned technology or technical attributes so far.

Of course, cybersecurity has a technical dimension, but it is a common mistake to reduce it to a pure technical discipline, while the key challenges large organizations have been struggling with over the years are at its interface with business and support functions, in terms of cultural acceptance or priority setting.

In my opinion, we have come to the point in terms of transformative urgency in many firms where cybersecurity leaders have to rise above the traditional technical content of their role.

They have to be just that: leaders, active, credible, and audible across all corporate silos, and not just technology experts.

35

Talent and Governance, Not Technology, Are Key to Drive Change around Cybersecurity

(24 November 2022)

You Are Not Going to Fix Your Cybersecurity Problems by Buying More Tech

For the last twenty years, large organizations have been spending significant amounts of money on cybersecurity products and solutions, on managed services, or with consultancies large and small.

Yet maturity levels remain elusive: McKinsey surveyed more than 100 firms in 2021[20] and found that 70% of their sample "had yet to fully advance to a mature-based approach." These results are regularly matched by similar reports and also by the anecdotal evidence we can see in the field every day.

Consensus amongst cybersecurity professionals seems to point towards low maturity levels being a consequence of under-investment in that space.

I have rarely seen that hypothesis thoroughly tested and would argue the problem is broader.

In essence, cybersecurity good practices have been well established for the best part of the last twenty years and, to a large extent, continue to provide in most industries an acceptable level of protection against most threats and an acceptable level of compliance against most regulations.

Over a period of time of such duration, security maturity levels should have developed naturally if they had been carried forward and fostered by genuine business protection values.

Clearly, in many organizations, it has not been the case, or not to a sufficient extent.

In 2019, the Security Transformation Research Foundation conducted a large-scale piece of research[21] analysing the semantic content of seventeen Annual Global Security Surveys from EY, looking at the frequency of keywords and the evolution of the language used.

The research shows very clearly two decades emerging:

The first decade of this century, dominated by *risk and compliance* considerations: Security being seen mostly as a balancing act between compliance requirements, risk appetite and costs;

The second decade of this century, dominated by *threats and incidents* considerations: Security becoming a necessary fire-fighting practice against constant attacks, in a context of massive technological change driven by mobile devices and the cloud.

None of those are positive drivers: The first one is restrictive and, taken to some extreme, has led to some security practices becoming mere box-checking or window-dressing practices; the second one is short-termist and technology-focused.

More importantly, both isolate cybersecurity from business cycles and business levers.

To me, that's the heart of the matter, and the main reason why maturity levels have remained low in spite of all investments:

Security was always seen as external to the business, locked in a compliance or a technology niche, where it was also alien (compliance and risk people focus on business aspects; technologists have always been incentivized to deliver on features and performance, not on controls).

This is the cultural cycle which has engineered a chronic problem of talent alienation and adverse prioritization, leading to execution failure around security programmes, the historic reluctance of senior executives to commit to large scale investments, and the continuing avalanche of breaches.

Now, things are changing: The "when-not-if" paradigm around cyber-attacks has taken root in many boardrooms, and the transformational urgency around cybersecurity practices has been evidenced in many firms by the Covid pandemic and the dependencies it created on digital services.

But it would be a mistake for the board to continue to believe that this is a mere technological problem that is going to be solved just by adding more layers of technology solutions (zero-trust, MFA, AI or whatever it might be).

Key here is to acknowledge the cultural and governance context in which the historic under-achievement of many firms around cybersecurity is rooted.

For genuine and lasting change to take place, cybersecurity now needs to be visibly linked to business values from the board down.

It means cybersecurity ownership being visibly and credibly established at Board level, and cybersecurity objectives being visibly and credibly driven from there, injecting raw business talent into the mix by showcasing that success as a cybersecurity transformation agent can be a career accelerator, and that those roles should not be seen as a dead-end or a second best.

For firms genuinely trying to break away from two decades of failure around cybersecurity, talent and governance have to be the real levers, not technology.

36

The Momentum behind the Role of the Chief Security Officer

(13 July 2023)

It Starts to Make Sense to Evolve the Role of the CISO and Return It to Its Native Technical Content

In many large organizations, defining and structuring a chief security officer role (CSO) is starting to make more and more sense.

The concept is not new and has generally been used to encompass all security aspects a firm may be faced with—physical and digital.

It is time to look at it under a broader angle in many large companies.

Broadly speaking, the role of the CISO (chief information security officer) has failed to drive change and build sufficient momentum around cybersecurity issues over the last two decades.

This is mostly driven by an excessive technological focus, which has imprisoned the CISOs in technical firefighting and prevented them from adequately reaching across the business and developing sufficient management and political acumen.

Today, as the penny is dropping across board rooms, and the “when-not-if” paradigm dominates around cyber-attacks, they are trapped in an impossible role where it is expected of them to be audible and credible across the depth and breadth of the enterprise, from boards and regulators to pen testers and developers.

No profile can reach effectively across a spectrum of skills that wide, and it starts to make sense to evolve the role by separating the components it has been accumulating over the years.

This is made all the more important by the increasing regulatory and reporting pressure, which has been mounting steadily for all businesses over the past decade across all industry sectors: It started around data privacy with the GDPR in Europe and many equivalent state regulations in the U.S. Reporting demands are now developing at federal level, and governance aspects are also coming under increased scrutiny.

This regulatory intervention is simply the result of devastating cyber-attacks, that have threatened or impacted key infrastructure components, and brought under broad daylight the extent of the disruption those types of events can cause.

As a result, senior executives have started to look beyond traditional business continuity approaches, to pay more and more attention to resilience concepts.[22]

All those aspects (cybersecurity, regulatory compliance, resilience) have one major component in common: they are cross-functional and require a reach across corporate silos to be effective and efficient.

I would add that on those three fronts, the risk dimension is increasingly becoming obsolete in my opinion: this is no longer about events that may or may not happen, but simply a business reality that has to be factored in the way the firm operates.

Those are the factors combining to build momentum behind a redefined role for the CSO, encompassing oversight of physical and cybersecurity, but also data privacy, operational resilience and their associated compliance and regulatory reporting obligations.

A role of that magnitude in most firms can only make sense and function from the top of the firm, as part of the most senior business leadership team.

It has to be seen as a senior management role, focused on building the necessary cross-functional channels, ensuring they remain active, and bridging across business and political issues by bringing sufficient gravitas and credibility around the matters involved.

It is—of course—a role for a seasoned executive, motivated overall by the protection of the business from active threats, able to take an elevated long-term view where required, over and above the short-term fluctuations of any business.

We are miles away from the current role of most CISOs (our starting point), but it does not make their job any less relevant.

To the contrary, it offers an opportunity to refocus the role of the CISO on its native technical content and give it a renewed currency by stripping off the corporate layers added over the years, for which its holders—most of them technologists by trade or background—were poorly prepared.

A dual reporting line to both the CSO and the CIO would then make sense for the CISO and ensure a degree of independent oversight in industries where those aspects around separation of duties are scrutinised.

This type of model is essential in my view to drive large-scale programmes, where cybersecurity maturity is low and urgent transformation is required across the cybersecurity practices of an organisation.

The combination of the top-down and cross-functional influence of the CSO with the technical reach of the CISO should be key to create and maintain the momentum required to deliver change, and break business resistance where it happens.

37

Is It Time to Accept That the Current Role of the CISO Has Failed?

(17 August 2023)

It Has Become Too Complex to Carry for the Profile of People It Attracts

The role of the chief information security officer (CISO) has been in existence for the best part of the last thirty years.

Infosec legends say that it was first created for Steve Katz at Citibank in 1995, and indeed it has had some form of operational reality for over twenty-five years in many firms, starting with the financial sector, pharmaceuticals, and energy firms, then spreading gradually to all industries over two decades.

I have been involved with the cybersecurity industry for the best part of that period, but, as far as I can remember, I have always heard CISOs complaining: Lack of resources, wrong reporting line, adverse prioritisation of security matters by the business, constant firefighting and burnout, talent and skills shortages... The list is long, but nobody seems to question why.

In fact, there are inherent problems with the historical construction of the role.

First of all, it was never conceived as a true C-level role. It probably originated in the minds of some organisation consultants, but it never developed any true C-level weight. Even if it may hurt some, it is my opinion that it was very rarely given to people with true C-level potential.

Second, it was almost always given to technologists by trade or background, although the underlying matter is unequivocally cross-functional and has always been: you cannot be successful around identity and access management for example without the involvement of HR and business units and the ability to reach credibly towards them.

As far as the evolution of the role is concerned, endemic business short-termism did the rest: As we established with The Security Transformation Research Foundation in 2019, for the first decade of this century, the prime focus of the role was on risk and compliance, cybersecurity being seen as a necessary compromise between regulatory obligations, risk appetite and costs. It is not uncommon to see organisations and professionals still stuck in that sort of paradigm, but it is broadly outdated.

For the last decade, with the emergence of cloud solutions, the acceleration of the digital transformation, and the accentuation driven by the COVID pandemic—not to mention the more recent supply chain disruptions or craze for generative AI—the world has seen an unprecedented increase in cyber threats. Most CISOs have been unable to get out of firefighting mode for a long-enough period to address the systemic changes they would need to put in place to truly move their companies forward.

For many, this constant level of stress has become simply the nature of the job. They think it is normal for them to be expected to be credible one day in front of the board, the next in front of regulators, the next in front of pen testers or developers, while at the same time, leading and managing their people and meeting the firm's reporting obligations in that space.

They don't seem to understand that it is simply impossible to do a good job at all those levels in today's context, that they are exposing themselves by accepting it, and that it is the root of their mental health issues, and the endemic short tenure plaguing the role, which, in turn, is the root cause of the long-term stagnation of cybersecurity maturity in many firms.

They become easy scapegoats when something goes wrong, and tomorrow may even be personally liable in court in case of breach depending how legislations develop.

After years of gradual marginalisation and in the face of endless breaches, I think it is time to start accepting that the current construction around the role of the CISO is not working anymore in many firms.

It has aggregated a mixed set of responsibilities and accountabilities without building up the right organisational and managerial momentum, and many CISOs are simply being set up to fail. The role has simply become too complex to carry for the profile of the people it attracts.

To break this spiral, the logic is now to split the role, stripping off the managerial layers it has accumulated over the years and refocusing the role of the CISO on its native technical content so that it can lead effectively and efficiently at that level, while at the same time bringing up a CSO role (chief security officer) able to reach across business, IT and support function to take in charge the level of corporate complexity cybersecurity is now amalgamating in large firms.

It is time to accept as well that the bottom-up constructions by which CISOs have tried to “convince” senior executives of the importance of cybersecurity over the years have mostly failed due to an excessive technical focus, and the lack of obvious success —aggravated by their short-tenures and in spite of colossal investments for some firms.

An elevated CSO role should be able to build a peer-to-peer dialogue with senior executives and board members, listening to their expectations and constraints, and embedding the protection of the business from cyber threats at the heart of their agenda.

That’s likely to be a sound way forward in many firms over the coming years, instead of propping up a CISO role that maybe has served its purpose, but now needs to evolve.

The CISO and the CIO

38

The Three Cybersecurity Governance Challenges of the CIO

(3 February 2015–21 April 2016)

How Does Information Security End Up in the Portfolio of the CIO?

Historically, the CIO has ended up in charge of information security in many organisations because many tactical measures required to deal with cyber threats lie in the IT field.

For decades, executive management has lived with the perception that information security breaches have a low frequency and low impact. To be fair, the size of the risk map that board members have to respond to has increased enormously over the past ten to fifteen years, and today, information-related risks are still just one small part of that overall risk map. Geopolitical and financial risks have escalated, as well as environmental risks, which have become more and more prominent in recent years. When coupled with endemic short-termist or compliance-obsessed management tendencies, cyber risks have often failed to be picked up on the board of directors' radar up to now.

Occasionally, the topic might have been escalated by auditors or regulators, but overall, it was seen as part of the normal way of running a large and complex organisation where many things could go wrong every day.

A number of very high-profile data breaches in recent years (Target, Sony, Ashley Madison, TalkTalk, etc.) have started to change that perception. However, many board members still tend to see cybersecurity breaches as something technical they don't really understand.

Can the CIO Make a Difference?

With the right attitude, the CIO can be a real driving force behind significant information security improvements.

In our opinion, it is not necessary to be overly concerned with separation-of-duties considerations. In most organisations, the CIO is a respected executive—as either a board member or reporting directly to a board member—and is entrusted with the management of large teams and very significant budgetary responsibilities.

The risk is often greater for an arbitrary separation of duties to fuel internal politics and paralyse effective decision-making.

What are the factors shaping the relationship between information security and the CIO?

First of all, the CIO needs to be control-minded for the relationship to function, or at least should have an interest in information security matters and some grasp of the concepts involved.

If the CIO is not personally or politically capable of looking beyond financial or IT delivery matters, information security will often be delegated down and, over time, turn into a mere box-checking exercise.

While this may randomly protect the organisation to a level that satisfies executive management, it will also perpetuate the poor-practice belief that cyber threats aren't really that important—with auditors and regulators continuing to run the control agenda.

This is a situation that we observe constantly in the field, with organisations failing to properly address the ongoing threats they face—in spite of spending huge sums of money on audit or compliance-driven programmes of work or in knee-jerk responses to incidents.

If the CIO is control-minded and wants to make a difference, he or she needs a clear definition of their information security role and a clear remit.

It's important to remember that information does not only exist in digital form. It also has a physical form, and more importantly, it is constantly manipulated by people as part of business processes. When it comes to personal information, there is often a complex legal framework to comply with, particularly for global organisations.

Protecting information requires concerted action at a physical, functional, and technical level. But the CIO can only be directly responsible for the technical aspects of information protection.

How Does a CIO Implement a Successful Approach to Information Security?

The CIO needs to send the right messages in three directions—upwards, downwards, and sideways—and will face key management challenges in each case.

Managing Upwards: How to Engage with Board Members on Information Security Matters?

CIOs will find that executive management is becoming more and more receptive to the cybersecurity messages being hammered out by politicians and the media. Board members might also have been scared by recent data breaches and the aggressive media coverage that surrounded them.

Many board members have started to understand that, even if significant information security breaches still have a relatively low frequency (all things considered), this frequency has increased dramatically over recent years. In addition to this, the impact information security breaches can have has become more and more difficult to quantify due to the increasing dependency on third parties and the tremendous amount of media and political interest that has been building up. Losses can easily run into the tens of millions, and more importantly, brand reputation and customer trust can be left irrecoverably damaged by cyber-attacks.

The message from the CIO to the board must be clear: Where the problem is rooted in decades of neglect, underinvestment, and adverse prioritisation, there can be no miracle solution—technical or otherwise. Avoiding these breaches, or dealing with them, will require coherent action over time—across the whole organisation. For this to be successful, each party involved (business units, HR, legal, IT, etc.) needs to have a clear understanding of its role and remit.

This is why a medium- to long-term strategy and a solid cross-silo governance model are essential to driving cybersecurity transformation. Ideally, it should also include a commitment from the board to medium- to long-term funding, in order to allow all parties to plan information security delivery over the necessary time frames.

The first challenge of the CIO is to drive this message upwards in the organisation—to the board of directors and its members.

Cybersecurity is also inherently a global problem, and only with a clear and unambiguous vision coming from the top can the CIO be successful at delivering complex technical security platforms across all operational divisions and geographies of a large organisation.

Managing Downwards: How Do You Close the Gap between Security and IT?

At the same time, CIOs must look without complacency at their own organisation.

Technologists are almost always trained and incentivised to prioritise delivering functionality, often seeing security controls as a pain point or a limitation to their work. There is no natural cultural fit between security and IT. As a result, information security is rarely seen as a powerful career path—and it can even have the tendency to alienate talent.

The profile of the individual who is going to drive information security across the CIO's organisation and the enterprise as a whole, the chief information security officer (or CISO), is fundamental.

Due to the inherent complexity and cross-silo nature of the topic, the CISO must be an experienced executive with significant management background and gravitas, as he or she will have to build internal respect and leadership in order to be successful.

The CISO will also face the task of addressing the short-term tactical problems that will unavoidably stem from incidents or legacy situations—while driving the medium- to long-term information security vision the CIO should be building with executive management.

These are attributes of seniority that are fairly rare, internally or externally. The CIO is not likely to find them among young executives, ex-consultants, or ex-auditors.

Acknowledging the specifics of the role and finding the right CISO is the second key challenge for the CIO—and the most difficult.

It will take time and may require the personal and political courage to look at current organisational arrangements and restructure them.

The reporting line of the CISO is also essential, with the lack of cultural fit between security and IT being a key element in that respect. In order to be taken seriously across an organisation, information security must be seen as a native part of the CIO's responsibilities—and it is absolutely essential for the CISO to have a direct reporting line to the CIO. Blending information security with the portfolio of another IT executive, or pushing the CISO role further down in the org charts, is simply a recipe for failure—fuelling the deprioritisation of information security matters and further widening the gap between security and IT.

But with the right seniority and profile, and at the right place in the CIO's organisation, the CISO—who should naturally navigate across corporate silos—can be a very powerful political ally for the CIO.

Managing sideways, how does the CIO lead themselves to success?

Finally, in order to be successful in establishing an effective information security practice, the CIO must remain focused and in control of their own cybersecurity priorities over the medium- to long-term period.

Where cybersecurity problems are rooted in decades of adverse prioritisation or underinvestment, there can be no quick fix. Change can only take time and relentless drive.

Historically, audit functions have strongly interfered with the control agenda of many organisations and driven numerous tactical decisions—often justified by the absence of any strategic security vision or interest coming from executive management. Now it may be other senior stakeholders stepping in, asking for knee-jerk action in response to some high-profile data breach happening elsewhere.

The problem is that these people can also lack real-life field experience, often causing them to single out arbitrary issues and ignore the cybersecurity bigger picture and how complex it can be to get things moving in that space. These arbitrary issues can confuse priorities and can easily cause a long-term information security plan to head off on a tangent.

The third challenge faced by CIOs is in tackling this issue. The CIO needs to manage the relationship with auditors and senior stakeholders firmly and intelligently in order to remain in control of the cybersecurity agenda.

First, the CIO must ensure that all parties are aware of the broader control agenda set for the whole organisation and of the vital need to work within it. But the CIO must also have the confidence, together with the personal gravitas and political acumen, to push back on arbitrary issues that do not fit within the broader control agenda.

All this can only work as part of a coherent medium- to long-term information security strategy and governance model—unambiguously signed off by all parties.

39

Cybersecurity and the Incoming CIO: What's Really Going On?

(22 September 2016)

Here is a scenario we are seeing far too often in the field:

A new CIO comes in, identifies security problems, then nothing serious happens.

At best, some tactical initiative would be pushed forward to answer outstanding audit issues, or a big gun of the industry would be called in to deliver countless slides, out of which some hypothetical "quick wins" would be enacted to calm the board about cyber risks.

Why so many incoming CIOs seem to be so cautious on cybersecurity at the early stages of their tenure, in the face of glaring internal issues and constant reminders of data breaches in the news, is a worrying question. Their answers are invariably the same:

- They have more pressing problems elsewhere.
- They have bigger fishes to fry.
- The business won't wear it.
- The budgets are too tight.
- A new organisation is due to be announced "next week" or "next month."
- They'll "come to it" in due course, "next year," or "once the new CEO has decided where priorities should be."

In most large firms, these have to be seen as poor excuses. The CIO would often have hundreds of staff in their teams, tens of millions in annual budget, and a significant direct sign-off limit consistent with their board-level reporting line.

In a context where everything runs in parallel and everything costs money, the truth is that addressing cybersecurity shortcomings from the start is often a mere matter of priorities for any new CIO—priorities and personal courage. The reality is that the underlying security problems are invariably complex and involve a combination of organisational, technical, and managerial issues:

- Legacy InfoSec teams buried in the org chart, poorly staffed, poorly skilled, and forced into constant tactical and technical firefighting.
- Expensive technical security initiatives half deployed and poorly sold to business and IT staff because they were always designed as point solutions to specific problems in the absence of any bigger picture and, as a result, perceived as a burden and a waste of money.
- Senior management very willing to accept cyber risk as a top risk for the firm but, at the same time, themselves

refusing to adhere to basic rules of security hygiene when it comes to mobile devices or passwords (rules that they are otherwise happy to impose on all other members of the staff).

Standing up to the board on those matters to tell them what they need to have, not just give them what they want, takes some gravitas but should elevate the role of the CIO, not diminish it. For most large and complex firms, if cybersecurity maturity is low because nothing structured has ever been done in that space in the past, a data breach is merely a question of time. And given current levels of media and political interest on these topics, gambling on it could be costly in a number of ways (financially or reputationally for the firm, personally for the CEO), as amply demonstrated by the TalkTalk data breach in the United Kingdom in **2015**.

Not only is waiting for something to happen a dangerous game, but it often leads to absurd knee-jerk reactions that simply perpetuate the preexisting short-termist approach to security without creating any fundamental change momentum.

Incoming CIOs should not be scared to launch into a cybersecurity transformation programme at the early stages of their tenure if they see a need, and good governance around cybersecurity is fast becoming "the most important criterion for an organisation to feel well protected," as highlighted by a short survey from recruitment firm Boyden collating feedback from thirty-six top CIOs.[23]

Of course, there may be legacy people problems to resolve, and these may take time, but overall, building a sound security organisation and operating model able to reach and operate across the whole firm is often the best start. Many security problems cut across corporate silos (into HR, legal, and business disciplines), and a strong CISO with true management experience—not a mere firefighter or a technology hobbyist—can be a strong ally for the CIO in broader transformational battles across IT or the business.

40
Why Reporting to the CIO Is Increasingly a Problem in Large Firms

(16 June 2016)

Our view, built on years of direct field experience, is that the reporting line of the CISO has to be at board level and must be driven by clear underlying objectives shared unambiguously by the CISO and their boss—whoever that happens to be in the organisation.

It could be a need to increase cybersecurity maturity. It could be a need to demonstrate compliance to regulators. It could be a need to demonstrate to shareholders that the right things are being done following a data breach. It could be all of the above, but in all cases, the boss has to be prepared and willing to throw their weight into the battle unambiguously and consistently.

In an ideal world, it's their boss's flawless commitment to cybersecurity values that the CISO does leverage on to drive change, coupled with their own gravitas, political astuteness, and management acumen.

In our opinion, this articulation is the strongest to deliver lasting change, and it is considerably stronger than multiple reporting lines or dotted lines often aimed at avoiding perceived "conflicts of interest" but in practice are poorly understood and highly vulnerable to internal politics.

However, it is also a construction that is coming under pressure in many firms when it comes to the relationship between the CIO and the CISO, and it is a direct result of the pressure being applied to CIOs by executive management to deliver "digital transformation."

Many CIOs struggle, frankly, with such pressure. One day they are told by auditors or regulators to focus on getting the basics right and keeping legacy systems going. The next day they are told by their board to be more "agile," to work faster, and to "do digital." And they have to square that circle with the teams they have—not necessarily best equipped in terms of skills—and often at the back end of several years of cost-cutting that might have introduced dysfunctional offshoring arrangements and opened the door to countless "shadow IT" situations within the business.

Where does cybersecurity fit in all this? Very often, the answer is quite obvious: it doesn't—until something goes wrong. And it is exactly in this context that maintaining a reporting line to the CIO is increasingly a problem for the CISO.

If the CIO is no longer able to prioritise cybersecurity all the time towards the top of the list because of the pressure of the "digital transformation," then the reporting line of the CISO must shift to another board member who can—and quickly.

This is a very serious matter precisely because the "digital transformation" itself is introducing, at a very fast pace, countless new cybersecurity issues—from customer data privacy considerations to the security of IoT devices. These are best addressed from the start instead of retrofitted later.

A strong CISO is key in times like these and can be an essential part to engineering cybersecurity as a competitive advantage. But they need to be highly visible in the organisation and backed unambiguously by a board member who cares.

41

Reporting Line of the CISO: What Really Matters

(4 May 2017)

Corporate Culture and the Profile of the CISO Are Key, Over and Above Any Arbitrary Organisational Consideration

It is astonishing to see the amount of interest still surrounding the reporting line of the CISO. The fact that it is still a topic of serious discussion among security professionals is teaching us a few things about the role and its perception:

Is the role properly established, identified, and accepted in organisations? Or is it (still) seen as some form of arbitrary (and bureaucratic) imposition by regulators?

In theory, there should be no debate in the face of a constant avalanche of cybersecurity issues in the news. The need to protect the firm from cyber threats should be obvious to the board.

One board member should own the problem and delegate the coordination and delivery of the necessary protective measures to one of their direct reports. Period.

At this point, there are several options available for the reporting line, depending on the cybersecurity challenges the firm is facing and its digital footprint. These lead to different role profiles for the CISO, which we have analysed in an earlier article.

The right reporting line is always the one that works and gets things done, not an arbitrary one that creates barriers, engenders politics, and hinders delivery (even if it ticks audit or compliance boxes).

In practice, however, things rarely work so simply. It is not uncommon to encounter problems in understanding around cybersecurity issues at board level, leading to adverse prioritisation. Equally, there are often skills issues at board level minus 1, leading the difficulties in appointing a CISO with the right profile for the role. Looking externally often fails (particularly in large firms) because of the intrinsically horizontal nature of the CISO role and the need to understand how the firm really works in order to navigate across corporate silos, be credible, and make things happen around security.

All this often leads to placing the CISO role by default in the portfolio of the CIO or the CTO, even if those are not board members.

This is not a problem in itself, particularly in firms that have a strong technological bias, and there are many good ways to make this work efficiently, as we have suggested in the past.

Many security professionals who have an interest in this topic seem concerned with issues in the separation of duties and the fact that conflicts of priorities may emerge between the CISO and their boss in those configurations.

It is true that CIOs and CTOs are coming under a lot of pressure in relation to the digital transformation, and some may struggle to dedicate time, attention, or priorities to security matters. But it does not make the option a bad one by itself.

Culture is key in all this, as well the personality and the gravitas of the individuals involved.

In today's world, if a CIO or a CTO is not capable of prioritising in favour of cybersecurity matters in the face of constant incidents across all industry sectors, frankly, it is likely that no one in the firm will, and wherever you place the reporting line of the CISO, you will be encountering similar cultural issues.

Those could be rooted in endemic short-termism or, very simply, in poor management or governance practices at the top. But if the CIO or the CTO is cybersecurity-aware and control-minded, then the CISO could become a very strong ally for them and help them forge a truly transformative vision.

Of course, the seniority and the gravitas of the individuals involved are essential. The CISO role is transversal and complex and needs to be given the right profile internally to attract the right senior professional. This is a role where real-life managerial experience is key to working autonomously, navigating around all pitfalls, and fighting the right political battles at the right time. All these aspects are probably more important than raw technical skills.

This is not a job for a junior consultant, a junior IT executive, or an ex-auditor, irrespective of their potential. This is a hard job that requires an experienced pair of hands with personal and political gravitas.

Issues around conflicts of priorities often emerge where both the CIO and the CISO lack that gravitas or political acumen: the CIO, not willing to face the business over security issues, and the CISO, not willing to confront the CIO over it. These are not intrinsic issues that are inherent to the reporting line but personal matters that relate to the managerial attitudes of those involved.

The CISO needs to be a credible field executive who really knows how the firm works, reporting to a control-minded senior executive at board level. Little else matters, and certainly not arbitrary separation-of-duties considerations.

42

Why Are We Still Talking about the Reporting Line of the CISO?

(10 May 2018)

The Right Reporting Line Is the One That Works—Period

Why are so many organisations and security professionals still worried about the reporting line of the CISO? This is one of the oldest and most consistent debates agitating the security industry, and it looks far from resolved.

It has been polluted for decades by arbitrary and simplistic views on "separation of duties" and alleged "conflicts of interest." But those views often come from sectors of the corporate spectrum with a fairly theoretical idea of how an organisation should operate and rarely reflect the reality of how large organisations function.

The truth is that people work with people and that strong organisations are bound by trust, not distrust.

So the reporting line of the CISO must be a means, not an end—a means to enable the security practice of an organ to deliver on its objectives, whatever those may be. And that, of course, implies first that the security practice needs to have clear objectives: a clear sense of purpose, a mission statement, an operating and governance model, and a medium- to long-term road map with clear milestones. It cannot be just a random list of projects driven by audit observations.

The reporting line of the CISO must be high enough in the organisation for the CISO to be visible, audible, and credible across all corporate silos, across all business units, all geographies, and with key vendors.

The solidity of the relationship between the CISO and their boss is paramount. It is the true cornerstone of the construction and the real key to success. It must be unquestioned and unquestionable. They must speak with one voice, share the same vision of what security means and needs to achieve, and have the same appreciation of the time frames involved.

Finally, the reporting line of the CISO must allow the right degree of independence and freedom for the CISO to remain able to act in all situations and arbitrate freely on conflicts and priorities. But that last point is only a parameter in this equation and must not rule alone.

Frankly, if security is not top of the list with the CIO, in a context where cyber incidents are at the top of the news several times a year (and often several times a month), it is likely that the CIO is simply the "tip of the iceberg," reflecting what the business units are pushing upon him. If that is the case, wherever you place the reporting line of the CISO in the organisation, you may find similar problems.

The key is to elevate the debate away from simplistic views on "conflicts of interest" and root it in the reality of the firm and the objectives of the security function. The reporting line of the CISO needs to be meaningful, not arbitrary, and positively determined and operated on a basis of trust between the CISO and their boss. It should be unambiguous, stable over the medium to long term, and positioned at a level in the organisation where action can be taken and resources prioritised. That means at board level or board minus one, *never* below.

These are the key factors. They will lead to different answers from one organisation to another, and that's perfectly normal. The right reporting line for the CISO is simply the one that works at enabling the security practice to do its job in the best possible way.

43

Cybersecurity and the Culture of Alienation

(13 August 2020)

Empirical, Bottom-Up, and Organically Developed Cybersecurity Functions Need to Evolve

The **2020** Information Security Maturity Report from ClubCISO makes for an interesting read.[24]

It compiles responses from one hundred of their members to a questionnaire sent in March **2020**, around the time of the COVID-**19** lockdown decision in the United Kingdom. Comparing results year to year is not entirely meaningful for such surveys, in the absence of any form of data normalisation (you have no guarantee that the panel responding is the same year on year), yet some interesting patterns emerge.

The typical respondent is a CISO working for a mid-sized or large organisation (**82%** have more than five hundred staff), headquartered in the United Kingdom or Ireland (**75**%), and has spent more than ten years in the InfoSec industry (**69**%; **60**% have been in their present role for less than two years).

Collectively, they paint a slightly uncomfortable picture: the picture of CISO roles and security practices still operating bottom-up, disconnected from the dynamics of the business. When asked which concerns most affect their ability to deliver against objectives, **49**% mention the culture of the organisation (as if they were not part of it); **36**%, the speed of business change (as if it were happening all around them but without them); and **33**%, the level of board support (although in response to another question, **58**% say they would like to report to board level).

It would be fascinating to ask some of the questions to the direct bosses of the respondents and compare results.

Of course, in such a context of alienation from the business, budgets are hard to get by for CISOs (**41**% mention budgets as a main concern, and **57**% mention insufficient staff). Frustration builds up and leads to attrition. When asked why they left their last role, **47**% of respondents mention "not seeing eye to eye with senior leadership" (!); not having sufficient resources to make their role a success (in their view, of course); or frustration with their organisation's approach to security.

But another shocking fact is that **89**% of respondents say they don't have a security operating model in place (**82**% say they are working on one at varying degrees). This element alone puts the rest of the survey into perspective. In the absence of a structured framework to work against, most cybersecurity practices can only operate "as they go along," in project mode or in firefighting mode.

How can you justify budgets and attract or retain talent without a referential to work against and in the absence of a clear governance model, roles, responsibilities, and to a degree, clear career paths? And again, how can you claim you do not have enough staff in the absence of a target operating model, detailing tasks and the resources required to deliver those tasks? It can only be a finger-in-the-air exercise, the very kind any half-decent CFO would smell miles away.

This kind of empirical, bottom-up, and organically developed cybersecurity function does not work and needs to evolve. What is required is structure, business acumen, and top-down engagement.

The emphasis on security culture throughout the report is valuable and meaningful, but it cannot be the only axis of action for the CISO. Security awareness has always been a low-hanging fruit and an easy sell for CISOs when they cannot find other levers. You can't go very wrong by distributing mouse mats and leaflets, and it does not cost the world. But this is not what culture change is about, and there cannot be any culture change that does not come from the top down.

The culture of alienation many CISOs have developed is probably comfortable for some; there is always someone to blame ("the business") and another juicy job to move into afterwards. But it does not help organisations and society at large.

To break this spiral of failure, the profile of the CISO needs to evolve, and the board needs to take ownership.

This is no longer just about tech—if it ever was. This is about protecting the business against cyber-attacks that have now become a matter of "*when,* not *if.*" This is no longer something you can push down in the organisation.

If the board does not see the need—or does not feel qualified—to step in, nothing will ever change for good around cybersecurity because it has simply become too complex and too transversal.

Bottom-up approaches will continue to pour cash down the drain, CISOs will continue to leave every other year out of frustration, and breaches will continue to happen.

If the board wants to set directions, they should drive, appoint someone they trust and can talk to (it does not have to be a technologist), and empower that person to build or rebuild cybersecurity practices across the firm, in the light of what the board wants and expects.

The COVID crisis is presenting most organisations with unprecedented situations, but it does not make cybersecurity less of a priority. On the contrary, cybersecurity—whether it is in support of remote working, e-commerce, or digitalised supply chains—will be a pillar of the "new normal."

Now is the time to deal with it strategically, and from the top down.

44

A Different Take on the Short Tenure of the CISO

(18 March 2021)

Looking Beyond Stress, Burnout, and Scapegoating Theories: What Is Really Going On?

A good piece from Dan Lohrmann on GovTech around the tenure of the CISO made me think.[25]

Overall, Dan's analysis is comprehensive, and the negative undertones behind the short tenure of CISOs match those in the Club-CISO **2020** Information Security Maturity Report, on which we commented last year.

Still, I would frame the topic slightly differently, and I think an element of reflexion is also required on the impact the short tenure of CISOs is having on the security industry at large and the evolution of the cybersecurity maturity of large firms.

First of all, many firms that never had a CISO before have opened up new positions across the last decade, and demand is strong from industry sectors that were never real players in the security space.

When I started attending security conferences over twenty years ago, most of my peers were in finance, Big Pharma, or the energy sector—regulated industries or industries where security has always worked hand in hand with safety and where safety has always been a pillar of the culture of the sector.

Today, most industry sectors have some form of security practice in place. Recruitment activity around CISO roles is significant and profitable for recruiters. There is a significant shortage of quality management profiles in that space; salaries are high and are on the rise.

To put it simply, good CISOs get headhunted—at least around me. Some offers are just "too good to turn down," and a number of them simply "follow the money." But for others, things are rarely as straightforward, and here I would go back to Dan's analysis.

The decision to change jobs is often rooted in a negative context, and the call from the recruiter is just the catalyst that starts the process. Again, this is clear in the ClubCISO **2020** Information Security Maturity Report.

Out of the seven responses presented by the report to the question "Why did you leave your last role?" (p. **19**), five are clearly and unambiguously negative (from the shocking "not seeing eye to eye with senior leadership," to "spending too much time firefighting," to "not being compensated sufficiently," to "being frustrated by the organisation's approach to security," to "not having enough resources or support to succeed").

Clearly, CISOs don't seem to be a very happy bunch, and their frustration appears to be rooted in some form of disconnect with their management.

That's understandable. Many CISO positions were created in response to rampant cyber threats across the last decade in industries that had never had such roles in place. They were created tactically with the operational objective of preventing breaches, by senior executives who didn't really understand the context and the transversal complexity involved in the cyber protection of large organisations.

It created situations where many CISOs struggled with limited resources and constant attacks and never managed to build a meaningful narrative with management beyond mere firefighting. They might have hopped from job to job, but they carried the problem with them, and over the past decade, many CISOs have not been able to develop the leadership and management skills that they would need to elevate the role to the next level.

In parallel, expectations from management have changed. In the face of constant breaches in the news, the penny has finally dropped in many boardrooms, and the "*when,* not *if*" paradigm around cyber-attacks has taken root. Many boards have reached the point where they are ready to make very significant transformative investments around cybersecurity, but in exchange, they would demand faultless execution and delivery from their CISO.

That's what is putting many CISOs under unbearable pressure. Over the past decade, they have been prevented, by constant firefighting, from developing the softer skills—the personal gravitas and political acumen—that are key to delivering complex initiatives in large firms.

To me, this is the context in which the short tenure of CISOs has to be seen. A survey by Nominet estimated it at twenty-six months in **2020**. Anecdotal evidence from my network seems to back this up. Having analysed the LinkedIn profile of fifteen of my contacts currently in CISO positions, I have reached the figure of thirty months, each having held three different CISO positions on average throughout their career.

It is time to start recognising the impact this CISO "merry-go-round" has had on the security industry over the past decade and on the evolution of security maturity in large firms.

You achieve very little in large organisations in two to three years, certainly very little that could have a lasting transformative impact—if that's what's required. At best, you kick-start some projects, but each CISO comes in with their own culture, priorities, and approach, and your successor may or may not follow in your footsteps.

Over time distrust sets in with senior management, who can't help noticing that breaches keep happening in spite of the investments made in that space. Security becomes a cost and a problem—an area that no ambitious executive, internally, would consider as a possible career step.

This distrust and the spiral of failure fuelled by CISOs' short tenures are at the heart of the problem here, and over the last decade, the situation has become self-perpetuating.

As we wrote back in **2018**, "Nothing will change until the profile of the CISO is raised and they start to see their role over the mid to long term."

To break this spiral, the board needs to own cybersecurity as a genuine board-level agenda item, elevate the topic and the role, build it up as a genuine career elevator to inject raw talent (probably from business circles), and create the conditions for trust to rebuild around business security objectives driven from the top down, instead of operational security objectives driven from the bottom up.

It may lead to the emergence of CSO types of roles, returning historical CISO roles to their original technical purpose. Now more than ever, this is crucial to driving real change across organisations made entirely dependent on digital services by the COVID crisis.

45

Time to Look at the Role of the CISO Differently

(2 June 2022)

What Is Now Required Is Political Acumen, Managerial Experience, and Personal Gravitas More Than Raw Technology Skills

In spite of being widely used, the role of the chief information security officer (CISO) has only had a few decades of existence and is still evolving.

Research from the Security Transformation Research Foundation[26] —based on the semantic analysis of the content of seventeen annual global security reports from EY between 2002 and 2019—points towards the role having already gone through two clear phases in its evolution, as it heads into its third decade of existence.

Fig. 8.

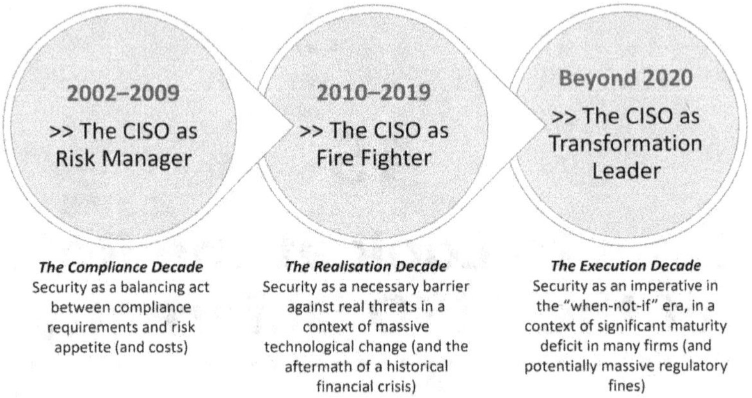
2002–2009
>> The CISO as Risk Manager
2010–2019
>> The CISO as Fire Fighter
Beyond 2020
>> The CISO as Transformation Leader
The Compliance Decade
Security as a balancing act between compliance requirements and risk appetite (and costs)
The Realisation Decade
Security as a necessary barrier against real threats in a context of massive technological change (and the aftermath of a historical financial crisis)
The Execution Decade
Security as an imperative in the "when-not-if" era, in a context of significant maturity deficit in many firms (and potentially massive regulatory fines)

The first decade of the century was essentially a "Compliance Decade." Security was seen as a balancing act between compliance requirements, risk appetite and costs; the CISO was mostly a risk manager.

The last decade has been effectively a "Realisation Decade," during which cybersecurity started to be seen as a necessary barrier against real threats, in a context of increasing cyber-attacks and data breaches (in number and scale), massive technological change and the aftermath of a historical financial crisis.

As a matter of fact, the last decade has been particularly complex for CISOs.

Not only the non-stop avalanche of cyber-attacks has prevented them from getting out of firefighting mode, but their role has also been challenged—and in many cases marginalized—at a number of levels:

The emergence of cloud technologies, coupled energizing the digital transformation urgency in many industries, has changed the roles of the CIO and the CISO. In many firms, the CIO now has to share powers with chief data or digital officers and, at the same time, deal with an increasing number of powerful service providers, enduring legacy technology and technical debt, and increased pressure from business units looking to gain a digital competitive advantage—something the COVID crisis has accentuated even further.

Over time, the historical role of the CISO, if it remains attached to the historical role of the CIO, runs the risk of being marginalized with it, becoming the guardian of an increasingly empty shell surrounded by an increasingly complex supply chain.

At the same time, large scale cyber-attacks have put cyber risk firmly on the board's agenda, but "Information Security"—the traditional perimeter of the CISO—is often seen as only one aspect of a much bigger problem: The board wants to see a fuller picture, encompassing the whole capability of the enterprise to sustain a cyber-attack and recover from it. In larger firms, this "resilience" concept tends to lead to the emergence of broader enterprise security functions which push down the historical role of the CISO.

This is deepened by the importance privacy regulations are also playing in shaping up the board agenda around security—in Europe with the GDPR and, gradually, through equivalent legislations throughout the U.S. and the world.

GDPR, in particular, has been a big topic in many firms over the last few of years. Tens of millions have been spent towards "compliance" in larger firms, and a good proportion of that went towards security-related measures, but many CISOs have failed to capitalise politically on the topic which has been treated—broadly—as a legal issue. The "data protection officer" roles and other "chief privacy officer" functions, which are emerging in relation with the implementation of the GDPR and other legislations, are likely to create an additional corporate layer "breathing down the neck" of many CISOs and altering their historical ways of working.

As the role heads into its third decade with a firmer transformative mandate to bring the cyber-attacks epidemic under control, business leaders must take a different look at it.

It is time to stop searching for non-existent profiles, expecting the CISO to be credible one day in front of the board, the next in front of hackers, the third in front of developers, and all the way across the depth and breadth of the enterprise and its supply chain.

Those profiles don't exist anymore, given the transversal complexity cybersecurity has developed over the past two decades. The role of the CISO has to be one of a leader, structuring, organising, delegating and orchestrating work across their team and across the firm—and across the multiple third-parties involved in delivering or supporting the business.

In essence, knowing what to do is reasonably well established and cybersecurity good practice—at large—still protects from most threats and still ensures a degree of compliance with most regulations.

But by focusing excessively on purely technical approaches to cybersecurity challenges, large organizations have failed to protect themselves effectively and efficiently, in spite of massive investments in that space over the last two decades.

This is essentially due to the cross-silo complexity of the problem which would require a mid to long-term focus to be properly addressed, and comes in conflict with endemic corporate short-termism, leading to execution failure.

Increasingly, in the face of non-stop cyber-attacks in large firms, the key priority around cybersecurity is now to get things done.

The role of the CISO is entering its third decade of existence and it is likely to be an "Execution Decade" with cybersecurity becoming an imperative, as the "when-not-if" paradigm around cyber attacks takes root in the boardroom.

But large organizations have to face their own inherent complexities and accept that the time has come to look differently at the role of the CISO in that context: this is no longer about throwing money at alleged tech solutions.

The role of the CISO is becoming a true leadership role, and what is required to get things moving is political acumen, managerial experience, and personal gravitas over raw technology skills.

46
The Curse of the Decade for Many CISOs

(6 April 2023)

It's Often Trying to Go Too Fast with the Wrong Leadership Baggage That Drives CISOs to Failure

The cybersecurity narrative on social media remains driven by the misleading messages of tech vendors and dominated by considerations of insufficient investments and challenges in convincing top execs. It has been the case for as long as I have been writing these columns.

In real life, many CISOs now face a very different situation.

The fact is that the penny has dropped in many boardrooms over the past few years, as we have written repeatedly in these columns: Cyber-attacks are now seen as a matter of "when," not "if," and this paradigm shift is engineering dynamics which are totally different to what CISOs might have experienced over the past decade.

In practice, it is not rare for the dialogue between CISOs and senior execs to shift overnight from "why do we need to spend this?" to "how much do we need to spend?"

This is seriously more common than one might think in field practice, and is generally triggered by incidents, near-misses, regulatory fears or more simply, a new executive taking up a top position and daring to ask the questions nobody wanted to ask before.

For the CISO, elevated at pace from a firefighter role to a transformative one, and often given substantial means (sometimes by the same people who were denying them before), the situation can become a curse more than a blessing.

Because now expectations are high, visibility is raised, and it is implied that execution needs to follow.

But execution often remains a challenge, in particular in large firms: cybersecurity is a complicated beast, intrinsically cross-functional, which requires reaching across silos and geographies—something large firms are not particularly good at in my experience.

Many CISOs, trapped in the technical firefighting of data breaches with inadequate resources throughout the last decade, have not been equipped at a personal level to face a gear change of that magnitude, and at that pace.

Many were technologists by background have remained technologists, in spite of their claim to "enable the business" or to "talk its language."

Nothing wrong with that, but transformational challenges require different skills to be credible and audible across the firm and drive the actual delivery of cybersecurity measures at the right place across IT, business units, and support functions.

Managerial acumen, personal gravitas, political finesse, real credible knowledge of the business—these should be the real attributes of the security transformational leader more than their understanding of zero-trust or quantum cryptography (or whatever the hyped topic of the moment happens to be).

Many burnout and mental health issues affecting CISOs are rooted in that type of mismatch, aggravated by frustration and short tenures: You simply don't achieve anything meaningful in a field as complex as cybersecurity in eighteen months to two years. And you don't learn much by leaving at the first hurdles in terms of management experience. And when the industry leads you to believe you are a "star" by allowing you to move from one job to the next always for more money up to some extravagant figures, you have the ingredients of a serious storm.

It might be counter-intuitive in the face of the transformative urgency, but CISOs facing those challenges need to take things slowly and give themselves time. It's often trying to go too fast with the wrong leadership baggage that drives personal and project failures.

Business leaders will generally understand that complex transformation takes time and value honesty and realism around timeframes.

The key for the CISO—as is often the case—lies in under-promising and over-delivering, splitting the delivery in manageable chunks and selling success along the way to build trust with stakeholders.

Trust and success, in turn, will become the true engine that builds confidence and drives the true dynamics of transformation.

The Role of the Board

47

When True Innovation Consists of Doing Now What You Should Have Done Ten Years Ago

(8 December 2016)

Year after year, major surveys highlight low levels of cybersecurity maturity across large firms and, increasingly, an even more worrying situation among smaller firms. The **2016** RSA Cyber Poverty Index is a good example of that trend.[27] It truly paints a grim picture but simply confirms findings that seem consistent across all large surveys—even if methodologies do vary.

Most of those surveys have another point in common. They are, in some form or another, organised or sponsored by heavyweights of the cybersecurity industry or large consultancy firms, who ultimately can be suspected of having an interest in accentuating negative traits in order to maximise their own sales.

But even if the results of those surveys have to be taken with great care for that reason, they do match an enormous amount of anecdotal evidence we come across in the field every day. Too many large firms—leaders in their field—are still struggling with fundamental basic principles of cybersecurity hygiene that have been regarded as good practice for ten to fifteen years and for which technical solutions and organisational processes have been in existence for as long:

- Monitoring of basic network security events
- Timely deployment of security patches on servers and desktops
- Timely removal of user accounts
- Periodic revalidation of access levels with business units

It cannot be suggested that solving those problems is easy in large firms, and to a large extent, the disappearance of the traditional business perimeter of the enterprise and the digital transformation of supply and value chains have made things even more complex.

But those good practices have been relentlessly pushed forward by auditors and regulators, as well as InfoSec professionals, for the best part of the last ten to fifteen years. Very large amounts of money have been spent with tech vendors on alleged solutions in those areas, so undoubtedly, it is concerning that so little progress seems to have been made by so many firms in those domains over such a long period.

The most common root cause is a constant short-termist approach by senior management, focused solely on alleged "quick wins," or illusory technical solutions to audit or compliance problems, at the expense of the more complex process and governance transformation issues that would have driven real change but would have required a longer-term vision and approach.

The technology industry has done little to break those dynamics. In fact, it has been happily riding that wave for a long time, and the trend shows no signs of abating. It also has a long-standing tradition of reinventing itself, and the cybersecurity sector is no exception. Most security vendors are now embracing emerging technologies such as artificial intelligence or machine learning, as well as more established platforms such as big data, and present them as "innovative" cloud-based delivery models that, in fact, have been in existence—for some of them—for over ten years.

They paint to their clients a situation where threats morph constantly and therefore new tools are constantly required, and it may well be the case to some extent in some industries. But the harsh reality is that many of their clients don't have the basic processes in place that would enable them to take full advantage of such products, and at best, they simply continue to buy those to put ticks in audit or compliance boxes, when it is not merely as a pet project for the CISO.

Many board members have woken up over the past few years to a situation they don't understand, being told all of a sudden that data breaches are simply a matter of time, often by the same people who have been telling them for years that everything was under control.

They need to realise that this is not just an external situation created by the acceleration of threats or some adverse economic or geopolitical outlook. Quite often, it is also the symptom of a serious internal problem rooted in decades of short-termism, adverse prioritisation of security matters, and a complacent "tick-in-the-box" culture around audit and compliance.

We are coming to a point in many large firms where true "innovation" in the cybersecurity space does not consist of deploying the latest tools but of going back to the governance drawing board to look at long-term actions and remove the roadblocks that have prevented progress in the past, redesigning fundamental security processes across IT, the business, and other support functions (such as HR) in order to rebuild proper and functional operating models conceived to protect the organisation once and for all.

48

Knee-Jerk Reactions to Data Breaches Are Damaging the Case for Cybersecurity

(12 April–19 May 2016)

Cybersecurity Transformation Is Not about Implementing yet Another Technology Product

Anybody who has spent a few years in InfoSec management has seen this happen. Following an internal near-miss or some high-profile security incident widely publicised in the media (such as the TalkTalk data breach in the United Kingdom), the same senior executives—who previously wouldn't bat an eyelid over information security issues—suddenly start panicking. Priorities shift. Immediate solutions are demanded. Money appears out of nowhere by the millions. Tech vendors are lined up. Some product is purchased that will allegedly fix everything. A box is checked, then normality returns.

Over the short term, only the tech vendors win—shamelessly—in these scenarios.

The CISO, if there is one, loses ground in most cases—unless they're just a technology hobbyist and they get another pet project to play with. Otherwise, they are likely to see their priorities turned upside down by the arrival of the new initiative and their ongoing projects being deprioritised in its favour.

This could be hugely demoralising for the CISO and their team, who might have worked hard for years to get some projects started that are now put on hold while other topics, which were repeatedly proposed and refused, are now being pushed forward by the same executives who previously turned them down:

- It damages the credibility of senior management with the cybersecurity professionals.

- It makes life more difficult for the cybersecurity team in their day-to-day interaction with IT teams, as they are seen as constantly "moving the goalpost."

- It perpetuates the wrong idea among IT communities that cybersecurity is just a topic you throw money at from time to time.

- In the long run, it alienates talent away from cybersecurity roles.

Broadly speaking, cybersecurity products tend to do what they are supposed to do, so the chosen technology solution may provide a degree of protection to the organisation, but only if it gets implemented properly. And that's often the key issue. The product would have been selected in an emergency to plug a technical hole, not necessarily on the basis of the most thorough requirements analysis or market research.

- It may not be suited to the company's environment (e.g., deploying internal security products while key IT assets are in the cloud, or deploying internet security products if your internet footprint is limited).

- There may be competing products or solutions already in place internally that could have been leveraged (e.g., in different geographies or business lines). Ignoring these alienates and demotivates part of the organisation and may deprive the initiative of invaluable field experience around the topic.

- There may be considerable process issues when trying to embed the new product into legacy practices (e.g., around identity and access management or patch management), potentially leading to escalating costs, deployment limitations, or project failure.

Overall, the knee-jerk decision may end up being an expensive "tick-in-a-box" exercise that achieves very little in practice.

Even for tech vendors, the situation may not be ideal in the longer term. As deployment fails or stalls due to technical issues, and value is limited by the lack of compatibility with people and processes, vendors may face dwindling revenue from subscriptions or cancellations of maintenance charges, which may damage the business models or investors' confidence.

Senior executives need to understand the dynamics they create where they demand instant solutions to problems that are, in reality, rooted in decades of underinvestment, adverse prioritisation, or complacency. And the CIO and the CISO need to have the management gravitas and the backbone to stand up to the board—with the right arguments—on those matters.

The harsh reality is that there can be no miracle solution, technical or otherwise, to such problems.

There may be a need for short-term tactical initiatives to demonstrate to the board, shareholders, or regulators that a new dynamic is being created around cybersecurity, but those have to be calibrated to the real maturity of the organisation around those matters and the genuine threats it faces. As importantly, it must be accompanied by a thorough examination of the cultural roadblocks that have prevented progress in the past.

A genuine and lasting transformation around cybersecurity can only come from the removal of those and from the definition of a long-term, transformative vision for the function—a vision that must come from the top and resonate across the whole organisation, not just IT.

49

The Six Questions the Board of Directors Needs to Ask

(7 August 2015–7 January 2016)

From a cybersecurity perspective, the **2015** headlines have been dominated by a number of high-profile data breaches: Sony, Ashley Madison, TalkTalk, etc. Those have put the cybersecurity topic on the board's agenda in many corporations and have also been drawing the attention of politicians.

Fundamentally, we believe that the board of directors needs to go back to basics on these matters. Time has now gone to continue approaching cybersecurity purely from a risk perspective. Risk is ultimately about "things that may or may not happen." When it comes to cybersecurity, the board should start from the premise that cyber-attacks are a matter of *when*, not *if*. It should shift the focus towards understanding and managing what is actually getting done to protect the organisation.

The board must not be allowed to believe that it needs to be involved simply because the cybersecurity topic is making headline news. The topic is making headline news because security breaches are occurring more and more often. This, in turn, is due to decades of complacency, neglect, or short-termist "tick-in-the-box" practices around the information and IT security space. The problem is not new, and those practices have resulted in low maturity and protection levels, which surveys keep highlighting year after year (for example, in the **2015** RSA Cyber Poverty Index survey).[28]

In large organisations exhibiting such low levels of cybersecurity maturity, it would be misleading to allow the board of directors to believe it's a simple problem to fix, or that it simply requires the board's supervision around a handful of key aspects. It is also misleading to allow the board to believe in ready-made technical solutions or that throwing money at the problem will solve everything, as McKinsey & Company recently highlighted in an article that echoes their **2014** findings for the World Economic Forum.[29]

"Cybersecurity is a high-stakes topic, so it is a CEO-level one," states the McKinsey article. However, the problem has some depth, and in many large organisations, where cybersecurity maturity levels are low, it could be rooted in ten to fifteen years of failure.

Understanding the true historical perspective of the problem and removing the roadblocks that have prevented progress in the past (people, resources, priorities—whatever they might have been)—these are the real issues that many organisations' boards of directors now need to confront and address.

Fig. 9. Cybersecurity: The Six Questions the Board Needs to Ask

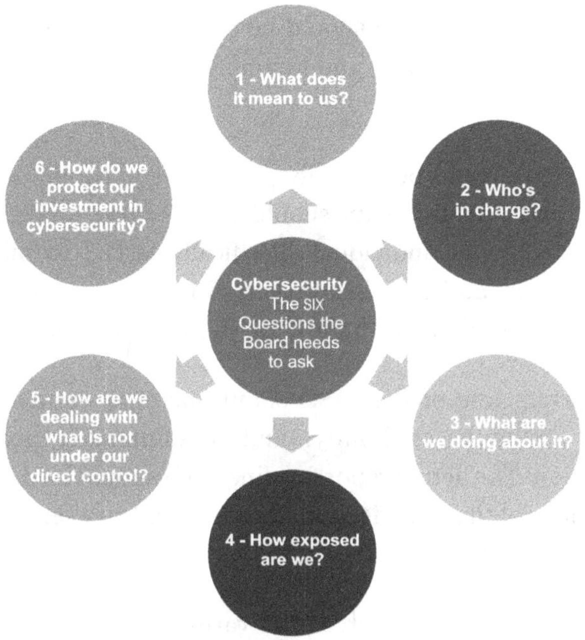

1. What Does It Mean to Us?

First of all, the board must form an understanding of the nature of the cyber threats that may target the firm.

Cyber threats do not target all organisations in the same way, and some industry sectors are more exposed than others. Cybersecurity results from the application of proportionate controls to protect the business against the cyber threats it faces.

Understanding these threats is key to success, and approaching the problem from a generic "one-size-fits-all" angle (or simply based on the content of media coverage) is dangerous and can lead to misguided judgements.

2. Who's in Charge?

Having established its own understanding of the concepts, the first concern of the board should be to ensure that cybersecurity responsibilities are clearly and unambiguously distributed across the organisation.

Cybersecurity should be formally part of the portfolio of a board member, and accountability should be cascaded down (directly or indirectly) to an individual specifically tasked to make sure the business is, and remains, protected from cyber threats. This responsibility would lie with the CISO in many large organisations.

The reporting line of the CISO should be clear—and at a level allowing visibility, credibility, and accountability across the organisation. The actual reporting line itself should be dictated by the priorities of the organisation ahead of arbitrary separation-of-duties considerations.

The repartition of roles across the various lines of defence and across corporate silos should be clear. A sound security governance framework and target operating model should document those aspects across IT and beyond—into HR, procurement, legal, corporate communications, and business units. They should cover, without complacency, the true geographical perimeter of the organisation and its dependency on third parties where relevant.

3. What Are We Doing about It?

Having established that a sound security governance platform is in place across the business, the board should ensure that key protective measures are (and remain) in place.

Starting with a sound appreciation of the threats the business faces (both internally and externally), a determination of the controls required to protect the business against such threats should naturally follow. These should be consolidated in a cybersecurity controls framework specifically tailored to each organisation.

Relying on recognised generic industry frameworks and good practice catalogues instead is often preferred (or recommended by some vendors), but the approach has its pros and cons. On one hand, it is a sound way of making sure that all angles are covered; on the other, it could easily lead to overengineering and overspending—particularly for smaller firms.

Fundamentally, the board should ensure that controls are proportionate to the threats the business faces; otherwise, their deployment could be challenged or costs may escalate. The board must look beyond which framework is actually being used to focusing on the way the controls it contains are effectively implemented across the organisation. Once again, it should also take into account the organisation's true geographical perimeter and its dependency on third parties where relevant.

4. How Exposed Are We?

The board should ask for periodic reports showing adherence of the organisation to its cybersecurity controls framework, and the primary focus should be on any deviations from this. Such deviations create opportunities for threats to target the business and cause harm, creating "risk"—in the most classical sense of the word.

The board should be concerned with any main issues—whether they're financial, organisational, or technical—that are preventing the implementation of the cybersecurity controls framework, ensuring they remain updated on what is being done to address these.

The key threats should be those to which the firm is the most vulnerable (i.e., those against which it is the least protected). Once the key threats are identified, the board should ensure that their organisation's incident response capability is regularly tested in those areas—if relevant.

The overall cyber risk posture of the organisation should result from the analysis of deviations from an established cybersecurity controls framework.

5. How Are We Dealing with What Is Not under Our Direct Control?

The board should be concerned with two very different aspects in that space:

1. Dependency on third parties. The board should be acutely concerned about dependency on third parties, across the business and IT, as we have highlighted several times above. Many controls in the cybersecurity controls framework will have to be cascaded down to (and implemented by) a variety of external firms, but the organisation may have no actual means to enforce these—even if a breach in the other party environment could cause catastrophic damage to the business. As such, effective vendor risk management could be of critical importance for some organisations.

   The board should start by building an understanding of the diversity and numbers of such vendors and of those on which the business is most dependent. This must not be seen as a mere IT issue, and it is key to approach it in terms of business processes. Following this, the board should build an overview of those vendors' levels of adherence to the cybersecurity controls framework—or, where relevant, of their unwillingness to cooperate with cybersecurity assessment efforts.

Finally, the board should ensure that unsatisfactory outcomes are being addressed, ensuring they remain updated on these matters. Board members also sitting on the boards of some of the offending third parties may want to take the matter into their own hands if and where they can.

Again, it is key to ensure that this is not turned into an IT matter and that all business relationships are in scope.

2. Media and political interest. The board should also be acutely concerned with the outcome of a cybersecurity breach spilling over into surrounding corporate areas, potentially contaminating their brand, customer trust, or shareholders' confidence.

   The dynamics of recent cases show that contamination often occurs as a result of aggressive media and political interest following breaches of privacy or service disruptions affecting the general public.

   While it is difficult to predict where media attention will be in relation to any particular service incident, the board can build an understanding of the amount of sensitive personal data the organisation stores and processes. The board should ensure it possesses a clear understanding of its legal duty of protection towards the privacy of its organisation's customers and staff, as well as the measures that are in place (or not) as part of the cybersecurity controls framework. The board of international organisations should also be aware that those obligations may vary from country to country.

In all cases, the board should ensure that the security governance framework is active across all relevant corporate silos and reaches into all areas that may be involved in case of a breach, and that those interactions are regularly tested.

6. How Do We Protect Our Investment in Cybersecurity?

The board should be aware that cyber threats evolve constantly and that there is no silver bullet solution, technical or otherwise.

Ongoing protection can only come from a strong control culture, embedded in the way the firm works. Such a cultural shift could take time, particularly in organisations where cybersecurity maturity is low to start with, so taking a long-term view and sticking to it is key to success.

Ensuring that key personnel (the CISO and their team, in many large organisations) remain in charge over the period is also key, and it means they may have to consider their tenure over a five- to seven-year horizon in many cases. Changing approaches every two to three years, or every time a new CISO comes in, is a recipe for disaster and could be very simply why so many large organisations still show such a low level of cybersecurity maturity.

The board should also ensure that its direct involvement in cybersecurity matters is clear, unambiguous, and widely publicised across the enterprise. The cybersecurity message from the board should, in turn, cascade down across the organisation through regular management channels. It is key for the staff to see that management (at their level) takes cybersecurity at heart. This type of bond is generally stronger, longer-lasting, and cheaper to establish than any type of engagement through awareness development campaigns, which often miss the point entirely by being too tactical or too technical.

Finally, having examined all aspects listed above, the board should consider the current level of cyber risk insurance protection the firm holds (if any) and whether it provides adequate cover.

The insurance question should come last, and the board should consider adjusting cover, if possible, to match the findings highlighted by the previous questions. The cyber risk insurance market is evolving fast, and products may be available today that were not available last time the board enquired.

50

Three Factors Marginalising the Historical Role of the CISO

(24 May 2018)

Is the CISO an Outdated Concept? And What to Do about It?

The last SASIG meeting in London on **8** May **2018**, examined the role and career of the CISO. It is hard to walk out of an event like this one without feeling that a number of things are seriously going in circles in the security industry.

The reporting line of the CISO—on which I presented–is one of those topics that have been discussed constantly among security professionals for the best part of the last fifteen years, but more generally, it felt like the role of the CISO was taken for granted as an established corporate concept.

In my opinion, that is far from being the case, and as a matter of fact, the role does encompass very different responsibilities from one organisation to another and is rarely a true C-level function. Far from being reinforced by the constant avalanche of cyber-attacks and data breaches of the past few years, it is marginalised by three long-term trends:

1. The Cloud, Digital Transformation, and Changing Role of the CIO

Information assets are changing; they are being used in new ways across new media and across an increasingly complex dematerialised supply chain. The CIO has to share powers with CDOs and must deal with an increasing number of powerful service providers and increased pressure from business units looking to gain a digital competitive advantage. Over time, the historical role of the CISO runs the risk of becoming the guardian of an increasingly empty shell surrounded by an increasingly complex web of supplier relationships, with little actual control over the real level of protection applied to sensitive information assets.

2. Resilience, Privacy, and the Consolidation of Broader Corporate Concepts

Large-scale cyber-attacks over the past few years have put cyber risk on the board's agenda, but "information security"—the traditional perimeter of the CISO—is often seen as only one aspect of a much bigger problem. The board wants to see a full picture, encompassing the whole capability of the enterprise to sustain a cyberattack and recover from it. In larger firms, this "resilience" concept tends to lead to the emergence of broader enterprise security functions that push down the historical role of the CISO, as McKinsey & Company rightly points out.[30]

Surprisingly, one point McKinsey & Company is missing in this article is the importance privacy regulations are also playing (at least in Europe) in shaping up the board agenda around security.

GDPR has been a big topic in many firms across the past twelve months. Tens of millions have been spent towards "compliance" in larger firms, and a good proportion of that went towards security-related measures, but many CISOs have failed to capitalise politically on the topic that has broadly been seen as a legal issue. The DPO roles and other "chief privacy officer" functions that will emerge over the years to come from the implementation of the GDPR are likely to create an additional corporate layer "breathing down the neck" of many CISOs and altering their historical ways of working.

3. Failure and the Price to Pay for the Cybersecurity "Lost Decade"

For many senior executives, the actual role of the CISO—in its historical sense—is still a mystery. It is seen as complex and technical, and it lacks a natural edge they could relate to. It feels like a "black art," always requiring more investments. At the same time, cyber-attacks keep happening and often seem to point out to the absence of basic protective measures that could have been implemented years ago.

This "lost decade" of cybersecurity investments has damaged the profile of the CISO position in the eyes of many business leaders. And indeed, many CISOs end up hopping from one job to another because they feel they can no longer achieve what they would like or are not being listened to. So the role of the CISO in its historical technology-driven perception is not outdated yet, but it is under threat and losing ground.

The firms looking to reverse this trend need to act at three levels:

- Elevate the personal profile of the CISO role by injecting real-life experience, managerial talent, personal gravitas, and political acumen.
- Decouple the role from its historical technical profile and stop following blindly the misleading agenda of the technology industry (those historical aspects of the role can be separated into an "IT security" function within the portfolio of the CIO or the CTO).
- And instead, turn the CISO function towards the new players in the field (CDO and DPO) and towards assisting the business units in all aspects of their digital transformation, dealing with third parties and the associated evolution of the threat landscape.

51
On Cybersecurity and Trust

(4 January 2018)

People Simply Trust Other People

This excellent November piece from McKinsey on cybersecurity deserves a comment: "A Framework for Improving Cybersecurity discussions within Organizations."[31]

The visualisation of the "trust gaps" between the board (the business, IT, and the firm) and its suppliers and government is a very strong and synthetic way of representing where roadblocks emerge that prevent security strategies from being properly executed, therefore leaving organisations vulnerable to cyber threats.

We highlighted the importance of trust in a broader GRC context in an earlier article and how dysfunctions breed when distrust sets in.

Of course, it is also true in the cybersecurity space. Let's take this opportunity to say this one more time: firms protect their key assets from cyber threats through the actual deployment of security measures. It's not having a security strategy or a plan in place that will protect your organisation, but it's actual implementation in the field, at the right levels, and across the true perimeter of the enterprise, taking into account without complacency the true geographical footprint of the company and its true dependency on vendors and third parties.

It is strategic execution that is key to protection from cyber threats; therefore, creating the conditions for execution to take place is paramount. These conditions revolve around trust and closing the "trust gaps" identified in the McKinsey paper. There are three key factors that will engender trust and close those gaps:

- Clarity of roles, responsibilities, and objectives around cybersecurity from the board down internally and with third parties.

- Simplicity of language in the formulation of those roles, responsibilities, and strategic objectives.

- And more importantly, consistency over the right time frames and the right budgetary allocations in terms of execution.

Transformation in that space can be complex and take time because it often affects people, their culture, and their real way of working. There is nothing more efficient at creating distrust on these matters than management changing directions or priorities every time something happens somewhere.

It is also essential to reflect on the role and profile of the key people leading strategic execution—in particular the CISO in the cybersecurity space. Large firms are plagued by the "ivory tower" head office functions that achieve very little in practice. Cybersecurity is no exception and is, all too often, one of those—except that the stakes are getting higher and higher every year and the time has come to create positive dynamics and break those deadlocks where they exist.

In most cases, navigating around the "trust gaps" and bridging them will require true leadership.

The CISO role will never be a job for a junior technologist, an ex-auditor, or a lifelong consultant. It requires true political acumen and gravitas. These attributes come with real-life field experience and in-depth knowledge of the firm, its culture, and its people that can only come from a substantial internal tenure and considerable managerial experience, in particular when it comes to influencing third parties.

Raising the profile of the CISO will often be key for many firms to efficiently bridge those "trust gaps." Because in the end, people will be key to the strategic execution, and people simply trust other people, internally and externally.

52

A Cultural Revolution and a Matter of Corporate Social Responsibility for Tech Firms

(10 March 2016)

For years, many technology firms have treated security and privacy matters as an afterthought. It was at best a necessary evil related to regulations and compliance; at worst, it was something you would window-dress on the day in front of those few clients who would ask the question. It was seen as something boring and expensive, at odds with functionality and preventing innovation and agility.

Of course, with the convergence of IoT, big data, and cloud technologies, the cards are now dealt quite differently, and many tech companies, large and small, are starting to realise that they are going to have to adjust their mindset to survive or make the most of the times ahead.

The convergence of those technology streams generates countless use cases in all industry sectors and has the genuine potential to transform our lives and create trillions of dollars of economic value, but it also requires a type of hyperconnectivity that multiplies attack surfaces exponentially and is highly vulnerable to cyber threats.

"Data" is currently treated by many tech firms as a free, limitless commodity, and many of these firms talk about it as if it belonged to them and they could do whatever they like with it. But in practice, they acquire it most of the time through ludicrously one-sided terms of business that nobody reads and from people (consumers, citizens) who have rights and expectations of privacy. It is only a matter of time until such practices start to be challenged.

The digital transformation of society will never realise its full potential as long as the trust of consumers and citizens is constantly being hammered by data breaches, cybersecurity incidents, and ruthless data monetisation by shameless vendors.

Technology vendors who want to stay in the game over the long term must take security and privacy seriously and turn that into a competitive advantage for the generations of customers who share those values. But it will be a massive cultural shift for many tech firms.

"Security by design" and "privacy by design" principles have been established for a long while, and they are still at the heart of what needs to be done to move forward:

Security features have to be treated, designed, and tested as a proper product functionality embedded as early as possible in the way the product works—not as an add-on.

The respect for customers' right to privacy has to be treated as a key business model parameter, not something you will compromise on to make the numbers add up.

Whether the current generation of executives, investors, marketers, and technologists running those firms is capable of understanding and delivering such shifts in values is a key factor. The fundamental need for controls and the ethical treatment of customers at the heart of those principles is probably not something they were taught at business school. But it is nevertheless the ability of those firms to embrace "security by design" and "privacy by design" concepts that will become the cornerstone of the digital transformation.

Fail to make the move, and at best, value creation will be reduced by several trillions (between **$1** and **$3** trillion by **2020**, according to McKinsey & Company for the **2014** World Economic Forum).[32] In practice, if it is the trust of the people that is irreparably damaged, it can be the dynamics of the entire digital transformation itself that may have to be reconsidered.

With so much at stake, it is becoming a fundamental matter of corporate social responsibility for tech firms to take security and privacy values at heart.

53

Cybersecurity in the "When, Not If" Era

(14 March 2019)

No Longer Just as an Equation between Risk Appetite, Compliance Requirements, and Costs

The "*when,* not *if*" paradigm around cyber-attacks is changing the deal completely around cybersecurity.

Many large organisations now assume that breaches are simply inevitable, due to the inherent complexity of their business models and the multiplication of attack surfaces and attack vectors that come with it. This realisation fundamentally changes the dynamics around cybersecurity.

Historically, cybersecurity has always been seen as an equation between risk appetite, compliance requirements, and costs. Compliance and costs were always the harder factors. Risk (difficult to measure and quantify) was always some form of adjustment variable.

Risk is about uncertainty. The "*when,* not *if*" paradigm brings certainty where doubt was previously allowed (or used to manipulate outcomes):

- cyber-attacks *will* happen.
- Sooner or later, regulators *will* step in.
- They can now impose *business-threatening* fines around the mishandling of personal data.
- Media interest has never been higher around these matters.
- Business reputation and trust in a brand *will* be damaged by high-profile incidents.

All the risk-based constructions that have been the foundations of many cybersecurity management practices are weakened as a result.

Compliance requirements remain (if anything, they are getting stronger as privacy regulators flex their muscles in Europe and the United States), and costs cannot be ignored. But "Are we spending enough?" has become a much more common question across the boardroom table than "Why do we need to spend so much?"

For CISOs, protecting the firm becomes imperative. This is no longer about doing the minimum required to put the right ticks in compliance boxes, but very often, it is a matter of genuine transformation. It forces them to work across corporate silos, look beyond the mere technology horizon (which is often their comfort zone), and also look beyond tactical firefighting (which often dominates their day-to-day).

Knowing what to do is often the easiest part. After all, good practices in the cybersecurity space have been well known for over a decade, and they still provide adequate protection against many threats—as long as they are properly implemented.

True cyber resilience can only come from real defence-in-depth, acting at preventative, detective, mitigative, *and* reactive levels, *and* across the real breadth of the enterprise, functionally and geographically.

The "*when,* not *if*" paradigm will often bring the board's attention and large resources to cybersecurity, but with those will also come scrutiny and expectations. The challenge really becomes an execution and a leadership challenge for the CISO.

In large firms where a major overhaul of security practices is required, establishing a sound governance framework and operating model from the start will always be a key factor of long-term success for the CISO.

Equally important will be the need to put people and process first and to identify the roadblocks that might have prevented progress in the past around cybersecurity matters.

Repeating the mistakes of the past would simply perpetuate the spiral of failure around security, as would an excessive or premature focus on tech solutions. There is no magical technology product that can fix in a few months what is rooted in decades of adverse prioritisation, lip service, and underinvestment. The CISO must appreciate that and place all transformation efforts in the right perspective. Change takes time and relentless drive, and there may not be quick wins.

Managing expectations and staying the course will always be key pillars of any lasting cybersecurity transformation.

54
What Cyber Resilience Is Not About

(25 April 2019)

Cyber Resilience Must Not Be Used to Legitimise Window-Dressing Practices around Cybersecurity

Although the theme is gaining momentum, there is a certain amount of confusion around what cyber resilience really means for organisations. For many, it is just another piece of consultant jargon, an abstract managerial concept with little real-life substance or meaning.

As a matter of fact, it is very real, and it is rooted in the "*when,* not *if*" paradigm around cyber-attacks, which is completely changing the dynamics around cybersecurity in many firms.

At the heart of cyber resilience lies a real application of "defence-in-depth" principles that have been well established for decades: acting at preventative, detective, mitigative, *and* reactive levels—

and across the real breadth of the enterprise, functionally and geographically. It is about the enterprise being enabled by the use of data and technology, while remaining protected from active threats.

It requires managerial and governance practices to be active across corporate silos and the supply chain (once again, functionally and geographically), and it cannot be dissociated from a broader approach to operational and corporate resilience.

It is hard to deliver at scale, and it presents many large organisations with significant cultural challenges. So the temptation is high for many to oversimplify it and focus only on alleged quick wins.

Of course, the "*when,* not *if*" paradigm implies that security breaches are unavoidable. But it does not represent a licence to ignore all protective, detective, and mitigative measures to focus only on the reactive ones. This is the type of simplistic approach to "resilience" that may put a few ticks in audit or compliance boxes, but in the long term, it can only aggravate security postures and lead to regulatory issues—particularly in the face of a worldwide tightening of regulations around the protection of personal data.

"Cyber resilience" cannot be limited to an annual desktop exercise with board members and corporate functions, during which they simulate how to react to a cyberattack, in order to minimise the impact on the share price, media coverage, or the reactions of customers.

All those factors are important, but "cyber resilience" must not turn into an excuse to legitimise a top-down window dressing culture around cybersecurity practices.

Corporate resilience is the ability of an organisation to continue operating in the face of disruptive events and to return to normal operations over time. It implies a deep knowledge of operational processes, their integration, and their interdependencies. It also implies a deep knowledge of the supply chain and its actors.

To operate efficiently in disrupted situations, it also requires a collaborative and positive culture that needs to be created and fostered from the top down.

All this is even more acute in cyber resilience scenarios due to their relative novelty, the speed at which the organisation often needs to react, and the technical complexity that may be involved.

Instead of being treated as another box-checking exercise and a quick win, cyber resilience must be embedded into the right corporate structures and used to channel a different culture from the top down around cybersecurity:

- A culture where cybersecurity (the need to protect the business from cyber threats) and the protection of individuals' privacy are not just matters of risk management or necessary evils imposed by compliance and regulations but key business concepts and, increasingly, matters of competitive advantage and corporate social responsibility.

- A culture that fosters the transversal nature of many security problems in large firms (looking across corporate is certainly much beyond the mere technology horizon), because the security measures needed to protect the firm are transversal in nature. Their execution is the only factor that will protect the business, and it requires transversal capabilities.

- Finally, a culture rooted in transparency around security breaches, because trust is the cornerstone of the digital economy and transparency is its foundation.

55

Cybersecurity: Revisiting the Questions the Board Should Ask

(2 August 2019)

One Board Member Must Be in Charge, and Their Pay Package Must Ride on It

In **2015**, in the wake of the TalkTalk data breach (which made a massive impact in the UK media and even got politicians involved), we first explored the key questions the board should ask in large firms around cybersecurity.

What a difference four years can make . . .

At the time, our line of thought was very much on making the board understand the exposure to cyber threats and what was being done to counter them, especially across the supply chain as the concept of a hyperconnected world bound by data and powered by emerging technologies was on the horizon.

At the time, the McKinsey Institute was estimating that emerging technologies could create up to **$20** trillion of economic value, out of which cyber threats could destroy up to **$3** trillion. Although we have seen no update on this research and its eventual accuracy, it cannot be denied that cyber-attacks have intensified and have been widely reported across the last five years—from Sony in **2015** to Capital One this year—with Equifax, British Airways, and Marriott reporting breaches in the last twelve months alone and not discounting the widespread Wannacry / NotPetya virus outbreak of **2017**, which impacted badly industrial and logistics giants such as Saint Gobain or Maersk.

Equifax has now agreed to a **$700** million settlement for its **2017** data breach, and the UK data privacy regulator is threatening British Airways and Marriott with a nine-figure fine under the United Kingdom equivalent of GDPR. So numbers are getting larger and larger, and it is hard to imagine a board member today in any large organisation who would be unaware of cyber threats.

Of course, priorities may vary in line with economic conditions or the general health of the business, but "cyber" is on the agenda of all boards and consistently rated as a top risk by many.

The last decade has undoubtedly been a decade of realisation for senior executives around cybersecurity. This is no longer about risk (things that may or may not happen) or compliance (boxes to tick and unnecessary bureaucracy). The "*when,* not *if*" paradigm has changed the game.

And with it the focus of the board has shifted towards execution, very often in exchange for significant investments in cybersecurity—in particular where initial maturity levels are low. This is no longer about understanding what's being done against cyber threats; it's about getting it done and getting it done now.

So frankly, our six questions from **2015** now boil down to two—in particular where a large programme of cybersecurity transformation is needed:

Who Is in Charge?

A board member must take direct accountability and responsibility for the security transformation programme delivery. Period.

This is no longer about wheeling in the CISO twice a year. This is about getting clear and accurate reports on progress at each meeting in return for the large investments consented.

So one board member must carry the can, preferably one closely associated with the operational challenges involved—not the head of risk or (with respect) the head of HR.

This is not about knowing which head will roll at the next breach but giving the initiative the right profile. Any large-scale security transformation programme can only be complex and transversal. In global firms, the international aspects could add a considerable dimension to the task. Without the credible and visible backing of the most senior sponsor, chances of success are significantly diminished.

At the same time, the task must convey a degree of accountability and must become a factor in determining the compensation level of the board member in charge—in stock and in cash and with retrospect. The situation that has surrounded the ousted CEO of Equifax will not be tolerated much longer by consumers, citizens, or politicians and can only breed adverse sentiment against the corporate world and further regulation.

What Are We Doing about It?

Here it is time to go back to the monitoring of good old-fashioned milestones against the deliverables of the programme of work.

What was meant to be done last month, and did it get done? No need for convoluted "return-on-security-investments" discussions or fuzzy risk models.

Of course, the detailed tracking of achievement should be done downstream from the board—in particular for large, complex, or global programmes. But the consolidated results should be clear, concise, factual, and delivered in person by the board member in charge.

Those two actions—personalisation and factualisation, underpinning a drive towards clarity and simplicity—will bring results over time, but here lies the main challenge for many boards and their members:

Thinking over the medium to long term and keeping steady orientations in the face of potentially changing business conditions is necessary to the success of any complex cyber transformation programmes because of their inherent transversal complexity (and also because in many cases, this is about catching up in a few years over fifteen years of lip service or underinvestment).

The board must be capable of driving a long-term vision for all this to work, even if "in the long term, we're all dead."

56

Cybersecurity: There Are Still Problems at the Top

(11 February 2021)

Only a Cultural Shift across the Boardroom Can Move the Needle

The survey released by BT Security in January **2021** is interesting, if only by the size of the population surveyed (over seven thousand people) and its triple focus on consumers, employees, and business leaders.[33]

But its findings are problematic—particularly what they reveal about the attitude of senior executives towards cybersecurity and the persistence of some problems at the top.

It starts well, with some stats broadly consistent with other surveys and anecdotal field evidence: **58%** saying that improving data and network security has become more important to their organisation in the last year and **76%** rating their organisations as "good" or "excellent" at protecting itself from cyber threats.

But these stats are hard to reconcile with others in the report. On page **7**, they mention that "fewer than one third of business leaders rate key components of their company's IT security as excellent" and that, broadly, they have "low confidence in the organisation's ability to deliver the fundamentals." Also, page **13** mentions the statement that "fewer than half of executives and employees can put a name to their CISO."

Without fuller access to the underlying data set, it is hard to draw hard conclusions beyond the fact that, clearly, an amount of confusion persists among business leaders around cybersecurity. How can you say that security is becoming more important and your organisation is well protected and at the same time be unable to name your CISO? And what does that tell us about the profile of the CISOs in those organisations?

Another aspect, typical of those surveys, is the emphasis on getting the security basics right and the importance of awareness development among employees.

To truly move the needle on those matters, you need to go beyond the obvious and start confronting the real underlying issues. This is something on which we already commented last year, in relation to several reports from the World Economic Forum.

Of course, getting the basics right and training employees are essential pillars of any cybersecurity practice, but the real question remains:

Why are we still here banging on about it?

Good cybersecurity practices, such as those mentioned in the BT survey (patching, access management, etc.) have been regarded as good practices for the best part of the last two decades, and large organisations that, collectively, would have spent tens or hundreds of millions on cybersecurity across that period should not be in such poor state. Period.

The underlying causes of that failure are rooted in adverse prioritisation by the business, short-termism, and internal politics. All factors point firmly towards problems of culture and governance at the top.

Until surveys such as this one, or the ones from the WEF we commented on last year, start tackling those issues, not much will move for good around cybersecurity.

The same can be said broadly around security awareness development. Of course, it's essential, but the "human firewall" has to start at the top of the organisation.

How can you expect staff to follow good practices and accept security constraints if they see senior executives constantly allowed to skip the rules?

There is so much a CISO and their organisation can push horizontally across the business or from the bottom up, and without a clear and unambiguous endorsement from the top, the best cybersecurity awareness programme can quickly turn into an expensive box-checking exercise. The example must come consistently from the top for any security awareness programme to stick and yield results.

So the CISOs are indeed "under the spotlight," but can they really "drive the reset" induced by the "speed and scale of the digital transformation triggered by the global pandemic" (page **13**)?

In the current state of affairs, probably not.

The attitude senior executives have had towards security in most organisations over the past two decades has driven towards

CISO roles a certain type of people. Most are technologists, consultants, or auditors by background; very few come from true business roles.

So before the CISO can "drive the reset," it is the role itself that needs a reset. "Enterprises urgently need to elevate cybersecurity leadership" (page **13**).

On that point, the BT survey is spot on. But it is easier said than done.

Once again, this is something that has to come from the top, and it may require a broadening of the traditional CISO portfolio towards continuity and privacy, effectively building up the role into an elevated CSO role able to reach across the organisation.

Such shift, supported at board level and coupled with adequate compensation packages and career profiling, should attract a different type of executive and drive change. This is the type of move we have been advocating since **2018** to address the challenges of the digital transformation and the increased demands on privacy compliance that came with GDPR.

But going back to the BT survey, to fix all this and get cybersecurity moving for good, you need to tackle the problem at board level, not at CISO level.

It is only a cultural shift across the boardroom that will move the needle.

57

The Three Biggest Mistakes the Board Can Make around Cybersecurity

(25 February 2021)

The Protection of the Business from Cyber Threats Is Something You Need to Grow, Not Something You Can Buy

The role of the board in relation to cybersecurity is a topic we have visited several times since **2015**, first in the wake of the TalkTalk data breach in the United Kingdom, then in **2019** following the WannaCry and NotPeyta outbreaks and data breaches at BA, Marriott, and Equifax, among others. This is also a topic we have been researching with techUK, and that collaboration resulted in the start of their *Cyber People* series and the production of the "CISO at the C-Suite" report at the end of **2020**.

Overall, although the topic of cybersecurity is now definitely on the board's agenda in most organisations, it is rarely a fixed item. More often than not, it makes appearances at the request of the audit and risk committee, after a question from a non-executive director or, worse, in response to a security incident or a near-miss.

All this hides a pattern of recurrent cultural and governance attitudes that could be hindering cybersecurity more than enabling it.

There are three big mistakes the board needs to avoid to promote cybersecurity and prevent breaches.

1. Downgrading It: "We Have Bigger Fishes to Fry."

Of course, each organisation is different, and the COVID crisis is affecting each differently—from those nearing collapse, to those that are booming.

But pretending that the protection of the business from cyber threats is not a relevant board topic now borders on negligence and is certainly a matter of poor governance that non-executive directors have a duty to pick up.

cyber-attacks are in the news every week and have been the direct cause of millions in direct losses and hundreds of millions in lost revenues in many large organisations across almost all industry sectors.

Data privacy regulators have suffered setbacks in **2020**. They have been forced to adjust down some of their fines (BA, Marriott), and we have also seen a first successful challenge in Austria leading to a multimillion fine being overturned (€**18** million for Austrian Post). Nevertheless, fines are now reaching the millions or tens of millions regularly. It is still very far from the **4**% of global turnover allowed under the GDPR, but the upwards trend is clear (as DLA Piper highlighted in their **2021** GDPR survey), and those numbers should register on the radar of most boards.

Finally, the COVID crisis has made most businesses heavily dependent on digital services, the stability of which is built on sound cybersecurity practices, in-house and across the supply chain.

Cybersecurity has become a pillar of the "new normal" and, even more than before, should be a regular board agenda, clearly visible in the portfolio of one member who should have part of their remuneration linked to it (should remuneration practices allow). As stated above, this is fast becoming a plain matter of good governance.

2. Seeing It as an IT Problem: "IT Is Dealing with This."

This is a dangerous stance at a number of levels.

First, cybersecurity has never been a purely technological matter. The protection of the business from cyber threats has always required concerted action at people, process, and technology levels across the organisation.

Reducing it to a tech matter downgrades the subject, and as a result, the calibre of talent it attracts. In large organisations that are intrinsically territorial and political, it has led to an endemic failure to address cross-silo issues for decades (e.g., around identity or vendor risk management) in spite of the millions spent on those matters with tech vendors and consultants.

So it should not be left to the CIO to deal with, unless their profile is sufficiently elevated within the organisation.

In the past, we have advocated alternative organisational models to address the challenges of the digital transformation and the necessary reinforcement of practices around data privacy in the wake of the GDPR. They remain current and, of course, are not meant to replace the "three lines of defence" type of models.

But here again, caution should prevail. It is easy—particularly in large firms—to overengineer the three lines of defence and to build monstrous, inefficient control models. The three lines of defence can only work on trust, and they must bring visible value to each part of the control organisation to avoid creating a culture of suspicion and regulatory window dressing.

3. Throwing Money at It: "How Much Do We Need to Spend to Get this Fixed?"

The protection of the business from cyber threats is something you need to grow, not something you can buy—in spite of what countless tech vendors and consultants would like you to believe.

As a matter of fact, most of the breached organisations of the past few years—BA, Marriott, Equifax, Travelex, etc. (the list is long)—would have spent collectively tens or hundreds of millions on cybersecurity products over the last decades.

Where cybersecurity maturity is low and profound transformation is required, simply throwing money at the problem is rarely the answer.

Of course, investments will be required, but the real "silver bullets" are to be found in corporate culture, corporate governance, and the true embedding of business protection values in the corporate purpose. It is something that needs to start at the top of the organisation through visible and credible board ownership of those issues and cascade down through middle management, relayed by incentives and remuneration schemes.

This is more challenging than doing ad hoc pen tests, but it is the only way to lasting long-term success.

58

Turning the Tables on Cybersecurity Budgets

(16 September 2021)

Time to Move Away from Bottom-Up Dynamics: The Board Should Decide on Priorities and Drive the Discussion

As we hit budget time again in many large organisations, it is still amazing to see the amount of content online dedicated to justifying cybersecurity investments or convincing the board.

This is difficult to match with field experience. As we have been saying repeatedly since **2019**, the penny has dropped or is dropping in many boardrooms, in the face of the non-stop epidemic of cyber-attacks we have seen over the past decade, which was even aggravated by the COVID crisis.

cyber-attacks are now seen as a matter of *when*, not *if*. This is no longer, strictly speaking, a matter of risk (something that may or may not happen and has a probability of occurrence) but a matter of certainty, and as a result, the attitude of senior executives has shifted with regard to cybersecurity.

Today questions around "Are we spending enough on cyber?" are more common across the boardroom than "Why do we need to spend so much?"

In many large organisations, the board no longer needs convincing that cybersecurity investments are required. The board needs to be given assurances that delivery and execution will follow, and in that respect, quite a lot of the arguments developed online around the topic seem to be going back several decades.

Board members and senior execs "have been there before" with cyber investment plans. Many large organisations would have spent millions or tens of millions with tech vendors and large consultancies over the past two decades, just to see a fresh-faced CISO (often the last one in a long line) coming back and asking for more money to buy more tech, arguing that threats keep morphing and that the world is about to end unless they buy more tech—all that backed by endless reports from tech vendors and their pet consultants.

CISOs—in particular, incoming CISOs—have to change their narrative to avoid unnecessary discussions. This is no longer about risk reduction or ROI with the board. In real terms, those ships have sailed long ago, and CISOs facing those types of questions must ask themselves the hard questions and face why.

The focus since the start of the COVID crisis has been on tactical and technical initiatives around cybersecurity, but those are rarely truly transformative, and many would just have added various layers of tech legacy on top of already-crowded security estates.

CISOs must start focusing on softer matters and showcase their ability to execute, because the priorities have to be on protecting the business now and in the longer term from real and imminent threats.

It has to start by demonstrating a sense of context, both in terms of business cycles (not all industries have done well throughout the COVID crisis) and security investment cycles. Very few organisations are pure green fields in terms of cybersecurity, and almost always, there will be a legacy of cybersecurity investments and practices to deal with. What happened to the last investments? Were they rightly targeted? What did they achieve (or failed to achieve)? What has prevented sufficient progress?

Showing an understanding of where roadblocks have been in the past, looking over the right time frames, and focusing on transformative initiatives that can actually be delivered in real life, given the business context and the available skills and resources, should be key to convince the board that new forces are at play and that a transformative dynamic is being established to avoid repeating the mistakes of the past.

This is likely to take the CISO into the fields of governance and culture, not technology (both within IT and the business), and those themes should resonate with the board and give them something they can relate to and address. Because fundamentally, this is what matters most.

The board needs to take ownership of the real cybersecurity agenda and start driving it from the top down, at their level, in terms they can understand and manage, removing roadblocks and looking beyond tech and pure tech matters driven bottom-up.

From that point, it should no longer be a matter of convincing the board of anything around cyber but of delivering on what they expect.

59

Cybersecurity: The Message That Never Makes It Up to the Board

(6 January 2022)

Cybersecurity Was Never a Purely Technical Problem; It Is Now a Leadership Imperative in Many Firms

For the past twenty years, cybersecurity ("information security" in its early days) has been seen primarily as a technical matter, to be solved by technologists using technology means.

In most organisations, it has never been "owned" as such at board level in spite of the tidal wave of cyber-attacks that have rocked most industries across the last decade and the false pretence by many that it's on their agenda.

In reality, it appears periodically at board meetings, sometimes as a matter of good governance pushed by independent directors or auditors and sometimes after an incident or a worrying near-miss.

But generally, it remains an operational matter and somebody else's problem—something the board is concerned about and is supportive of, but something the board is not prepared to consider on its own as board-level material as such.

At best, it has been seen historically as part of the enterprise risk-management practice. Nowadays, with the "*when,* not *if*" paradigm around cyber-attacks taking roots, it tends to be seen as part of a broader VUCA agenda, and that is not a bad thing as, indeed, the accumulation of cyber-attacks we have been seeing in recent years do form part of those patterns, in particular those that can be related to state-backed actors.

But quite often, there are also concerns about competence around those matters across the boardroom table. Is the board sufficiently digitally savvy to fully appreciate what is at stake and the right actions to take?

These concerns need to be qualified when it comes to cybersecurity. Firstly, because specific competencies can be brought in if required—that's just good governance and something the board can manage. Secondly, because cybersecurity was never a purely technical problem, and that's the message that has failed to make it up to the board over the past decades.

Fundamentally, the time is coming for senior executives to realise that the predominantly technical approach to cybersecurity that has been prevailing over the past two decades—on its own—is failing to protect large organisations from cyber-attacks. Not just because cyber threats keep morphing, but because large organisations have become too complex—functionally, geographically, and politically—to effectively deploy protective technical measures across their depth and breadth and across their supply chain, in spite of the billions spent collectively on tech vendors and large consultancies.

Now more than ever, it is dangerous to continue seeing cybersecurity only in its technical dimension. It downgrades the problem and prevents real, long-term solutions from emerging, among other reasons, because it alienates real talent.

Only defence-in-depth can protect large organisations from cyber threats, effectively layering controls at people, process, and technology levels in a structured way, supported by accountabilities and responsibilities spanning the entire enterprise and all its silos (IT, HR, business units, geographies, senior management, etc.).

Putting in place a protective architecture of that type becomes a matter of governance and often requires an amount of culture change around the concepts of control and business protection.

It is not primarily about buying more tech but about the embedding of cybersecurity (i.e., the protection of the business from cyber threats) within a broader controls framework and within the culture of the organisation.

Only top-down dynamics can make this happen, and it is a genuine board-level competency to have the leadership, the gravitas, and the political acumen required to drive it.

Delegating it down to technologists has failed and will continue to fail because most technologists are trained and incentivised to deliver on functionality and efficiency, not on culture change or control mindset.

The board has no reason to feel embarrassed in taking ownership of what has become, fundamentally, a leadership matter in most firms—in particular where cyber maturity is low and urgent transformation is required. It is the only way to make it happen.

60

Revisiting the Questions the Board Should Ask (One More Time . . .)

(14 April 2022)

Three Axes of Discussion to Build Up a Cybersecurity Agenda at Board Level

This piece in the HBR caught my attention: "**7** Pressing Cybersecurity Questions Boards Need to Ask," not least because I wrote on the same theme and framed it in the same way at least on two occasions in **2016** and **2019**.[34]

The scene setting around the "five things directors need to know about cybersecurity" is spot on and echoes many aspects we have been endorsing and writing about at Corix Partners since **2015**.

But when it comes to the "seven questions," I am left slightly confused about who is meant to be asking them and to whom. I assume this is a board member asking the others and expecting answers probably from C-suite representatives across the table, but I miss three elements:

- **First of All, I Miss a Clearer Reference to the Cyber Threats the Business Is Facing**

This is not just about knowing what key assets have to be protected, but also about understanding who and what could target them to cause harm to the firm (also how and to what extent).

In fact, only a sound appreciation of the cyber threats involved can determine the nature and level of cyber protection required. You don't defend yourself in the same way against rogue insiders motivated by financial gain or state-backed actors motivated by stealing your IP.

It is the role of the board to understand the level and nature of cyber threats the business is facing and position them on a broader picture encompassing all other threats (e.g., environmental or geopolitical) and in the context in which the business has to operate, often dominated by volatility, uncertainty, and ambiguity.

- **Second, I Miss a Reference to Cybersecurity Maturity Levels**

This cannot be a one-size-fits-all exercise. In spite of the non-stop avalanche of cyber-attacks of the last decade, not all organisations have reached an advanced level of cybersecurity maturity, and many have struggled with the deployment of protective measures due to adverse prioritisation by their business.

Understanding where the firm is on the maturity spectrum and looking without complacency at the root causes that have prevented progress in the past should be key for the board.

After all, good cybersecurity practices have been well established for over two decades and, to a large extent, still provide a degree of protection against most threats.

Waking up today to a low level of cybersecurity maturity should not be treated as "normal" by the board. The underlying causes have to be confronted. They can be financial (underinvestment); cultural (adverse prioritisation, business short-termism); or organisational (low reporting line of the CISO, absence of operating model). The most likely is that they will involve a combination of the three and possibly other elements.

Understanding those should be key to position the questions the board needs to ask at the right level—in particular when it comes to assessing the adequacy of the investment required and targeting action to the right places.

• Finally, I Miss a Broader Reference to the Governance Framework

Within which cybersecurity measures have to be deployed and executed. This is taking me back to my **2016** and **2019** pieces, and frankly, the "who's in charge?" question is still very relevant. To be more precise, it should be, "Who's in charge of what?"

The board is justified in pushing that agenda because of the escalating levels of cyber threats, coupled with the escalating complexity of the modern enterprise and its supply chain.

This is not about deciding whose head will roll in case of a breach but understanding how roles and responsibilities for cyber defence are documented and allocated across the board, the C-suite, and the firm at large.

This can no longer be left to semiformal arrangements and vague job descriptions. It goes way beyond having incident response plans and testing them, and it is not about "wheeling in" the CISO twice a year in front of the board either.

Accountabilities and responsibilities for cybersecurity need to be attributed formally across the firm from the top down at the level of each relevant stakeholder and set in role descriptions, against which objectives can be defined and compensation determined.

Formalising cybersecurity roles and responsibilities would drive the formation and the backbone of a security operating model, against which investments can be justified, progress tracked, and maturity measured.

In conclusion, and revisiting one more time the questions the board should ask around cybersecurity, I would suggest three axes of discussion, to build up the right agenda:

- What cyber threats are targeting us?
  Which assets are they targeting? What harm can they cause, and how?

- How mature are we at defending ourselves against those threats?
  If maturity is not at a level deemed satisfactory, what are we doing about it?

- Who is in charge of what in that context?
  How are organisational arrangements structured and formalised, in a way that would give the board assurance that cybersecurity investments do deliver the expected level of protection, progress is tracked, and maturity maintained or improved?

We are also reaching a point of urgency in many firms where cybersecurity matters can no longer be explained away or delegated down by the board.

Where that is the case, one board member should own and drive such an agenda. If the skills required to understand the situation are perceived as lacking at board level, then they need to be brought in, permanently, temporarily, or on an ad hoc basis.

This is the only way to move things forward around cybersecurity where bottom-up approaches have failed and a strong top-down push is required.

61

Why Cybersecurity Is Now a Board-Level Leadership Imperative

(11 August 2022)

Supporting Cybersecurity and Promoting It Has Now Become a Plain Matter of Good Leadership

We are not hearing enough about the short tenure of the CISO.

Regular studies place it in the region of two years, and anecdotal evidence from my own network, based on the analysis of the profile of fifteen current CISOs, points towards thirty months.

In my opinion, it is often the symptom of serious underlying issues and the cornerstone of long-term stagnation for many cybersecurity practices in large firms.

We have to look beyond the most commonly invoked reasons: Lack of resources, disconnect with management, and constant firefighting leading to mental health issues and burnout.

All three aspects, in my opinion, point towards the profile of the CISOs themselves.

Not all organisations are doing well and not all organisations are well managed, but it is hard to imagine one where senior executives and board members would be insensitive to cybersecurity issues, given the level of media coverage of the past decade and the non-stop occurrence of cyber-attacks.

Actually, "are we spending enough on cyber?" has become a far more common question at these levels over recent years than "why do we need to spend so much?"

In such context, CISOs failing to obtain the resources they deem necessary to do their job, should ask themselves where this is going wrong.

More often than not, the problem is rooted, not so much in the amounts involved or the storytelling by the CISOs, but in the excessively technical focus of the demands, and the trust deposited by senior executives in the CISOs themselves with regards to their ability to execute on what they are asking.

Let's not forget that the role of the CISO is rarely a board-level construction engineered top-down; at best, it has evolved bottom-up out of a technical context; in most cases, it is still a technical construction rooted in IT matters.

Over the past decade, many senior executives and Board members in large firms would have seen several generations of CISOs coming up with grandiose plans asking for millions to spend on tech firms and tech products, before disappearing after a few years having achieved very little in practice.

It is hard to get things done in real terms in large firms on a complex topic such as cybersecurity, which cuts across all corporate silos, in particular where maturity levels are low and radical change is required. It requires time, persistence, and relentless drive.

On cybersecurity matters, the penny has dropped years ago in the boardroom around the "when-not-if" paradigm, but CISOs need to understand how much this is changing the nature of the agenda for senior execs.

All of sudden, this is no longer just about risk—something which may or may not happen—or putting ticks in compliance boxes at minimal cost; it becomes a plain matter of business protection and as a result, the actual execution of protective measures becomes paramount.

But CISOs have been poorly prepared by the last decade for the type of management challenges involved in this shift.

They continue to understand "when-not-if" as meaning "whatever-we-do-we-will-be-breached" and to see the value they bring as being rooted simply in the short-term tactical and technical firefighting of cyber-attacks, and not so much in the actual implementation of good practices with the view of delivering a degree of long-term and lasting protection across the firm.

That's the root of the disconnect between CISOs and many senior executives: they are often prepared to consider large investments around cybersecurity, but they expect to be given a sense of perspective, credible execution to follow, and some degree of protection to result from it—not just constant demands to buy more tech, covered in technical jargon, every time something happens...

All this breeds frustration; frustration breeds mutual distrust; distrust breeds unwillingness to commit resources; this is the vicious circle which feeds short tenures.

In practice, short tenures breed long-term stagnation: you don't achieve a lot in large firms in two to three years; quite often, very little gets done beyond tactical measures and alleged technical low-hanging fruits; almost always, projects which have started are aborted or left unfinished, as the next CISO has other views, or business priorities have changed.

To break this spiral of failure, in particular where maturity is low and things need to change, the board needs to take ownership, assign clear responsibility for cybersecurity to a senior executive they trust at their level, and start driving the topic top-down with a sense of long-term perspective, looking beyond the day-to-day of the business.

Board members often object that they simply don't have the skills to do that, but in my opinion, it is a misconception, and they must not stop at that hurdle. Cybersecurity is not just a technology problem—it never was.

It is a problem rooted in culture and governance, which happens to have a technology dimension like almost everything large enterprises do.

Getting the governance right from the top down around cybersecurity is a plain leadership matter which fits perfectly in a board agenda, and the necessary start to embed the right business protection culture in each and every corporate silo.

Middle management needs to see the right attitude, the right example and the right message coming consistently from the top around cybersecurity, and in most cases, given the right support, they will follow.

Good cybersecurity is quite simply good business; it protects the firm and its customers and builds resilience; supporting it and promoting it has now become a plain matter of good leadership.

62

Why Would You Expect Your Current CISO to Sit on The Board?

(15 June 2023)

Research Suggests Only 14% of CISOs Appear to Have the Skills Required, but Does It Really Matter?

A recent survey by IANS Research[35] highlights that only 14% of CISOs appear to have the skills required to sit at board level.

The findings have been widely relayed on social media and commented on as if they were a surprise, but frankly, why should we be expecting anything else?

Most CISOs I come across are still technologists by background and by trade, and their personal development over the past decade has been heavily conditioned by the constant firefighting of cyber-attacks.

Those are not the type of situations where you can be expected to build up the type of political acumen, management experience and personal gravitas that would be required to be credible in senior executive positions.

In these columns, we have been writing for years about the need to elevate the role and look for a different profile for the CISO to allow board-level engagement to take place.

That's the only lesson I would take from the IANS survey: It does not make sense to expect most current CISOs to take a seat at board level, and it could even be counter-productive to elevate arbitrarily unprepared individuals to that type of position. They have a role to play elsewhere in their organization, and there is nothing wrong with that.

If you want to inject cyber competence at board level ahead of forthcoming SEC reporting obligations (that's the background of the IANS piece), you should look elsewhere: there is no reason to expect that the first person you should consider appointing at board level to cover cybersecurity matters should be your current CISO.

First of all, it is key to acknowledge that cybersecurity is not—never has been—a purely technical discipline: that's the first message the board needs to hear and acknowledge.

Cybersecurity is fundamentally cross-functional, and its values have to permeate through all corporate silos.

This is not just a matter of culture and awareness, but critically a matter of control and governance—that is, in essence, the spirit of the SEC regulatory intervention in that space.

In that sense, the executive carrying the topic at board level should be a control-minded individual credible at driving cross-functional execution, respected by support and business functions and capable of facing regulators with sufficient gravitas.

It is a dated and dangerous view to consider that the same individual should also have a deep technical understanding of the underlying matters.

Dated, because, as mentioned above, cybersecurity was never a purely technical subject.

And dangerous, because you might end up looking for a profile that simply doesn't exist, waste time, and end up appointing a useless "jack-of-all-trades"

What is required here is true leadership, in particular if cybersecurity maturity is deemed to be low and transformative efforts are required across the business.

The board is a governance body; it has a duty of oversight. What needs to be embodied at board level is the value of controls and key governance and reporting mechanisms ensuring the actual execution of protective measures across the firm.

Nothing else. The board needs to own the topic in its own way, at its own level, in its own language.

It can rely on the expertise of independent directors, bring in additional ones if needed, or specific ad-hoc expertise, but is not the place for deep technical debates and the cybersecurity technical knowledge must be structured and developed elsewhere in the organization.

At board level, embodiment is key: there cannot be any doubt across the firm that cybersecurity is on the board's agenda, and it needs to be reflected in the role titles of relevant board members and the composition of their portfolio.

Having a chief security officer position, for example, at that level sends that type of message and is increasingly what many firms should be considering, instead of pushing up their CISOs into untenable positions.

63

Framing the Role of the Board around Cybersecurity Is No Longer about Risk

(19 October 2023)

Business Protection from Cyber Threats Must Be Rooted in the Reality of the World We Live In

The role of the board with regards to cybersecurity is a topic that keeps coming back and is often addressed in simplistic terms in my view.

I don't think it makes sense to look for "one-size-fits-all" answers to the problem, given the number of parameters at play.

Macroeconomic conditions affecting the business at large, industry-specific aspects of the threat and incident landscape, and in particular the history of the company with cybersecurity and its cyber maturity levels (actual or perceived), are all aspects that should affect the attitude the board takes with regards to the matter.

I wrote on the topic on three occasions: first in 2016, in the wake of the widely publicised TalkTalk data breach in the UK; then again in 2019, following the 2017 Wannacry & NotPetya outbreaks as well as a number of high profile breaches (Equifax, Marriott, British Airways to name a few); and finally in 2022, in response to a piece in the HBR that had attracted my attention.[36]

It is relatively easy to address the problem from a post-breach perspective, as I was doing in 2016 and 2019: the emergency context creates a natural agenda for board members to follow, which they would have encountered in a number of similar crisis-related situations.

It is more difficult to set the tone in a context where the "when-not-if" paradigm around cyber-attacks is turning them into an ongoing reality.

There is also an amount of confusion, in my opinion, in many pieces on the topic with regards the role of the board from a corporate governance perspective, and particular in relation to the role of the executive or leadership team (i.e., the group of people around the CEO actually running the firm and delivering on its strategic and operational objectives). I must admit I might have been guilty of that myself in the past to some extent, and this article is also about re-formulating some positions I took in earlier pieces.

Fundamentally, the board has a duty of oversight over the executive. It should, amongst other things, ensure that the business is adequately protected from all existential and critical threats, not just cyber threats. It is a duty the board has towards shareholders, but also employees, customers, regulators and in some cases, society at large for critical national operators.

So in a first instance, the board should ensure it has a sound appreciation of the threat landscape the business is facing, in terms of potential threats agents, their motivations, degree of sophistication and potential targets.

In some cases, this knowledge and these considerations would have been there for a long time on the board's agenda. After all, global threats did not appear overnight. But this assessment needs to be kept up to date, in particular in relation to cyber threats, and if specific knowledge is missing on some aspects, it needs to be brought in through independent directors or special advisors.

But in all cases, this is something the board needs to develop in their own terms and in their own language.

Then the board should look for unequivocal accountability within the executive team for the protection of the business. And this should go as far as impacting remuneration and compensation for the executives involved.

This may be hard to establish in the face of growing and personal liabilities, but it is not something that should be delegated down, below the executive team, in particular when it comes to cyber threats on the basis that they might be "too technical." As I was writing back in 2022, this is no longer about "wheeling in the CISO twice a year" after something has gone wrong or to put a tick in some compliance box.

The reporting between the board and the executives in charge should be framed in relation to the history and maturity of the firm with regards to its protection from the threats it faces.

For example, irrespective of past accountabilities, it seems unthinkable that cyber threats would not have appeared on the board's agenda in recent years, given the amount of media coverage around some breaches, and the fact that each and every large organisation would have faced some form of incident or near-miss at some stage.

Having set an unequivocal level of accountability with one executive for cybersecurity, the board may want to revisit the history of the firm with regards to cyber protection, to ensure that mistakes are not repeated, that funding is sufficient and overall, that the right timeframes are set and respected, in particular over the mid to long-term horizon if large scale transformative efforts are required around cybersecurity.

We start to see a list of topics emerging, broadly matching my earlier pieces, around the "key questions the board should ask," but more than ever, executive accountability is key in the face of current threats to start building up a meaningful and powerful top-down dialogue around cybersecurity.

Readers may notice that I have not used the word *risk* even once in this article.

Ultimately, risk is about things that may or may not happen: in the face of the "when-not-if" paradigm around cyberthreats—and increasingly other threats as well—it is essential for the board to frame and own business protection as a topic rooted in the reality of the world we live in, not some hypothetical matter which could be somehow mitigated, transferred or accepted.

This is not just a matter of language but a matter of mindset, and it is absolutely key to building meaningful engagement from the board down and across the firm around cybersecurity.

The Fabric of a Successful Security Practice

64
The Key Steps towards a Successful Information Security Practice

(10 June–3 September 2015)

This series deconstructs eight commonly held views on information security that CIOs would have encountered. It highlights the key governance and leadership rules CIOs and CISOs should follow to build and deliver a successful information security practice.

1. Think of Information Security as a Control Function and Not as a Support Function

Information security within a large organisation is often simplistically seen as a support function, and as such, many stakeholders expect it to help streamline or "enable" the business. The reality is, information security needs to be seen as a control function, and rules (which may be perceived as restrictive) are a necessary part of ensuring its effectiveness. CISOs must have the management skills to effectively communicate the threats facing the information assets to all stakeholders across the business, and they must get everyone on the same page when it comes to ensuring the appropriate controls are put in place to protect these assets.

2. Create a Sense of Reality around the Threats, and Do Not Focus Only on IT Aspects

A commonly held view among information security communities is that businesses don't care enough about information security, and decisions are often made from a convenience or avoidance perspective. However, a disproportionate focus on technical details and IT issues by the security teams themselves is often to blame for the disengagement with the subject. It's down to the CISO to effectively communicate to the business the real threats faced by information assets, how this could translate into real consequences across the organisation, and how protective controls can prevent this from happening. If the level of risk (resulting from the presence or absence of controls) is presented in a language that the businesses can understand, the CISO will build a meaningful dialogue with them that should drive the right decisions.

3. Focus Resources on the Proper Implementation of Key Controls and Sell Success

It's often believed that information security is a chronically underfunded practice and budgetary limitations are a barrier to its success. However, research by the World Economic Forum has shown that many large organisations, in fact, spend more than **3%** of their total IT budgets on cybersecurity.[37] Despite this, few have reached an acceptable level of cybersecurity maturity. Instead of requesting budgets to fund new technical initiatives, CISOs should tilt the magnifying glass and focus the resources they do have on the proper implementation of key controls that have been mapped for a long time and alone can be highly successful in preventing most cyber-attacks. Implementing demonstrable controls will give the business confidence that real protective measures are being put in place and that the spend is justified.

4. Pin Tactical Initiatives against a Long-Term Information Security Road Map

Within information security communities, the CISO is frequently regarded as a "firefighter," working mostly in a reactive manner around cybersecurity incidents and attacks. This approach is often further fuelled by management's short-term obsession with audit and compliance issues. While reacting to breaches or acting on regulatory demands will always remain a priority, especially as cyber threats continue to evolve and regulation increases, the key focus should be on addressing the root cause of the underlying problems. The CISO must pin tactical initiatives against the backdrop of a long-term, transformative information security road map and think beyond mere technical and tactical solutions. But to be truly successful, the CISO must also have the gravitas to influence lasting change and the personal skills to drive security transformation.

5. Assign Information Security Responsibilities and Accountabilities

Countless security awareness programmes follow the train of thought that information security is everyone's business—across the organisation. While it's true that everyone in an organisation can do something at their level to protect the business against threats, it cannot be "everyone's responsibility," as this attitude can quickly derive towards becoming "nobody's responsibility." The CIO must ensure that the CISO is accountable for ensuring that the appropriate controls are in place across the organisation, backed by a sound information security governance framework. They must ensure that accountabilities and responsibilities are cascaded down to all relevant stakeholders across all silos (e.g. HR, legal, business units, third parties, etc.).

6. Operate Information Security as a Cross-Silo Practice and Not Just as a Technical Discipline

Information security practice is regularly considered a purely technical discipline. However, information exists in both digital and physical forms and, more importantly, is constantly manipulated by people during the business day. While technology should undoubtedly play a strong role, in many industries, a stronger focus on the other elements of information security is often required. In order to implement an effective information security practice, CISOs need to establish a controls-based mindset across all silos of their organisation.

7. Operate Information Security as an Ongoing Structured Practice and Not Just a Series of Technical Projects

Information security practitioners always seem busy with technical projects. In fact, information security should be there to provide continuous and long-term protection to the business. Therefore, it should not be approached just as a series of tactical projects with a set start date, end date, and checklist of deliverables. All technical projects and tactical initiatives within an organisation's information security practice should be seen as forming part of a structured practice and aligned with a long-term information security strategic road map—aiming to achieve an information security vision and deliver lasting change across the organisation.

8. Operate Information Security to Focus on People and Process Supported by Technology, Not Just the Implementation of the Latest Technical Products

In order to "keep up with the hackers," as technology evolves and cyber-attacks become increasingly more advanced, many believe that business protection is derived primarily from the implementation of the latest technical products and solutions. While it can be tempting to believe that the latest technology products are going to be the "silver bullet" needed to keep the business safe, in reality, there's often more to consider. It's critical that the information security practice addresses any weaknesses in the organisation's functional structure (people and processes) before turning to technical products as potential solutions.

65

Think of Information Security as a Control Function and Not as a Support Function

(7 May 2015)

There is a commonly held view across information security communities that information security should be an "enabler" to the business. This is simply the wrong debate and one that CIOs and CISOs must avoid. Information security results from the application of controls around information to protect the business from the threats it faces.

The "security as an enabler" cliché is often used in contexts where information security functions have historically promoted approaches perceived by business or IT communities as arbitrary and negative (i.e. "disabling"). But it is a cliché also applied broadly to many support functions in a large organisation (IT, HR, procurement, etc. as an "enabler"). It simply means that the business expects support functions to make it work better and not to impose arbitrary or bureaucratic barriers.

But information security is more complex than that, and it cannot be seen just as a support function, ensuring that business processes run safely. It needs to be a control function, mandating protective measures and ensuring that they are implemented. It is there to protect the business from real and active threats. This is no more (or less) enabling than roofs over heads or locks on doors, and saying no to some individuals is sometimes necessary to protect the business as a whole.

The CISO must have the personal, professional, and political gravitas to communicate effectively the reality and seriousness of the threats to all business stakeholders. The need for protection should follow as a natural consequence. Proportionality and common sense should prevail throughout (i.e., ensuring the adequacy of controls in proportion to the threats), and all decisions about controls (including budgetary and financial decisions) should be made in the context of a structured information security governance model.

66

Create a Sense of Reality around the Threats, and Do Not Focus Only on IT Aspects

(14 May 2015)

Another commonly held view across information security communities is that the business doesn't really care about information security. Businesses often end up making decisions about controls from a convenience or cost-avoidance perspective without really understanding the information security context and the risk.

Very often, it is not that the business does not understand the need to protect information but that the CISOs and their teams focus too much on the technical details. At best, it perpetuates the bad practice of treating information security as a mere IT discipline. At worst, it damages relationships as the business is just not interested in this level of detail.

Risk is a consequence of the absence or deficiency of controls. The business can only manage risk on the basis of a clear understanding of the threats it faces and the real controls that are in place to protect it from those threats. Controls work in layers, with some counteracting the absence of others.

It is down to the CISO to communicate this to the business, creating a strong sense of reality around the nature of the threats the business faces and the natural need for protective controls. In turn, the CISO should ensure the proportionality of controls (in relation to the threats), and the business should drive action as it sees fit (and understand the consequences).

To be successful in building up this dialogue, CISOs will have to look beyond pure IT security matters to talk to the business in management terms and in terms of business processes supported by technical solutions (not the other way round).

The business will generally understand if spoken to in its own language. Breaking silos across business, IT, and other communities (HR, legal, insurance etc.) to deliver real, effective, and efficient controls platforms and ongoing support around those is key to success for CISOs.

But ultimately, risk can only be signed off through the right governance mechanisms once all relevant aspects have been taken into account, not on a "piecemeal" basis. If the threats faced by the business are real, and the mandated controls are proportionate, a technical "waiver" (possibly poorly understood) signed off by one business stakeholder does not remove any risk. It simply creates a controls gap that can be exploited and exposes the organisation. It must be recorded, regularly reviewed, and where relevant, escalated as part of a structured information security governance model.

Some information security practices have developed over time a proper "cottage industry" around such "waivers." This is not right and should not be endorsed by auditors and regulators as a valid risk-management mechanism on its own.

If the business is constantly challenging the proportionality of the mandated controls or the real nature of the threats, then the CISO must look with great care at the structure of their own policies and practices and consider the necessary adjustments.

In all cases, a clear information security governance framework should be in place—assigning roles, responsibilities, and accountabilities for all stakeholders across business, IT, and all relevant communities. This allows a meaningful dialogue to take place around those issues and the right decisions to be made at the right level—including any budgetary or financial considerations, without complacency (i.e., taking into account the true geographical perimeter of the business and all relevant partners and suppliers).

67

Focus Resources on the Proper Implementation of Key Controls and Sell Success

(21 May 2015)

Another commonly held view across information security communities is that information security is critically and chronically underfunded and that obtaining the budgetary allocations it deserves is always difficult.

In fact, many large organisations (greater than $5 billion market caps) claim to spend in excess of 3% of their total IT spend on cybersecurity,[38] and on the whole, large firms have invested very significant amounts over time in information security.

Most of them would have had information security practices in operation for years, but according to the same report, in spite of the amounts invested, **79%** have not yet achieved a recognisable level of cybersecurity maturity. This was highlighted in our February **2015** analysis of the World Economic Forum report published on Computing.co.uk.[39]

The business appetite for more investment is frequently limited by the absence of tangible results, as CISOs and their teams constantly ask for more technical resources to drive new technical initiatives. However, properly implemented essential controls can actually prevent approximately **80%** of cyber-attacks—according to the UK GCHQ.[40]

What information security teams critically need is to focus their significant resources (budget and people) towards the real, proper, and demonstrable implementation of those key controls. Focusing on *people* and *process* as well as *technology*, rather than constantly following the latest technology trends, can prevent breaches.

This is about vision, priorities, and results—not just resources. The business will generally give a budget if they have the confidence that real protective measures will be delivered. CIOs and CISOs must sell success internally against the backdrop of a clear, long-term information security vision and within the context of a clear information security governance model.

It should be natural for the business to want to protect itself against real and active threats and to give resources to a person and a team that can articulate a clear vision in that respect—creating a sense of direction and inspiring confidence that things will get done.

68

Pin Tactical Initiatives against a Long-Term Information Security Road Map

(28 May 2015)

Another commonly held view across information security communities is that the CISO can only be a firefighter because of the virulence of cyber threats and the endemic short-termist obsession of management with audit and compliance issues.

As mentioned in the previous article in this series, **79%** of large organisations have not yet achieved any recognisable level of cybersecurity maturity, and cyber threats are continuing to evolve at an increasingly faster pace. So it is understandable that many organisations face immediate problems stemming from incidents or near-misses.

Those must be always addressed and will always require a degree of priority, but successful CISOs must look beyond this and address the root causes of these problems. They must pin those tactical initiatives against the backdrop of a long-term, transformative information security road map and think beyond mere technical solutions to cover all relevant people and process aspects as well.

Failure to achieve this—and reliance on short-term audit or compliance-driven objectives without addressing the underlying cultural or structural issues that have created problems to start with—can only perpetuate an endless project-driven cycle of firefighting and breed bad practices.

In most large organisations where current cybersecurity levels are low, the role of the CISO must be one of a change agent, and the CISO must be prepared to stay in charge for the time it will take for real change to take root. In most large organisations, this will involve (at least) an initial transformation cycle of several years, followed by a consolidation cycle of several years. The CISO must be incentivised to keep their position for that long. Governance and culture are key to driving lasting change, and any change momentum can be devastated by the untimely withdrawal of key personnel.

Lasting change can only stem from a clear, long-term information security vision and be built around a clear information security governance model. This should assign roles, responsibilities, and accountabilities to all stakeholders across the business, IT, and all relevant communities—without complacency (i.e., taking into account the true geographical perimeter of the business and all relevant partners and suppliers).

A clear, long-term information security road map should also allow CIOs and CISOs to fend off arbitrary audit observations and remain in control of their own priorities.

The CISO must have the right blend of technical and management experience to achieve this, coupled with personal gravitas and political acumen to drive change. These are attributes of seniority that are fairly rare, and finding the right profile is key to success.

69

Assign Information Security Responsibilities and Accountabilities

(4 June 2015)

Another commonly held view across information security communities is that information security needs to be everybody's responsibility.

This is the cliché against which countless security awareness development programmes have been justified, and while there is an element of truth in the fact that each employee can do something at their level to protect the organisation against threats, this is true across the board and is not specific to information threats.

In practice, most awareness programmes are missing the point by focusing excessively on a technical message to the detriment of the emotional message. Employees will only change their attitudes to protect the organisation if they care about it to start with. To be effective over the long term, awareness programmes should insist primarily on those emotional aspects—in a way, similar to public campaigns targeted at anti-alcohol abuse or road safety have been structured—and develop the protective bond between the employee and the company. And measuring progress should be built in from the start, through the definition of key indicators and internal focus groups or polling methods.

Of course, this is far more complex (and costlier) than distributing leaflets or mouse mats—and it would force the CISO to work across silos with HR and other corporate functions. Results are hard to predict, let alone return on investment, and can only be rooted in the corporate culture of each organisation. While well-designed, long-term awareness programmes can be an element in the machinery that drives change, when structured around an opportunistic technical angle—and without metrics to measure progress—they can be a catastrophic waste of money.

The CIO must not look at those as any kind of "silver bullet" to deliver change in the security space, even in very large organisations where it seems nothing else could be practically delivered on a global scale due to complex geographical or business spread (and in actuality, those very aspects could make awareness programmes even more difficult to drive).

Driving change in the information security space is complex and takes time. It can only stem from a clear, long-term vision and from the clear assignment of accountabilities, responsibilities, and reporting lines at the top—backed by the right HR provisions in terms of performance management and rewards for key actors.

Information security cannot be just "everybody's responsibility"; over time, it may just become "nobody's responsibility." It needs to be "somebody's responsibility," and that person can only be the CISO.

The CIO must ensure that the CISO is clearly and unambiguously accountable for ensuring that the right controls are in place across the organisation, backed by an information security governance framework that ensures that accountabilities and responsibilities are cascaded down to all relevant stakeholders.

70

Operate Information Security as a Cross-Silo Practice and Not Just as a Technical Discipline

(11 June 2015)[41]

Another commonly held view across information security communities is that information security needs to be primarily a technical discipline.

At face value, this view doesn't make sense because information exists in both physical and digital forms, and more importantly, it is constantly manipulated by people as part of business processes. While most business processes are increasingly dependent on technology, this is not true for all of them (across industries), and certain ones will not benefit greatly from the use of technology.

The role of the CISO will always need to have a technical dimension as a large amount of information is processed through technology and threats often target technology directly. The CISO must understand the technical context to a sufficient degree in order to remain credible when facing IT stakeholders.

However, information must be protected at physical, functional, and digital levels, and a successful information security practice needs to operate across the various silos in the organisation in order to protect the business. Therefore, the CISO will also need to have a significant understanding of the business so that they can communicate with the business leaders in their own language. It is essential that the CISO builds trust in the information security practice with all the stakeholders (business, IT, HR, legal, compliance, etc.).

Consequently, in most large organisations, the day-to-day activities of the CISO will be geared primarily towards management and governance, and the CISO absolutely needs to have the management experience, personal gravitas, and political acumen to influence across the business and IT. A clear, long-term vision, governance, and target operating model around information security is the only way to make CISOs successful in the long term and enable them to generate and maintain change momentum.

To be successful in information security requires a controls-based mindset that reaches into all aspects of an organisation in order to appropriately protect the business. This can only be done by looking beyond the technical aspects and cutting across all the traditional silos within the organisation.

71

Operate Information Security as an Ongoing Structured Practice and Not Just a Series of Technical Projects

(18 June 2015)[42]

Another commonly held view across information security communities is that an information security practice needs to drive technical projects.

In the previous article, it was highlighted that information security needs to be a cross-silo practice rather than a purely technical discipline. The necessary controls around information are required to protect the business from the threats it faces and have to form part of that mindset instead of it being seen as a necessary evil or an occupational hazard. Some will be delivered through IT platforms and others through physical measures, functional measures within business processes, or managerial methods.

Therefore, it does not make sense to consider information security just as a series of technical projects. One of the key attributes of a project is that it has a start date and an end date with a number of clearly defined deliverables. If information security is merely structured as a series of projects, then it will be focused on the delivery of specific items rather than an ongoing structured practice that provides continuous protection to the business.

Technical projects must form part of a strategic road map—required to achieve an information security vision that will deliver lasting change to both the business and the information security practice. Otherwise, there can be no guarantee that these projects will be properly organised or joined up.

There is no magical tool or method to achieve that, and it is dangerous to believe that a technical approach alone can deliver it.

Ultimately, a successful information security practice needs to be an ongoing practice, structured around a clear target operating model that architects all activities performed across the function. The CISO has to be the catalyst to make it happen and deliver cost-effective protection to the business. The CISO must drive a security mindset across the firm and cannot be just another IT project manager.

72

Operate Information Security to Focus on People and Process Supported by Technology, Not Just the Implementation of the Latest Technical Products

(25 June 2015)[43]

Another commonly held view across information security communities is that, given the current level of cyber threats, business protection is primarily driven by the implementation of the latest technical information security products (in order to "keep up with the hackers").

Given the complexity of the cyber landscape—and the speed at which both technologies and the related threats are evolving—it is clear that technical information security products are essential to assisting in the protection of information assets. However, it is often easy to forget that information assets do not have a single digital dimension and that, ultimately, it is the combination of digital controls and people's actions—coupled with the right physical and functional processes—that forms the strongest line of defence.

Therefore, to create an effective protection framework for information assets, it is critical for solution architecture and design to focus on people, process, and a clear definition of roles and responsibilities among all stakeholders—before looking for specific technical information security products.

It is all too easy to believe that the latest information security technology is always a "silver bullet" to protect the business. The key to not falling into this trap is to properly understand the threats that you are trying to protect your business against and to focus always on the most appropriate controls to be implemented. What is it that a particular new line of technology will achieve? Can it be practically deployed across the organisation? And will it actually improve the protection of the business, or is it just somebody's "pet project"? Not all controls need to be technical in nature, and sometimes procedural controls will be both more effective and efficient to implement.

Technology vendors are all too keen to sell their products and highlight the benefits that may be derived, but this often ignores the complexities of actually implementing the product across the complete scope of a large organisation.

This all too frequently leads to a situation where a product only ever gets partially implemented and can have a number of potentially damaging consequences:

- The business may be unaware that the complete implementation has failed and so will falsely believe that it is better protected than it actually is.
- When made aware (in particular if this is a recurring event), the business may question the value of the information security function that could erode the CISO's credibility or their ability to secure future budgets.
- The information security team is likely to be frustrated that they have not completed the implementation and don't have visibility or control across the entire organisation.
- The vendor is unlikely to be happy in the longer term because the customer may question recurring charges or the purchase of additional products.

Always following the latest information security technical trends can be dangerous for CISOs. It may assist in putting ticks in audit and compliance boxes, but it also detracts resources from the implementation of essential controls. As mentioned in an earlier article in this series, these essential controls can prevent approximately **80%** of cyber-attacks according to the UK GCHQ. Technical solutions have existed for many years to enable the essential controls, and the CISO's priority must be to ensure that they are properly put in place in support of the right processes.

Making It Work in Real Life

73

Cybersecurity Transformation Is Rooted in Governance and Culture, Not Technology

(23 February–14 April 2016)[44]

Compliance- and audit-oriented "tick-in-the-box" practices are still underpinning many InfoSec strategies. Huge sums of money are being spent on supposedly "one-size-fits-all," reactive solutions to one-off threats. However, such a firefighter mentality is at odds with the holistic, preventive protection that an efficient twenty-first-century InfoSec strategy requires.

Cyber threats have become increasingly salient for most organisations, with potentially fatal consequences in terms of operations, finance, and reputation. The board must realise the growing ubiquity of such threats and the hard, cold fact that cyber-attacks are no longer a matter of *if* but a matter of *when*.

This Is Not Just a Technology Problem

Your organisation forms the most efficient shield against potential threats, and as such, a transition towards an effective InfoSec governance is the only way ahead. A clear, simple, and consistent security mindset must be embedded at every level of the organisation. For many large organisations, this is no longer a matter of awareness development, but a profound matter of cultural change.

Rome was not built in a day, and neither will be a lasting InfoSec culture. As with any organisational change, it will always be a medium- to long-term journey.

For most of the Roman Empire's glory, the protection of the City of Rome was deemed a secondary issue, which could be addressed on an ad hoc basis with interventions by the Roman army. It took the Romans more than three hundred years—and the pressure of a growing crisis due to barbarian threats—to finally decide to build the Aurelian Walls as a consistent and lasting security strategy for their city. They took four years to build, but they protected the city for almost two centuries.

As cybersecurity transformation experts, we feel a lesson can be drawn from history. Most organisations' current approach to InfoSec is, in many regards, very similar to that of overconfident Roman emperors: short-term-oriented, overly expensive, and inefficient in the face of growing threats. Good practices have existed for decades and will go a long way to protect against those threats, but they need to be in place.

In that respect, for many large organisations, driving cybersecurity change starts by looking back and removing the roadblocks that have prevented action in the past. All those (underinvestment, adverse prioritisation, complacency) do challenge governance and cultural practices up to board level. Addressing them is a complex management exercise—and definitely not an IT matter.

74

Getting Real Business Value out of Cybersecurity Assessments

(14 January 2016)

Seven Real-Life Tips for Cybersecurity Practitioners and Senior Executives Who Want to Look Beyond Technical "Box-Checking" Approaches

Cybersecurity assessments can be conducted for a variety of reasons. More often than not, they are performed in response to regulatory concerns, third-party requests, or executive management questions following a widely publicised data breach (the "could-it-happen-to-us?" type of scenario). They are also often ordered by incoming senior executives trying to understand the true nature of the security landscape around them.

Key in this context is to create an assessment dynamic that will produce reliably actionable results, instead of a mere "tick-in-the-box" exercise that middle management could manipulate to justify existing IT projects or the status quo.

There are countless software assessment tools that can be used in that space, but it is key to start from governance, process, and methodology before looking for the right automation tool.

The most common mistake with cybersecurity assessments—in particular in large organisations—is to design an assessment practice around the capabilities of a software tool. Business value will not come directly from any software functionality but from the assessment's relevance, the true engagement of key stakeholders, and their trust in the validity of the results.

Relevance will come from understanding the legacy context in which the assessment is rooted. Engagement and trust will come out of honesty, competence, transparency, and independence of the assessors from any legacy situation.

In order to generate a true transformational dynamic out of this, a number of key management rules have to be followed.

Fig. 10. The Cybersecurity Assessment Cycle

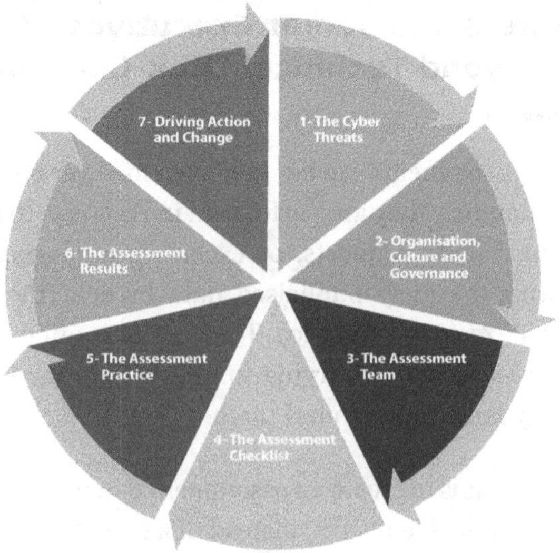

1. Cybersecurity Assessments Must Start from the Start: What Are the Cyber Threats the Organisation Faces?

The assessment practitioners should start by "doing their homework" (instead of relying on generic, ready-made statements) and identifying threat agents, attack vectors, and attack surfaces in the actual context of the organisation being assessed.

They should look without complacency at the true geographical footprint of the business and its dependency on third parties, as well as industry dynamics around threats and recent attacks.

On that basis, they must assemble a number of compelling war stories to open the eyes of executive management (if necessary) to the real nature of the cyber threats their business is facing.

2. Understand the Existing Organisation and Its Culture to Build a Clear Governance Framework Surrounding the Assessment from the Start

Getting the governance context right from the start is also fundamental to engineering acceptance of the assessment results and, ultimately, driving corrective action by the right stakeholders at the right level.

The assessment sponsors must be clearly identified. The assessment practitioners must understand without ambiguity whom they are working for and what the sponsors' objectives are; how the assessment's results are going to be used (e.g., reporting into risk and compliance or audit committees); and by whom, for what purpose, and at which frequency. The internal culture surrounding "controls" at large must also be understood.

The purpose and context of the exercise must be clear: Assessing compliance? (Against what?) Assessing risk? (What does that mean?) Assessing maturity? (According to which model?) Is this going to be a "one-off" or a periodic exercise? What are the time frames involved?

The actual scope of the exercise and the key stakeholders must be clearly identified: Who is in charge of what? Is there one specific individual identified as being in charge of cybersecurity?

Practitioners must understand, as much as possible, the roles—past and present—of the various parties in relation to the existing cybersecurity posture of the organisation being assessed and their reporting lines. Again, they must not underestimate the true geographical footprint of the business and its dependency on third parties.

On the basis of the analysis detailed above, a clear steering committee format, membership, and meeting schedule should be defined and signed off by all parties to oversee the assessment exercise over the required time frames (multiple committees may be required at different levels for large organisations—equally, existing committee structures may be reused where relevant).

3. Assembling the Assessment Team: Balance Experience with Common Sense and Inquisitiveness

The team can be structured around internal resources or rely on external consultants, but in all cases, it must be totally independent of the pre-existing cybersecurity organisation and any legacy situation or arrangement.

Assessment team members must have a degree of knowledge of the cybersecurity field, but they do not need to be all subject-matter experts, and they must not be all technologists.

They must have enough experience to spot nonsense and understand what to challenge and where to stop. At the same time, they need to have the inquisitiveness to dig in the right areas or look behind the curtains.

Fundamentally, they must be empathetic and be able to build trust with stakeholders by showing them they understand their constraints.

4. Assembling the Assessment Checklist: Firmly Root Your Assessment in Existing Material—Good or Bad; Do Not Trust Ready-Made Checklists

Practitioners must start from existing internal material in terms of policies, procedures, and guidelines to build their assessment checklist instead of relying on ready-made material. Most large organisations would have had information security practices for years, and practitioners should find a vast amount of existing internal material in that space:

- If the existing internal material is too large or too complex, simplify it.
- If it's too vague, enrich it with the right amount of (relevant) good practice.

But in all cases, traceability to pre-existing internal material must be regarded as paramount.

It should give stakeholders a sense of continuity, coherence, and value of their past efforts where relevant. Ignoring valued pieces of existing documentation that might have taken vast efforts to assemble or replacing them with arbitrary, external good practices can only alienate stakeholders.

But practitioners must also assess upfront the pre-existing governance model surrounding all internal material collected. How was it assembled? By whom? When? When was it last updated? What are the internal validation processes surrounding it? How was it communicated to relevant stakeholders?

They must tailor their assessment checklist to focus on the sponsor's objectives and the purpose of the exercise (e.g., compliance versus risk versus maturity assessment, as highlighted above) while respecting the following:

- The validity and relevance of pre-existing material (ensuring such material remains traceable throughout)
- The prescribed time frames and your own resources (both may be constrained by the budget available to perform the exercise)

Simplicity, industry relevance, and clarity of language must rule throughout.

This type of exercise will bring the assessment practitioners in contact with the key cybersecurity players (typically, the CISO—or equivalent—and their team) and will give them an important vehicle to win their trust by showing they understand their capabilities and constraints. This degree of trust (between the assessor and the assessed) will be fundamental to the accuracy and honesty of the assessment itself. From the accuracy of the assessment will be derived the results' relevance and actionability and, from there, the genuine value of the exercise to the business as a whole.

5. The Practice of the Assessment Itself: Listen, Listen, Listen

Cybersecurity is a complex topic, where problems are often rooted in decades of short-termism, underinvestment, adverse prioritisation, or excessive focus on arbitrary technical solutions at the expense of sound governance practices and common sense.

In any large organisation, the assessment practitioners are likely to come across a complex historical context and often a vast amount of technical and personal legacy. It is essential to capture—or at least understand—the "softer" (human) aspects:

- Practitioners should analyse their checklist and group subjects by themes.
- They should identify relevant stakeholders, book meetings in advance, and meet with them on their turf (preferably face to face) to form a personal bond, even if it forces them to travel.
- They must not follow the structure of their checklist to the letter. Instead, they should ask open questions, let the stakeholders talk, and *listen, listen, listen* before reassembling the stakeholders' input to match the intended output of the checklist.

Practitioners are also likely to find situations where a number of initiatives or projects are already underway in the cybersecurity space. They must understand their scope, their context, their degree of advancement, and the stakeholders involved.

They should record fairly without burying bad news and give due credit to unstructured practices where they are efficient.

Overall, the assessment team must be kept small and compact, even for large-scale assessments. Meeting notes should be recorded ASAP and shared with other members of the assessment team.

Validation must take place transparently with key stakeholders throughout the assessment and step by step. It will ensure they buy into the overall approach, drive a common interpretation of the assessment checklist, and ultimately, engineer a stronger acceptance of the findings.

Analysing and Presenting Results: Do Not Catch Senior Management Unaware

The assessment practitioners must understand upfront what works best in terms of presentation format for the organisation being assessed (i.e., the type of format that is already being used that senior management would recognise and be comfortable with).

Assessment results must be formally linked to the threats identified upfront and work underway. Initiatives and projects, good or bad, must be acknowledged.

The strength of graphical models should be used to allow "what-if" scenarios to be visualised, typically around quick wins (should there be any) or projects already underway.

Again, simplicity and clarity of language must rule throughout. The focus must be on hard facts and the hard reality of the assessment results, instead of fuzzy numbers, arbitrary "ROI" calculations, and other highly disputable business justifications.

Fundamental to results acceptance is not to catch senior management unaware if results are bad. Nobody likes to be "embarrassed" publicly in meetings. Instead, senior assessment team leaders should book briefing sessions ahead of key validation meetings with relevant stakeholders and allow them to voice their views in private.

7. Creating Change Dynamics and Driving Real Action

Real and lasting change in the cybersecurity space can be complex and take time to be delivered. It is fundamental to put actions in the right perspective in terms of time frames and build on work underway—good or bad—as much as realistically possible.

The focus must not be purely on technical solutions. Technology should support and enable sound security processes. Large organisations facing complex cross-silos problems (e.g., in the identity and access management space) must resist the urge to build security processes around technical platforms for the sake of winning time. This is rarely the case, and many large companies have been getting it wrong for the last fifteen years (in many instances pushed by shameless vendors).

Equally, the focus must not be on looking for arbitrary quick wins, as there may not be any. Instead, the focus must be on looking into the past for roadblocks that have prevented progress and finding ways to remove them or circumnavigate them, challenging the organisational status quo if necessary. People and organisational structures in place may be unable to lead change, and it could be that changing those is the right place to start.

Most cybersecurity problems will be rooted in culture, governance, and process. This is where corrective action should be rooted too to be successful.

Building a support coalition among business leaders is fundamental to ensuring funding over the medium to long term. The approach highlighted above—clear governance established upfront with all stakeholders and constructive assessment leading to genuine findings acceptance—should lead to it naturally.

75

Cybersecurity Awareness Programmes: Are They Really Working and What to Do about Them

(24 February 2022)

When Some People Say They Don't Know What to Do around Cyber, You May Want to Ask Them Where They Have Been for the Last Ten Years

For a number of years, I have been puzzled by the high idea some cybersecurity professionals seem to have that their job is about convincing other people: convincing users that they need to do certain things to protect themselves and their data, convincing the board that they need to invest more to protect the business, etc.

There is also the prevailing sentiment across cybersecurity communities that those are rational arguments, to be won through facts and figures.

Somehow, there seems to be the sense that employees don't know what to do around cyber and that the board does not understand. They need to be educated or trained about it, it needs to be explained to them, and cybersecurity needs to be brought to their level—up or down.

All too often, the argument is framed in technical terms, irrespective of the target audience and the business environment and culture in which they operate.

This approach is flawed at two levels in my opinion:

First of all, I think the argument wherein employees and executives need to be educated around cyber is losing ground and credibility. The last decade has seen a non-stop avalanche of cyber-attacks at all sorts of levels—personal as well as corporate. Most of the enterprise communities would have been exposed by now to some of those incidents and would have built up an amount of knowledge around what they mean and how to deal with them.

Large organisations—and public agencies—have had cybersecurity practices and have been running security *awareness* campaigns in some form or another for the best part of the last two decades. Frankly, when some people say they don't know what to do around cyber, you may want to ask them where they have been for the last ten years.

Fundamentally, we have to question why the messages the cybersecurity professionals have been trying to push collectively over the years don't seem to leave an imprint.

My view is that, beyond the technical aspects I mentioned above, we have also been framing the messages in a way that is too functional and too rational while we are dealing in fact with a situation that is mostly cultural.

We have to assume—and this is my second point—that we may be dealing with cognitive biases and an emotional attachment to the firm and its values that require a different approach.

The key here is to find ways of embedding cybersecurity—and business protection at large—in the cultural fabric of an organisation. This is not something cyber professionals can engineer by themselves and push bottom-up or sideways. To a large extent, it needs to be seen as coming from the top.

Fundamentally, it is a natural human instinct to protect what you care about: your home, your children, etc. Employees, like executives, cannot say anymore that they don't know what cyber risk is about because of the avalanche of cases we have seen over the last decades.

For them to react to it, cybersecurity needs to be framed in their culture and by their peers and, more importantly, in the real context of their jobs. It cannot come from an outsider like the CISO or, to a lesser extent, the CIO.

To put it negatively and forcing the trait, you can spend as much money as you like around cybersecurity awareness if people see managers and senior execs constantly flaunting the rules—and being allowed to do it.

If the corporate culture is toxic and employees are not happy in their jobs and in their relationship with the firm and its management, do not expect cybersecurity and the protection of the firm's data assets to be on anybody's radar. Trying to engineer positive dynamics around cybersecurity will be costly and will probably not lead very far.

Broadly speaking and looking at it from a long-term perspective, we have to consider that those types of awareness programmes—driven bottom-up or sideways by CISOs and CIOs—have not worked well enough over the years, beyond putting—at great cost—a proverbial tick in compliance boxes. They have been tried and tested in all sorts of formats over the past two decades, and we wouldn't be here writing about this if they were working as they pretended to be.

So things need to change, and the first step is to stop repeating the mistakes of the past.

Senior execs must take the lead around security awareness and drive it from the top down consistently towards their people, in their own language, and in their own ways—at the level they believe to be pertinent for the firm.

If they don't see the need or remain in denial about it, I think we have passed the point where we should expect cybersecurity professionals to "convince" them.

In the face of non-stop cyber-attacks, we have now entered the realm of corporate governance, and I think the board should simply mandate it. I would see it as a duty for independent directors to ensure it gets done.

If skills remain a problem at that level, then appointing a cybersecurity specialist at board level should be considered, but that's now the only way—in my view—for this to start moving forward.

76

Managing Risk or Managing Risks?

(2 February 2017)

The Keys to a Successful Second Line of Defence

There are many risk-management methodologies in existence, but it is not uncommon to come across large firms still following simplistic, dysfunctional, or flawed practices today—particularly around operational risk management.

The main issue with many of those approaches is that they are plagued by a fundamental theoretical issue that goes far beyond semantics. There is an abyss between managing "risk" (broadly defined as "the impact of uncertainty on objectives") and managing "risks" (events or scenarios that may have an undesirable outcome).

But many practitioners, when faced with the challenges of establishing a second-line-of-defence type of function, still follow the path of least resistance and start with the arbitrary definition upfront of a series of "risks" that are generally collected through workshops with senior executives in the business. In practice, that's where many aspects start to go wrong, driven by a short-termist business agenda or a complacent "tick-in-the-box" management culture around compliance.

The dynamics of those workshops often revolve around "What keeps you awake at night?" type of discussions, which force the participants to imagine situations where something could go seriously wrong and hit the firm. Participants generally engage with the process based on their own experience and ability to project themselves. Almost always, they draw on past experiences, things they have seen at other companies (in other jobs), or things they have heard of.

Rarely are those stories based on hard facts directly pertinent to the firm and its problems. It often results in organic and very rich exchanges but also leads to an avalanche of scenarios, unstructured and often overlapping. The lack of rigour in the approach also results, in most cases, in a considerable language mix-up, with the description of the so-called "risks" combining shamelessly threats, controls, and other elements—internal or external.

Then follows a second phase, during which participants are asked to estimate how likely those scenarios are to affect the firm and what the resulting financial loss could be.

The first part ("how likely those scenarios are to affect the firm") is plagued by a fundamental confusion between frequency and probability (in many cases, this is entirely by design—i.e., participants being asked, "Could this happen weekly, monthly, annually?").

Again, participants tend to engage with the question by drawing on past experiences (the "bias of imaginability" theorised by Kahneman) or things they have seen elsewhere, irrespective of the actual context of the firm itself. At best, it results in "educated guesses"; at worst, we end up in a purely "finger-in-the-air" territory.

The assessment of the potential financial losses is often more reliable, as this is an area where most of the senior executives involved would have more experience, and as long as the monetary brackets are wide enough, they are likely to put the various scenarios in the right buckets.

At the back of that, a risk "heat map" is drawn, a number of action plans are defined, and a budgetary figure is put on each (in terms of the investment required to have an impact-of-the-risk map). This is the point where risk is either "accepted," "mitigated," or in theory, "transferred."

In practice, the impact of the proposed scenarios on the risk map is often estimated and rarely quantifiable, and the whole process is simply used to drive or justify a positive or negative investment decision or to present an illusion of science to auditors or regulators.

The agreed actions are then given to a project manager or to a programme office to supervise, often with some form of progress reporting back to a risk committee put in place, with all sorts of convoluted KPIs and KRIs wrapped around it.

This whole approach is certainly better than doing nothing, but it is flawed at a number of levels. Essentially, it is vulnerable to political window dressing from start to end, and the various estimations made by senior executives along the chain (willingly or unwillingly) can be used to adjust to any internal political agenda (e.g., presenting a particular picture to regulators, limiting expenditure, and not having to confront boards or business units with an inconvenient truth).

Fundamentally, the "risks" being (allegedly) "managed" may have nothing to do with the actual reality of the firm, and even the "management" aspects may be disputable—in particular if the governance around the actual delivery of the agreed action plan is weak or inefficient (or, at the other end of the scale, bureaucratic and overly complex). This is more about "doing stuff" (at best) than "managing risk" because of the colossal amount of assumptions made along the way.

There are three aspects that need to be addressed for those methods to work better and deliver proper results in terms of real "risk management." Talking to senior executives and running workshops with them is a good start, but they should be focused on "threats" (not "risks") and on the "assets" the "threats" may target. Focusing on threats and assets brings advantages at two levels:

- First, it roots the language of the discussion in the reality of what is at stake, instead of hypothetical scenarios.
- Second, by following simple threat-modelling practices, it offers a structure to guide the discussion with some rigour:
    - Who are the people or organisations who could cause you harm (the threat agents)?
    - What are their motivations? Their level of sophistication? The attack vectors they use? The attack surfaces they look for?
    - What could they do to you?

By combining and ranking these factors, you arrive to a number of key scenarios that are rooted in the reality of the firm and its context, and in the process, you have forced the executives involved to face the reality of the firm, the world it operates in, and its real viciousness.

But for the result to be truly representative and meaningful, it is also essential to ensure that all stakeholders are involved across all geographies and corporate silos (business units, IT, legal, HR, procurement, etc.) and to include key external business partners where business processes or IT facilities have been outsourced.

Asking executive management to place the resulting scenarios in broad financial loss buckets is a good step that is likely to work well, as we indicated before, and could be kept. But the assessment of any form of probability of occurrence or potential impact should be dissociated from the discussion with executives at this stage and, again, firmly rooted in the reality of the firm through an independent assessment of the actual presence or absence of the necessary protective measures.

This is essential in focusing management on the fact that "managing risk" is about protecting the firm from undesirable outcomes. It is achieved through the actual implementation of tangible measures that are known to protect and can be determined upfront based on the identified threat scenarios; mandated by policy or adherence to good practice; and enforced through good governance, internally, and with third parties.

Fig. 11. The Risk-Management Cycle

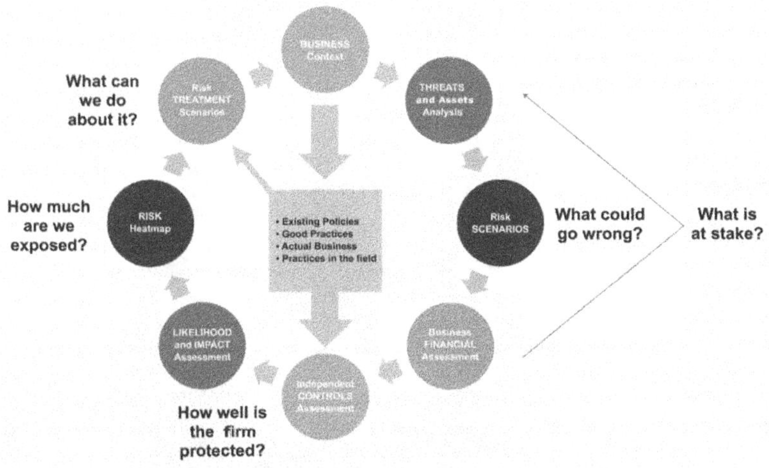

It is then possible to compare those risk-treatment scenarios and determine the most attractive for the firm. It also becomes possible to track and visualise progress in a quantifiable manner.

It is easy to argue that the governance issues around the actual delivery of the agreed risk-treatment actions still remain (in particular for larger firms) and that the two approaches are fundamentally the same (one qualitative and the other quantitative). But the quantitative approach is truer to its purpose ("managing risk"), considerably richer in terms of managerial levers, and far less vulnerable to manipulation and window dressing.

77

The "Three Lines of Defence" Model Only Works on Trust

(20 April 2017)

It is no big secret that the "three lines of defence" model underpinning many GRC practices in large firms is poorly understood and poorly applied at grassroots levels.

Anecdotal evidence we observe in the field every day suggests that many organisations operate it in a variety of hybrid fashions, knowingly or unknowingly, and they experience a range of dysfunctions that seriously limit the value the model is designed to bring.

These dysfunctions all revolve around the same problem in our experience: a form of defiance between the parties that builds up over time and is rooted in inconsistencies, lack of clarity around reporting models, language issues, and a lack of overarching investment coherence at board level.

For example, it is not uncommon to find situations where first-line controls are fundamentally weak or missing in some areas. This is something the second line must identify and report on, but at the same time, the second line cannot become prescriptive with regard to the implementation of the relevant first-line controls (even if the actual nature of the second-line controls themselves may always influence the determination of the first-line controls to be put in place). In those situations, it is unavoidable that first-line stakeholders may feel singled out and exposed, particularly in the following instances:

- Those deficiencies are going to be reported in the simplistic format of a RAG report to a body of management where they are not represented.
- The topic at hand is genuinely complex, multidimensional, and rooted in decades of adverse legacy (and may be impossible to explain in simple terms to senior executives coming from a totally different background).
- The same issues were not identified in an earlier targeted audit performed by the third line.

Their management is clearly pushing them towards other priorities, sometimes coupled with aggressive cost reductions.

It is easy to look at this list and think that most of it revolves around ordinary, day-to-day political dysfunctions that are common to many large firms and impossible to avoid to a large extent. After all, the "three lines of defence" model is not designed to avoid those issues but to highlight them so that they can be treated (maybe).

But it remains unavoidable that, over time, these dynamics create the conditions for distrust to build up at the interface between the lines of defence, in particular if personalities don't match or where differences in personal backgrounds create language issues or other barriers.

Distrust breeds window dressing, and in the long run, it could bring data quality or relevance issues that may seriously skew risk reporting and mislead investors or shareholders.

These situations are generally hard to unlock, with second- and third-line functions often entrenched in dogmatic separation-of-duties considerations.

There are two lines of action to treat the problem:

- Heads of risk, compliance, or internal audit should ensure that counterparts across the lines come from a similar background and professional culture. For example, the second- or third-line staff should have faced the same day-to-day challenges as their first-line counterparts at some point in their career and should, therefore, relate to those more naturally and more practically. Using only lifelong auditors or lifelong consultants to staff those layers often creates the conditions highlighted above.

- Where first-line maturity is really low towards controls and first-line stakeholders are genuinely struggling with the concepts involved, heads of risk, compliance, or internal audit should sponsor the setup of a separate "controls architecture" function (independent from their respective teams) that would assist stakeholders in that respect.

Separation of duties is important, and it is often looked at dogmatically by regulators. But an overarching principle of efficiency has to prevail, in particular where senior management is genuinely driving a culture of change around controls. In an earlier post, we have highlighted how this principle of efficiency could be applied (e.g., where the InfoSec function is structured within the portfolio of the CIO).

Hybrid models can work and bring value around GRC—more than watertight and dogmatic separated models—but as long as the dynamics of trust and efficiency are preserved.

78

Cybersecurity: How Do you Build a Transformational Dynamic?

(19 October 2017)

Security Is Not about "Enabling" the Business but "Protecting" It

At the end of a keynote speech I gave at the excellent CIO WaterCooler LIVE! event in London on **28** September **2017**, on security organisation, governance, and creating the dynamics for change around cybersecurity, I was asked a challenging question on which I would like to elaborate:

It is true that it is one thing (complex enough) to lead and deliver the cybersecurity transformation of an organisation that has reached the point where it knows it needs to change, but it is another thing (equally complex) to create the condition for such realisation to take place.

Where the business mindset is rooted in short-termism and senior executives are unable to look beyond quick wins and the figures for the next month or the next quarter, how do you get them to the point where they realise that without a greater emphasis on security controls, their business will eventually fall victim to cyber criminals, that cyber-attacks are fast becoming a simple matter of *when* (not *if*), and that the associated impact (financial and reputational) is increasingly impossible to quantify?

I don't think this is a battle that can be won through a rational engagement. Essentially, it is rooted in breaking down deep cognitive biases, a situation that has been well analysed by Nobel Prize laureate Daniel Kahneman among others.

In a purely bottom-up approach, it is my opinion that many CISOs are simply wasting their time trying to articulate how security could be a "business enabler," or trying to calculate some hypothetical "ROI" on security investments. More often than not, these exercises only add a vernacular of business language over the same old tech storyline, and when it comes to ROI calculations, those are often open to considerable margins of errors or plagued by untested and unverified modelling techniques. It has reached the point where it knows it needs to change, but it is another one—equally complex—to create the condition for such realisation to take place.

In my opinion, this is not the way you break those cognitive biases, and the problem needs to be approached over time in a completely different manner.

Where security maturity is low but the business is incapable or unwilling to prioritise in favour of much-needed long-term security transformation efforts, the key is for the CISO and the CIO to act at two levels:

First, they must keep their head down and, on a daily basis, continue to deliver on those tactical projects the business wants them to drive. They must be successful at that. They must develop a positive and successful relationship with their business. They must be seen as adding value (whatever value means to the stakeholders).

At the same time, and in parallel to those delivery efforts, they must constantly focus their language towards the business on the reality of the threats it may be facing, not on risks that, ultimately, will always be something that may or may not happen for the business—something you can transfer, mitigate, insure against, not necessarily something you need to *do* something about.

And they should stay well clear of cliché-esque business jargon ("security as a business enabler!") or business concepts they don't master properly ("ROI of security!").

They should stick to their core competencies (that's where they will be successful) and always bring the discussion back to the field of reality. After all, cyber threats are real, virulent, and targeting almost all business sectors. Cybersecurity doesn't have to excuse itself for existing!

Data breach after data breach, incident after incident, newspaper article after newspaper article, the CISO and the CIO need to push those real-life events towards business leaders, picking the right battles and right timing with each executive.

It will require time, political acumen, and a true sense of subtle communication with each business leader, but over time, it will chip away at the defences and create the sense with business leaders that threats are real and internal controls insufficient to ensure adequate protection.

Protecting what you care about is a natural thing for most people, and it should gradually shift priorities towards security matters, to where before they were structurally stacked against those objectives, even in the most complex business situations.

But the CISO and the CIO must also build their own credibility up throughout the exercise, as it is their trustworthiness and ability to deliver the must-needed change that will be tested, and that comes through a demonstrable ability to navigate the political complexity of the firm.

A complex task indeed, in particular in large organisations—not one that needs vague business jargon but strong and determined leadership.

79

The Shifting Debate around Security Metrics

(7 June 2018)

Driving Security Transformation Is Becoming Key, Not Justifying Investments

The age-long debate around security metrics and dashboards seems very much alive within the CISO community, but it is often positioned in an outdated historical perspective. For many CISOs, it seems to be still about "justifying investments" or articulating some form of "return on security investment."

For CIOs and many other C-level executives, those ships sailed long ago. The large-scale cyber-attacks and data breaches of the past decade, coupled with the change in privacy regulation they triggered, have put cyber risk on the board's agenda, and the "*when,* not *if*" paradigm resonates with many board members.

On security matters, "Tell me how much we need to spend," and "Are we spending enough?" have become more common questions around the boardroom than, "Why do you want to spend so much?"

So why are we still hearing some form of disconnect between the CISOs and their bosses on the topic? Trust is at the heart of the problem here and also the nature of the relationship between the CISO and their boss.

Many CIOs don't have any problem justifying security investments in the face of non-stop cyber-attacks. But they know as well that it is getting things done that will protect the firm, not just committing budgetary resources, so the CIO asking the CISO, "Show me what return we will get for such investment," is sometimes a way of saying something else:

- I don't understand why you want to do this.
- I am not sure this is the right thing to do.
- I don't think you will deliver it on any meaningful scale.

It is often a challenge that is born out of some form of distrust. In our experience, where there is complete and total commonality of views between the CISO and their boss around what needs to be done on security and there is full trust around the execution of a common security road map, those issues don't arise, and the question of "return on security investments" is never asked.

The debate around security metrics—like the whole approach to building and managing a successful security practice—needs to shift from a short-termist, project-driven approach to a long-termist, road map–driven one.

In such a context, you mainly need metrics upstream to build and sell the long-term security road map. Those have to be rooted in the reality of the challenges the firm is facing and backed against a sound appreciation of the threats it faces.

Security measures—and the associated investments they require—will protect the firm from real and active threats. Their implementation will modify the cyber risk, cyber maturity, or cyber compliance posture of the organisation (depending on what the main drivers are at the executive level). That's what the associated metrics need to capture and show.

They can be assessment-based metrics but need to be linkable to actual actions, and the methodology must reflect where necessary, in particular in relation to third parties, the lack of availability or reliability of assessment data.

Visualisation is also a key factor. It is essential to put actions in the right long-term perspective and to give management the sense that there is a real purpose behind security measures. This should be accompanied as well by the right governance and operating model to give management assurance around the actual execution of the proposed road map.

Fig. 12. Example of Risk-Treatment Road Map

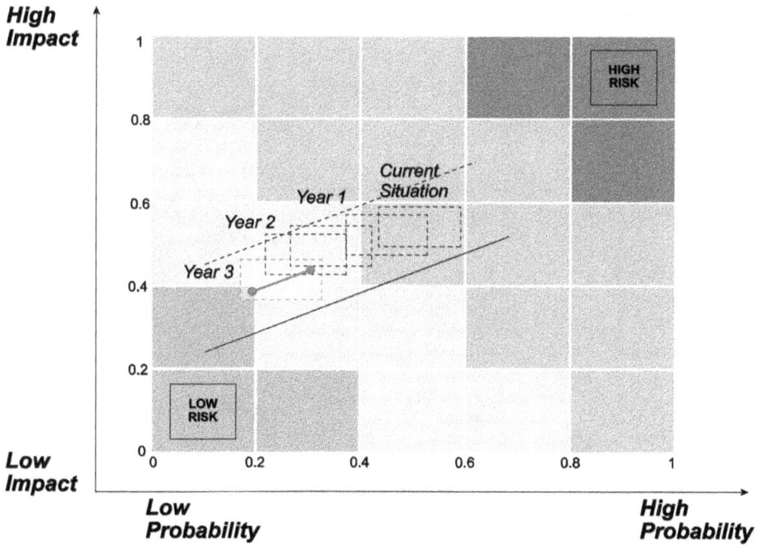

In the example above, the size of each rectangle reflects the uncertainty around data availability or quality, and the evolution of the score for each year would have been associated with actual measures (e.g., year **1**—implementation of an identity and access management model; year **2**—implementation of a vendor risk-management model; etc.).

You will also need metrics downstream to show actual progress against the road map, but those should be standard programme management metrics, and many large organisations will have well-established methodologies in place in support of that.

Overall, selling success will be key. Going back to the original scoring model used to build and sell the road map will give senior executives a sense of continuity and management solidity.

Way beyond the justification of ad hoc investments and pet projects for the CISO, metrics have to be at the heart of the sound security practice, but they must be focused on tracking progress in time in support of a long-term, transformative vision.

80

What to Look Out for When Hiring a New CISO

(21 June 2018)

The Traditional Role of the CISO Is Changing

It is being challenged by emerging new regulations, such as GDPR, that are impacting all industry sectors and the arrival on the scene of the new role of the DPO in many firms.

It is being marginalised by long-term digital transformation trends, which are changing the historical role of the CIO, and the emergence of broader corporate concepts (such as resilience), which are bringing out a more holistic way to address business protection matters from the board down.

At the same time, the CISO role has never been more important, in the wake of non-stop cyber-attacks and data breaches.

Hiring a new CISO could be hard for many firms, and finding the right person will involve a careful approach articulated around the following principles:

The Broad Profile of the Role Must Be Clear: Firefighter, Figurehead, or Change Agent?

First of all, the hiring manager must be clear about the nature and objectives of the role and the context in which the hire is taking place. It could be that the firm has never had a CISO before. It could be that a new role is being created, for example, at group level. It could be that the departing CISO was perceived as highly successful and that their departure is a big loss. It could be that the departing CISO had been in the job for many years but had achieved very little in practice.

At the high level, the hiring manager must define the broad profile of the role—firefighter, figurehead, or change agent?

In all cases, security is becoming a far more complex and transversal matter, and getting results will mean that the CISO will have to work across corporate silos (with IT, HR, other support functions, business units, and geographies). The managerial complexity of the role and the level of experience required to be successful must be acknowledged.

Management Experience Is Paramount, More Than Raw Technical Knowledge

The role of the CISO is no longer some form of a low-grade tech job. Even more, it is no longer a role for a junior executive, a lifelong consultant, or an ex-auditor. It will require grit and true field experience to achieve anything—and preferably a good amount of knowledge of the industry sector and corporate politics. Those only come with real-life management experience.

Judging by what we see in the field, an internal assignment is generally more productive, and less risky, as the new CISO will know the firm and will be known to key stakeholders. But it means that the CISO role must have a truly senior profile to attract the best internally, the incentives package and role visibility have to be right, and the reporting line must match all those factors.

The new CISO does not have to be a technologist or someone already in a CISO role. As a matter of fact, the key will be in their ability to articulate the business value of security, and that should come more naturally to business leaders. Control-mindedness, personal gravitas, and political acumen are likely to be important success attributes for the CISO, probably as important—if not more—than their raw technical knowledge of the security field.

Think Outside the Box, and Take Your Time

This is definitely the type of search for which thinking outside the box could be rewarded, and where most will come—in terms of long-term success—from the personal profile of the individual involved.

Overall, take your time. It is likely the role will be difficult to fill, and rushing into appointing someone "because you need to" will only lead to mistakes. Use an interim CISO if necessary until the right person is found, but you must not hire in a hurry.

This is all the more important for organisations that have never had a CISO before or those that have been stuck in a decade-long spiral of failure around security matters.

It is also essential for those creating a new CISO role, for example, at group level or those moving towards a CSO type of organisational model, as highlighted here by McKinsey & Company.

The CISO role has never been more important. The firms that fail at appointing a new CISO are those that rush and push an inexperienced techie into a poorly defined role.

Positioning the role accurately in relation to the firm's objectives around security, thinking of it as a senior leadership role, and taking the time to find the right leader are the keys to long-term success.

81

The Four Pillars of a Lasting Cybersecurity Transformation

(8 November 2018)

Simply Throwing Money at the Problem Is Rarely the Answer

Many CIOs and CISOs would have come across this situation after an incident, a serious near-miss, or a bad audit report. Suddenly, money and resources—which were previously scarce—appear out of nowhere, priorities shift, and senior executives demand urgent action around cybersecurity.

It is probably the dream of many CISOs to one day inherit such a transformational challenge where money is, apparently, no object. In practice, however, it can also be a curse if you fail to deliver.

What are the key factors in driving successful transformation around cybersecurity?

Setting the Right Time Frames

First, the CISO must assess without complacency the true nature of the transformation required, the depth of commitment of senior management, and the time frames that would be required to deliver real and lasting change–independent of stakeholders' expectations.

This is the first area where the CISO will need to manage expectations with senior executives. Change takes "the time it takes," in particular where culture and behaviours are involved, and some aspects associated with cybersecurity transformation could be complex, disturb existing business practices, and lead to substantial projects (e.g., around identity and access management or data leak prevention).

In our experience, the complete top-down reengineering of an entire security practice can take up to three to five years in any large organisation. Nobody can be expected to achieve anything significant in six months to a year if initial maturity levels are very low; two years may not be enough either.

The first management challenge of the CISO is to get senior stakeholders to understand that fact. This is about a real commitment to change at least as much as it is about resources and the ability to think strategically over the medium to long term. Not all senior executives or board members are capable of doing that. The CISO will have to find the right allies and use their influence to get the message across.

Merely "fixing" illusory quick wins never amounts to lasting transformation.

The realisation of the time frames involved will be rooted in the appreciation by senior management of the tasks involved, and such appreciation needs to be backed against a sound and meaningful assessment of the starting point.

From there, a transformative vision and road map can be drawn by looking towards the right horizon.

Focusing on Clear Transformative Themes and Explicit Goals

In situations where the organisation needs to face fundamental change around cybersecurity, it will be essential to set clear and simple objectives for all parties.

Trying to fix everything at the same time, irrespective of interdependencies, the inherent complexity of some issues, and possibly over unrealistic time frames will simply lead to confusion and failure.

Instead, the CISO should start by assessing dependencies between the various parts of the transformative road map and group action around broad themes, which in turn will focus on priorities and investments.

Those themes should be clear, simple to articulate, and structured around explicit goals and milestones.

Delivering through an Empowered Senior Team

Although there will be projects involved in delivering the transformative road map, the ultimate objective is to create a sustainable and self-standing transformed security practice. To this end, the reengineering of their team needs to be the first task for the CISO so that transformation can be delivered through the reshaped team and not only through contingent project resources and consultants.

Defining the right team structure and operating and governance model should be a top priority for the CISO, involving all relevant stakeholders across IT, business, and support functions and also involving all relevant geographies and third parties.

Staffing the new team should follow and start top-down so that the CISO can delegate the transformative burden to empowered senior direct reports. Once established, this layer of management will take on the duties to staff the rest of their teams and deliver explicit parts of the transformative road map. Finding those people—internally or externally—in the current recruitment market could be tough and take time, so starting as early as possible in this phase should be key for the CISO.

From there, the delivery of the transformative road map can start, but it will be equally crucial for the CISO to ensure that all key personnel are incentivised to stay the course as there may be rough waters ahead.

Sticking to the Plan

Establishing realistic time frames, setting clear goals, and finding the right people to drive the transformative efforts through a structured team are key. In parallel, the CISO should continue to get all parties on board behind the right transformative road map. This phase could easily take up to six months, but it is essential to long-term success.

There may be quick wins, or there may not be. The CISO must resist inventing some where there are none and must also avoid knee-jerk reactions that may only damage the long-term case.

One thing this is not *about is implementing more tech—at least not upfront.*

There is no magical technology platform or service provider that can be, on its own, the answer to a fundamental transformative challenge around cybersecurity.

Technology will, of course, have a role to play in the transformative effort in most organisations, but the CISO and their team must come to that in due course and, in the right context, set up the right transformative vision, road map, and operating model. Jumping at tech solutions and tech vendors upfront cannot be the first thing to do.

The overarching challenge for the CISO behind all this lies in getting senior management to see that a long-term change is rooted in a long-term vision and long-term planning that takes time to establish.

It may be a hard sell in the absence of tactical quick wins, and a lot will rest on the trust between the CISO and their boss, as well as the personal profile, managerial experience, and political acumen of the CISO.

Given the complexities involved, which are not just technical but also often rooted in culture and governance, delivering lasting change will always require a structured approach and a relentless drive to succeed.

Simply throwing money at the problem in the hope of making it disappear, without proper consideration of those matters, simply leads to failure and can only aggravate the perception of the senior stakeholders that security is just a cost and a burden.

82

The Business Value of Cybersecurity

(22 November 2018)[45]

Tangible Business Metrics Are Key but Hard to Find

Cybersecurity is rising as a key issue on the radar of virtually all organisations. According to a recent AT Kearney report, cyber-attacks have been topping executives' lists of business risks for three straight years. This concern is also driven by security and privacy becoming increasingly valued by customers and by regulators stepping into the topic (GDPR in Europe, California Consumer Privacy Act of **2018**).

Beyond this, it is now becoming crystal clear that cybersecurity—beyond good practice and good ethics—is quite simply good business. As a recent Cisco study made clear, cybersecurity will help fuel (and protect) an estimated **$5.3** trillion in private sector digital value at stake in the next ten years. This is the kind of numbers boards cannot afford to overlook.

Tangible estimates like this one, however, are painfully rare in the cybersecurity space. Indeed, concepts relating to cybersecurity are both multifaceted and very elusive—making them notoriously hard to measure. Furthermore, good cybersecurity is defined by the absence of breaches or losses. Observing what is not happening is a challenging—if interesting—endeavour.

A stringent example of this measurement problem can be found in a recent BCG research on "Total Societal Impact." To their credit, cybersecurity is mentioned fairly extensively throughout the report as a key component of a firm's ESG (environmental, social, and governance) strategy—although not consistently across industry sectors.

The issue arises when it comes to quantifying that intuition. The BCG, for example, reports finding a significant link between "securing business and personal data" and a firm's valuation. Looking into the appendix of the report, the problem lies in the fact that this concept seems to be operationalised through a series of somewhat vague dummy (**0/1**) variables. Examples of such metrics include *whether* "measures to ensure customer security" have been taken or *whether* an information security management system has been implemented.

This is not only overly simplistic (hiding key nuances in levels of cybersecurity maturity across firms), but it also encourages "tick-in-the-box" approaches to cybersecurity that have plagued the field for ages. Tellingly, no quantitative results are actually presented for cybersecurity in the report.

This lack of details around the quantification of the tangible value of following cybersecurity best practices is a problem. In fact, we believe it is an important reason why the issue is still shifting in and out of most boards' radars. Gut feeling alone does not make for a strong-enough case. Top executives are increasingly asking, "*Show me the data.*"

Beyond the fact that measuring success in cybersecurity is very hard, another issue is the stringent lack of meaningful data.

This is a really big problem in the field of cyber insurance, for example, which struggles to fit its traditional actuarial models around the scarce data it can get a hold of. The reason for that is quite simple: most organisations are still very reluctant to share what they perceive as highly sensitive cybersecurity data (assuming they even have them to start with).

We also talked about this problem in the context of training defensive AI for cybersecurity, but this scarcity of reliable InfoSec data hinders generally much-needed research and results.

Being able to show key stakeholders in business terms what exactly the tangible value added is of cybersecurity will be key in finally anchoring the topic at the right level of organisations.

Money—and data—talks, and boards usually listen. But we're not there yet, and cybersecurity looks definitely like a promising path for data-driven research.

83

The Two Factors Killing GRC Practices

(31 January 2019)

Excessive Complexity and Lack of First-Line Integration Render Many GRC Metrics Useless

Many CISOs complain of communication problems with their business. They are not being listened to. They are not getting the budget they think they should get. They feel their business prioritises against security too often.

It has been a recurring theme among information security professionals for the best part of the last fifteen years, and it is rooted in a wide range of factors, among which the profile of the CISO is often a dominant limitation.

Many CISOs are simply too technical. They know they need to bridge the gap with their business, but they often return to their comfort zone at the first opportunity. For them, "threats" are often translated into malware, phishing, and hackers, while the business wants to hear insider fraud or intellectual property theft.

This often leads to the CISO role being ring-fenced and limited to its first-line technical remit, while GRC functions develop in the second line of defence. But those functions themselves very often struggle to develop meaningful conversations with their business around cybersecurity.

GRC teams tend to have an ivory-towered view of the problem and rely on ready-made, overly complex methodologies loosely related to the reality of first-line activities.

They rush into buying some tech platform that is supposed to "enable" the GRC process, but in reality, the jargon of those products and methodologies is often meaningless to the business. Impact assessments and risk assessments can be inextricably complex. The quality of the data collected is often questionable as a result, and many of those approaches never scale up for good in large firms due to the sheer human cost of deploying them.

The lack of hard-wiring for first-line activities makes the GRC metrics produced artificial and unusable in practice to recommend, justify, or manage the first-line investment. If, in addition, the scope covered is limited due to deployment or acceptance issues, the overall value of such metrics can be highly disputable—beyond the proverbial "tick-in-the-box" that they will invariably provide.

None of that helps the business understand and manage its cyber risk posture. Over time, distrust sets in, and as the "*when,* not *if*" paradigm around cyber-attacks takes root in the boardroom, senior executives need to find a way out.

It can only involve refocusing GRC practices towards simplicity so they can be effectively and efficiently deployed on a large scale across the real breadth of the firm—and possibly towards its supply chain.

It will also involve refocusing GRC practices towards a proper and meaningful integration with first-line cybersecurity data so that GRC metrics reflect the reality of the first line of defence.

The "*when,* not *if*" paradigm makes the board increasingly willing to invest to ensure the protection of the firm from cyber threats, but it also shifts priorities towards measuring progress and ensuring things get done.

In many firms, the equation between governance, risk, and compliance around cybersecurity is becoming heavily weighted towards the *G*, and GRC functions must adjust as a result, both in terms of internal structures and in terms of interactions with other stakeholders.

In particular, the first line and second line must work together on this. They must trust each other and look beyond absurd and arbitrary "separation of duties" concepts to produce meaningful data for the business, around which meaningful decisions will be made to protect the firm.

84

The Hard Truth around Cybersecurity Awareness Programmes

(10 October 2019)

Five Key Points to Drive Culture Change around Cybersecurity

Culture and governance are key to driving change around cybersecurity behaviours, but too many awareness programmes focus simply on superficial technical gimmicks. Let's start by deconstructing three clichés that have been dominating the security awareness arena for the past decade.

Cliché 1: Cybersecurity Is Everybody's Responsibility

At face value, this is truly a very dangerous argument to manipulate. To answer it using another cliché, there is a fine line between something being everybody's responsibility and the same thing becoming nobody's responsibility.

The key here is to acknowledge that while each employee may have a role to play in securing the firm's assets, those roles do vary from function to function, and failure to communicate with each staff member in meaningful ways in the context of their own job will simply not work. Telling HR staff, who receive CVs by email every day, not to open attachments is a waste of time.

Also, it is essential to acknowledge that the level of engagement of each employee around cybersecurity will depend entirely on the level of engagement the employee has with the firm, its culture, and its values. It is a natural instinct to protect what you care about. Conversely, it can be a hard job to convince disengaged staff, or staff who see senior management constantly being allowed to skip the rules while they have to adhere to stricter measures.

So it may well be that in some form, *cybersecurity is everyone's responsibility*. But the message cannot be generic and has to be structured appropriately. In addition, the example has to come from the top and must be relayed without exception by all middle-management layers for the message of good practice to work through the fabric of the firm.

That's often the most common flaw of many cybersecurity awareness campaigns. They are owned by the cybersecurity team and structured horizontally towards all staff instead of being owned by a board member and structured to cascade vertically through line management. Ownership for cybersecurity has to start at the top. Period. One board member should be visibly in charge, and part of their compensation package should ride on it, as we advocated in an earlier article.

HR management should be involved as well, and they have a key role to play. Specific key responsibilities and accountabilities around cybersecurity should be distributed across staff members and articulated formally in role descriptions. Staff should be incentivised through compensation and by middle management to address those aspects of their roles as an integral part of their job, not as a piece of meaningless management jargon.

Readers may think this is just idealistic and cannot work in most firms, because those layers of management simply would not be interested or would not understand cybersecurity sufficiently to articulate a meaningful vision around it.

They may well be right in many cases, but it is also the role of the CISO to stimulate, structure, and support that type of engagement.

Of course, firms looking to engage in that type of top-down approach to cybersecurity awareness development will need to have the right CISO in terms of personal profile, personal gravitas, and management experience or may need to evolve their security organisation to bring in a broader CSO role.

Those necessary exchanges between the security leadership team and senior management will constitute a fundamental awareness programme just by themselves, but any security awareness development campaign can only be truly successful with a visible and credible board member as a figurehead.

If senior management (including HR management or middle management) is not prepared to engage in a meaningful manner with the fundamental aspects of good security practice, any message anybody may try to drive towards the staff could simply prove to be an expensive waste of money.

Cliché 2: People Are the Weakest Link

They may well be, but the key is to understand why and how in the context of each firm, before jumping to ready-made solutions, in particular with tech vendors.

It has to start from a sound examination of the threats each business is facing. The insider threat may well be a widespread, high-ranking business threat in financial services, not so much maybe in logistics or retail.

Of course, in all firms, there will be people who have access to sensitive business information and who may be tempted or coerced in certain circumstances to leak it out. But the key here is to understand and address their potential motivations in doing so.

Quite often, those motivations will be rooted in corporate culture, management styles, and governance problems—many areas you are not likely to address through a "traditional," tech-focused cybersecurity awareness programme.

It is worth repeating this one more time: staff will protect the firm with a natural instinct if they care about it and share its values and purpose economically and, increasingly, socially as well.

If that sense of care is not there, if the corporate or management culture is toxic, if the employees don't have a sense that they know where the business is going—either because it is not well managed or because its industry sector at large is not doing well—a broader communication initiative addressing staff disengagement is required, and specialised or siloed awareness programmes focusing simply on cybersecurity are not likely to succeed.

The key will be to bring staff on board with a valid corporate purpose they can understand and endorse. The need to protect the firm, in general, as well as its information assets could be one aspect but immersed into a broader campaign aimed at developing a real sense of belonging with employees.

Here again, HR, corporate communications, and senior management at large have a key role to play. One senior executive must visibly own and drive the initiative. Once again, this cannot be siloed and left to the CISO and their team.

Cliché 3: This Is All about "Awareness"

How can it be that some firms—and their CISOs—still believe that their staff, apparently, do not *know* what to do to protect their organisation from cyber threats?

Many people, at an individual level, have experienced fraud attempts or virus attacks. Data breaches and cyber-attacks are constantly in the news, and many online platforms and service providers have strengthened considerably various of their security measures (e.g., around multifactor authentication). Increasingly, people are getting used to those additional layers of security in their everyday life.

More importantly, good security practices have been well established for two decades and have not evolved that much. "Don't write down your password" means the same now as it did ten or twenty years ago. And large firms have spent collectively hundreds of millions across the last two decades on so-called "security awareness" programmes, not to mention governments and their agencies.

So where did it go wrong with those programmes?

The problem is that most of those—over time—have focused too much on making sure people simply *know* what to do around security and not so much on giving them incentives to *act* on it or dealing with the roadblocks preventing staff from enacting good practice.

Just "knowing" what to do to protect your organisation is simply not enough; only the right actions and behaviours can protect the business, so "awareness" by itself is never going to be sufficient without incentives to act and, where necessary, culture change.

In addition, as detailed above, many of those programmes have often fallen short of expectations by being too generic and not rooted in the right cultural context.

Fake phishing campaigns are a good example of where it goes wrong. They have been all the rage for the past few years, but often they contribute to the build-up of a "nasty" culture around cybersecurity. Employees feel tricked and embarrassed, and those are not emotions that are likely to build a favourable ground in which to root good security practices.

Sending random emails, forcing people to follow online training programmes, putting up posters, or distributing mouse mats may well put ticks in compliance boxes, but what does that achieve in real life?

Success criteria ("what good looks like") remain vague, qualitative, or anecdotal in many campaigns (for those that are not designed as a purely box-checking exercise to address some cheap audit point).

That shouldn't be the case, and as a matter of fact, the issue of metrics should be central to any cybersecurity awareness programme and built in from the start. But it is a really difficult topic, which is why it is frequently sidestepped.

The only way to address this in a meaningful manner—for firms large enough to do this—is to fall back on traditional marketing and polling methods:

- Build representative panels of employees across the firm.

- Measure their level of “security awareness” through questionnaires and interviews, in a structured way, prior to launching the campaign.

- Design the campaign to be centred on key findings highlighted by panels and interviews, and deploy it.

- Measure levels of security awareness again and compare.

Of course, as well as difficult, this may be expensive, and priced in from the start, it may well push any programme out of an acceptable budgetary bracket.

But cutting out the metrics aspects, on grounds of costs, from a cybersecurity awareness programme should bring out a real management question to address:

Is it worth spending large amounts on an initiative of that nature, knowing and accepting from the start that you won’t be able to measure its success quantitatively?

Five Key Points to Build a Successful Cybersecurity Culture Change Programme

In summary:

- A board member must visibly own the campaign and act as a figurehead, with the involvement of HR, corporate communications, and the cybersecurity team. It can only work top-down. Accountabilities and responsibilities around cybersecurity must be clear.

- Stay clear of empirical and ready-made solutions. Start with focus groups, questionnaires, and interviews, and measure upfront levels of staff security maturity and engagement with corporate values.

- Centre your campaign on the findings of the initial survey, and define success metrics from the start based on measured maturity levels. Your scope may need to be much broader than just cybersecurity to deliver on staff engagement if initial levels are low.

- Make the messages specific, achievable, and rooted in the real life of each team, driven by line management, *not* the CISO and their team.

- Build incentives for staff to *act*. It cannot be just about *telling* people what to do.

85
In Defence of Maturity-Based Approaches for Cybersecurity

(24 October 2019)

It Doesn't Make Sense to Oppose Maturity- and Risk-Based Approaches to Cybersecurity

This interesting piece from McKinsey has made me think and deserves some comments: "The Risk-Based Approach to Cybersecurity."[46]

The risk-based approach itself that it promotes has solid foundations and is, in fact, nothing new. Actually, in many ways it echoes the model we at Corix Partners have been developing and delivering with clients and associates for the past ten years.

But I don't think it makes sense—or, indeed, helps the industry move forward—to oppose maturity-based approaches and risk-based approaches. And the characterisation of maturity-based models as "a dog that had its day" is frankly excessive.

The assumption that risk-based approaches are somehow more advanced than maturity-based ones and represent an "evolution" of cybersecurity practices is highly disputable, and the quantification of maturity-based approaches as leading to overengineering and overspending by a factor **3** compared to risk-based approaches is simply misleading (a footnote actually refers to the costs mentioned as "illustrative and extrapolated from real-world examples and estimates").

As a matter of fact, those two approaches are just different ways of managing, driving, and measuring action around cybersecurity in different situations and different firms. One does not have to be superior to the other. The keys are elsewhere: the approach one firm decides to follow has to be right in relation to the firm's management and governance culture and its objectives around cybersecurity. Those will vary naturally from one organization to another, and from one management team to the next.

One trend we are observing more and more is actually the weakening of traditional risk and compliance drivers around cybersecurity with senior executives. The "*when,* not *if*" paradigm around cyber-attacks is strongly taking root in many boardrooms, and many firms are committing very large amounts to large-scale transformative security programmes. But in return, the board expects execution and protection, and they are holding CIOs and CISOs accountable for both.

In those situations, risk often goes to the background, delivery takes centre stage, and maturity-based approaches generally work well—as long as they revolve around a clear set of capabilities to be developed through the delivery of clear, tangible actions to achieve a clear target maturity level.

This is not an approach that will work well only in situations where initial maturity levels are low. It can continue to work throughout the maturity spectrum up to advanced levels. As long as the capabilities and actions required to develop them are backed against the firm's objective around cybersecurity and the real threats it is facing, there is no reason to assume that it would lead to a greater degree of overengineering—and overspending—compared to other approaches.

As a matter of fact, whether a firm takes a maturity-driven route or a risk-driven one to ensure it is well protected from cyber threats, none of that changes the nature, reality, and virulence of those threats and, as a result, the nature of the measures the firm needs to have in place to be well protected. Those necessary protective measures may end up ordered or prioritised differently, in order to improve maturity or reduce risk, but barring political manipulation by stakeholders, they will be the same and will cost the same.

The chosen approach simply needs to be right to give the executives in charge the levers they need to understand and manage the firm's cybersecurity posture.

It is our experience that simplicity, clarity, and consistency are often the real factors behind successful approaches, and at that game, maturity-based models often win because they can be action-driven from the start, faster to put in place, and less vulnerable to window dressing by stakeholders.

86

Does the Role of the "Virtual CISO" Make Any Sense?

(28 November 2019)

Outsourcing Something Simply because You Don't Understand It Is Rarely a Good Start

Faced with constant reports of cyber-attacks in the media, most small- and mid-sized organisations have woken up to the reality of cyber threats over the past few years. Many still don't really know what to do to protect themselves and turn to "virtual CISO" services for assistance.

While this is better than doing nothing or relying blindly on the security of cloud providers, those externalised, part-time services—often delivered remotely—are rarely the magic bullets they pretend to be.

And let's eliminate upfront any language ambiguity. The idea of a "virtual" solution to a concrete problem created by real threats is dangerous, and the "virtual CISO" shortcut is definitely one the security industry should try to eliminate. Beyond marketing and hype, either you need a CISO or you don't, but their role (and their actions) cannot be "virtual" to counteract real threats.

Moving on from those considerations, the concept of an externalised, part-time, and partly remote CISO role is generally attractive to small- and medium-sized organisations for numerous reasons:

- First, rightly or wrongly, they often see cybersecurity as a complex technical matter and feel that they do not have the right skills in-house. At the same time, they also think they do not need a full-time security role given their size. Of course, both aspects of that statement are disputable. It is not rare to find IT analysts with cybersecurity as their hobby who could make perfectly suitable CISOs in small firms, and the scale of the role depends on the maturity level of each firm, its regulatory obligations, and its security ambitions.

- Second, an externalised role is seen by many as a cheaper and more flexible task-driven stepping stone for them to understand what the CISO job really entails and the value it can bring, before committing further.

- Finally, for some, externalising the position is also a way of ensuring a degree of independence with regard to internal politics.

Those last two aspects are defendable and may lead to positioning the role at a level where it really adds value. But organisations must also consider the following points to avoid taking a wrong direction:

"We can't afford a full-time role," is an excuse often heard around the appointment of a so-called "virtual CISO."

But this is not just about what one organisation can "afford." Anybody who has spent enough time in the security industry would know that money appears out of nowhere at the first sight of an incident—or of an audit point in some firms.

And how can you determine how much to spend on security until you really understand what you need to do to protect yourself and meet your regulatory obligations?

Outsourcing something simply because you don't understand it is rarely a good start.

The decision around right-sizing and externalising—or not—the role of the CISO must primarily be about what one organisation wants and needs to achieve around cybersecurity and the message it wants to send to its ecosystem on that matter.

Having a CISO of some sort will always be better than not having one when it comes to demonstrating adherence to security values, but relying on an externalised part-time service could send a weak confidence signal to customers, partners, or potential investors.

Then it is worth considering the real nature of the role itself, even in small- to mid-size organisations. It cannot be reduced to tasks and projects. The "security by design" and "privacy by design" principles are becoming the norm, and to work well, the role of the CISO must be embedded within operational processes.

In small and medium firms, those processes are simpler than in larger structures and rely on people who simply know each other and work together.

Developing an inner knowledge of the organisation and its culture is always going to be key for the CISO in small firms, and it will definitely be harder to establish if the role is externalised and delivered on a part-time basis or remotely. At best, it could take a long time to deliver value; at worst, it could simply become useless.

Finally, organisations deciding to take that route must also consider the portfolio of other clients their externalised CISO would be supporting. This is absolutely essential to avoid conflicts of interest (e.g., up and down the supply chain) and risks of confidentiality breach (e.g., towards competitors).

Overall, beyond any cynical "box-checking" and before jumping to ready-made conclusions, small and medium firms should consider the following questions to determine the type of CISO they need:

- What's their initial level of cybersecurity maturity?
- What's their ambition in terms of maturity development?
- In which regulatory framework do they operate? And how is it likely to evolve over the short to medium term?
- What is the level of cybersecurity maturity of the supply chain or the ecosystem around them?
- What are the levels of cybersecurity expectations of their customers, partners, or investors?

It's only by looking at their own cybersecurity context in that way that they will be able to right-size and position a CISO role that will work for them.

87

A Real-Life Take on the Cybersecurity Skills Gap

(17 September 2020)

The Security Industry Must Rebuild Its Narrative to Attract More Raw Talent at All Levels

You don't have to go far these days to find security professionals complaining about skills shortages and countless media outlets relaying their views. But there are at least two sides to this argument, and the situation requires a more balanced approach.

First of all, there is no doubt that the cybersecurity industry still has an image problem. It often carries a dated tech-heavy narrative and ends up being perceived as an obscure and complex technical niche, something reserved for nerds and geeks. When the excellent ladies of the CEFCYS in Paris published their first guide to the cybersecurity professions earlier this year, they titled it "I Don't Wear a Hoodie, yet I Work in Cybersecurity."[47]

In fact, the security industry has never managed to make itself attractive, and in turn, the lack of awareness around the diversity of security roles breeds a lack of relevant training courses and educational opportunities.

The absence of clear security career paths is also a real problem at all levels when it comes to attracting new talent. What do you do once you have been a security analyst in a SOC for a few years (or a CISO for that matter)? You should not have to be condemned to hopping across similar roles all the time, but credible alternative role models are cruelly missing. How many CISOs have actually become CIO, COO, or CRO?

However, this is rarely what people refer to when they talk about the "cybersecurity skills gap." They often refer to problems in staffing large security initiatives or security operation centres, and here the so-called skills gap is often a fig leaf hiding different problems.

Many security leaders—particularly in large organizations—are stuck with legacy operational processes around identity management, security monitoring, incident handling, or threat intelligence—which are mostly manual, labour-intensive, repetitive, and built around countless tools (twenty on average, according to a recent Cisco report).

Attracting and retaining young professionals in such jobs can indeed be hard. It is even harder in the absence of clear career paths and role models, as we highlighted above.

Also, many large organisations, faced with large-scale maturity problems and urgent security transformation challenges, are trying—unrealistically—to fix all their problems at the same time. But building a monstrous programme of work requiring—in theory—tens of additional FTEs, and ignoring all dependencies between tasks and cultural aspects, is not how you change things.

You would struggle to staff it in any specialised industry—and to deliver it. This is just bad planning, and it is fuelled by the tech industry and large consultancies.

So does all this reflect a real shortage of skills—or a shortage of appetite from the leadership to tackle the reengineering of legacy security processes to make them attractive and better suited to the expectations of a younger workforce? Or is the alleged shortage of skills simply an excuse to hide poor management and the greed of the security ecosystem?

Ultimately, all those aspects are just the different sides of the same problem. To attract more raw talent into the security industry (at all levels, security management included), you have to make it more attractive in a credible and meaningful way—at all levels.

To help with that at an analyst level, the leadership should focus on decluttering the cybersecurity estates and automating processes intelligently to allow a smaller number of analysts to work more efficiently, creating a more stimulating—and less boring—environment for them.

At the middle and senior level, the focus should be on building role models and career paths, showcasing real, meaningful, and credible bridges across cybersecurity roles and other roles—at least across the broader GRC spectrum but ideally across the entire management spectrum. Looking beyond tech is absolutely key in that space. There is no reason why a CISO would not come from a business role.

Professional bodies and industry bodies have a role to play here to rebuild that narrative and help the security industry become more attractive and move forward.

These are the themes I have been exploring with the techUK cybersecurity team and that have been summarised in this report released in December **2020**.

88

Cybersecurity Automation Is Key to Fight the Skills Gap

(29 April 2021)

To Start Building Solutions to the Skills Gap Problem, It Is Key to Look at It in All Its Dimensions

The debate around the cybersecurity skills gap continues to ride fairly high on the security industry's agenda, but to start building solutions, it is key to look at the problem in all its dimensions.

The cybersecurity skills gap problem has its origins in three interlocking factors:

There is undoubtedly a growing demand for cyber skills, rooted in long-term trends towards the digitisation of many industries and the avalanche of cyber-attacks we have seen over the past ten years, both aspects greatly amplified by the COVID crisis.

Many organisations—large and small—that had never had an InfoSec function before now have one or are building one. Many organisations that didn't know what a pen test was are now getting regularly tested. We need far more cybersecurity analysts, developers, testers, and managers than ever before, and education and training programmes are struggling to keep up with the growth of the demand and the diversity of the roles.

But you cannot end the analysis at this point and conclude that the solution lies entirely in attracting and training more people. Because the problem has at least two additional dimensions you also need to act on.

Many large organisations tend to respond to the growing cybersecurity emergency by scaling up legacy operational processes and with the perpetuation of a culture that believes that the solution to all cybersecurity problems is technical in nature and requires more tools. This is fuelled not only by countless tech vendors and large consultancies, but also by many CISOs being technologists by trade and by background and hopping from job to job, carrying with them the same technical recipes. This has led to a proliferation of tools—poorly integrated, often partially deployed or implemented—that simply embeds manual steps within security operational processes in many large firms and dramatically increases their demand for resources and skills.

This is also attritive in nature, in particularly at analyst-level and many entry-level cybersecurity roles, because it results in jobs that are excessively repetitive and boring, with limited career development options. So attracting and training more people is key to fixing the cybersecurity skills gap, certainly in the long run. But if you can't keep them in the industry (because you give them boring jobs to do and no career path), this has the potential to become a self-perpetuating problem.

To break this cycle, and in parallel to increasing long-term efforts around training at all levels, the security industry must look at the medium to short term, accelerate on automation and tools integration, and focus on decluttering legacy tooling landscapes and operational processes to give fewer analysts more exciting jobs where they can develop more and bring more value.

It is certainly more difficult for CISOs than just hiring more people. But jumping straight at AI-driven solutions (which may be immature or overhyped) is not the answer either—only a continuation of the same tech-driven obsession that has led to the proliferation of security tools in the first place.

Now more than ever, the key to driving a successful decluttering and automation project around cybersecurity is keeping things simple and focusing on people and process first, then technology.

89

A Few Big Hacks in the United States and Everybody Is Talking about Ransomware Again

(17 June 2021)

Defence-in-Depth Is Key, but Why Are We Hearing So Little about It? Time for a Few Hard Truths

Frankly, this is starting to become embarrassing for some security professionals. In these columns, we have been writing about ransomware since **2016**, and even at the time, it was reasonably established as a topic and already a subject of events and conferences. We revisited it in **2019** in light of an event in Paris targeted at SMBs, in which we participated. Since then, it has grown monumentally, and its impact has increased even further with the pandemic. Now even cyber insurers are starting to change their tune about it.

Meanwhile, some in the security community continue to go around in circles, looking for straight answers or technical silver bullets. Should you pay the ransom? Is it all about backups?

It's time for a few hard truths.

The debate around paying or not paying the ransom is typical of the confusion that reigns, amplified by increasingly contrasted messages from public authorities (who seem to be resisting making ransom payments illegal) and cyber insurers (who might have played an ambiguous game in the recent past).

There is no "Robin Hood" story line here; this is not about robbing the rich to feed the poor. Paying ransoms finances organised crime. Period. Paying or not should be a reasonably plain matter of business ethics.

Let's consider the following scenario, as a matter of comparison:

You are the CEO of a business that has been heavily affected by the COVID crisis. You were not in an ideal shape pre-COVID, and competition was already hitting hard at you. You have struggled to keep going and find finance throughout the crisis. You literally have a few months of runway ahead of you before having to have a difficult discussion with creditors, possibly leading to laying off people in big numbers.

An opportunity presents itself to open a new market in an emerging country. It is a solid opportunity, and you have been aware of it for years, but you have stayed away from it. Access to the market involves paying large sums to corrupt officials, in a regime that is openly recognised by international agencies as being involved in drug and people trafficking.

What do you do?

My point is simply, you must see the debate around ransomware and the payment of ransoms in the same ethical light, because ransomware is cybercrime. It is deluded to see paying the ransom as some form of economic trade-off and a regular business transaction.

Now, everybody can understand that it is a hard decision to make when your business is actually down, but it should still be guided by ethical considerations and an increased level of support of public authorities towards the victims, something we were already pushing for in **2019** in support of small businesses.

Making ransom payments illegal without adequately supporting victims could make things worse, as the Cyber Threat Alliance rightly argues.

Having said that, protecting yourself can be hard, especially if you are just waking up to the problem now, well past the eleventh hour.

There is no silver bullet. Period.

The only thing that can protect you is defence-in-depth, and it can take years to put it in place properly at the level of a large enterprise if you're truly starting now.

- Yes, you need to educate your staff about phishing and opening up attachments. But by itself, that's not enough; human mistakes are unavoidable.

- Yes, you need to filter emails upstream to remove any suspicious content. But by itself, that's not enough; some may still go through.

- Yes, you need to deploy security patches in a timely manner across your entire estate. But by itself, that's not enough; you will always miss a few across large estates.

- Yes, you need to take and maintain regular backups so that you can return to business quickly. But by itself, that's not enough; by then the deed would have been done and your business would have been affected—and by the way, the life of most CIOs is full of backups that didn't work.

You need to act in a concerted manner across all those levels, and many others, to achieve true protection. This is not just about having a rehearsed incident-response plan ready, with lawyers and PR people lined up.

Cynically, many recent ransomware incidents are challenging in a harsh way the way security has been prioritised in many industry sectors over the years and how the focus on technology, point solutions, and low-hanging fruits fails to protect the large enterprise in real terms.

This cannot be reduced to a matter of insufficient investments. Large firms have spent billions collectively on cybersecurity over the past decades. It's an excessive focus on pure tech solutions, coupled with execution failure, that is at the heart of the situation many organisations are now facing.

This is also a challenge for some CISOs—and tech vendors and large consultancies—who would have effectively accepted and endorsed the "risk appetite" decision of business leaders, unwilling to understand and challenge the fact that this is actually driven by cognitive biases, that "risk appetite" goes out of the window at the first sight of real problems, and that there cannot be a proper discussion around "risk appetite" without a genuine appreciation of the threats targeting the business and the protective measures the business has in place—or not—to protect itself from those threats.

The hard truth is that good practices—known for decades—can still protect against ransomware if properly deployed, in layers, across the real breadth and depth of the modern enterprise.

True defence-in-depth is complex. It requires a coherent vision, the right governance and operating model, and the right skills at the right level across the enterprise. But it simply works at creating a protective shield; siloed vision and point tech solutions don't.

90

The Problem with Cybersecurity ROI

(5 August 2021)

CISOs Being Asked Those Questions Should Look Beyond the Topic Itself and Face the Underlying Issues It Might Be Hiding

If the reporting line of the CISO is the oldest ongoing topic of discussion among cybersecurity communities, security ROI is probably the second oldest.

In reality, it hides several endemic problems that have been plaguing the security industry for the last two decades.

First of all, it downgrades cybersecurity to a mere matter of investments—which would have to be justified—implying that lack of funding and lack of resources are at the heart of low security maturity levels and the cyber-attacks epidemic we have been seeing for the last ten years.

In fact, problems have largely been elsewhere. Large organisations have committed billions collectively to cybersecurity over the period; it's governance and cultural issues that have led to adverse prioritisation and execution failure.

While it may be the case that some organisations have not invested enough in relation to the threats they face, the security ROI discussions are often the sign of arbitrary programmes of work driven bottom-up by a CISO, either replicating recipes applied elsewhere or listening to the sirens of some tech vendors, when not simply pushing their own pet projects.

Cybersecurity did not appear overnight with the COVID pandemic. Any large organisation will have a history and a legacy of some sort in that space spanning two decades.

Understanding the investments made in the past—what has worked, what hasn't (and the reasons why)—and showing decision makers that lessons are being learnt around past execution failures would be more important to building trust than a financial ROI calculation that will be invariably plagued by disputable assumptions and estimates, leaving it vulnerable to internal politics and horse-trading around numbers.

Because very often, trust (or the lack of it) is at the heart of the context here, particularly when the ROI question comes top-down onto the CISO. Many CISOs take it as a normal business question and a natural justification to give, while in fact, it tends to mean, "I am not sure I understand what you are trying to do and why you want to spend so much."

It is a rare concern at the top these days, in the face of non-stop cyber-attacks and data breaches. Boards are often more concerned with demonstrating they are spending enough on cyber.

So the persistence of the cybersecurity ROI debates is to be seen in my view as a symptom of the distrust, a lack of positive engagement between the CISO and senior stakeholders, and a defence mechanism on their part.

Any large organisation would have spent millions or tens of millions—if not more—on cybersecurity over the past decades. You cannot blame senior execs for being suspicious when they see in front of them yet another investment plan in that space.

Instead of jumping straight into a financial ROI debate where they are likely to lose credit, CISOs who want to drive large-scale, transformative programmes around cybersecurity should focus first on building trust with senior stakeholders and solid communication channels with all of them, working across silos towards business units, geographies, and support functions (such as legal, HR, or procurement, as well as IT and their suppliers).

Even if they are working towards the delivery of a long-term, large-scale road map, they should split it into cheaper, more manageable chunks to demonstrate their execution capabilities with simple and achievable tasks, addressing business expectations before getting to meatier (and more expensive) matters.

By then, their own clarity of vision and their ability to execute should carry them sufficiently to avoid arbitrary—and often useless—discussions around ROI.

That's the key to discussions around cybersecurity ROI. They shouldn't be happening at all in the current context, given the non-stop avalanche of cyber-attacks we are seeing worldwide.

CISOs being asked those questions should look beyond the topic itself and face the underlying issues it might be hiding.

91

Cybersecurity: The Constant Confusion between Tool and Process

(11 November 2021)

There Are Real Issues in the Security Operations Space, but Buying More Tools Won't Help

The **2021** survey from TrendMicro paints a slightly frightening picture of the state of security operations in large firms: twenty-nine monitoring solutions in place on average and analysts stressed out, unhappy, drowning in alerts, and spending **27%** of their time dealing with false positives and ending up ignoring or turning off alerts.[48]

All these are to be taken with a reasonable dose of caution, coming from a tech vendor active in that space, but also matching anecdotal evidence we see in the field regularly.

As always, with those, the conclusion of the survey is that you need to buy more tools to solve all highlighted problems (those sold by the people who commissioned the survey, of course). Nobody in the cybersecurity tech industry seems to see the irony behind that type of report.

Still, they put in perspective some real issues in the security operations space.

The tool-proliferation problem is real and ancient, aggravated by the COVID crisis that has accentuated short-termist and tactical tendencies and engineered countless knee-jerk reactions around cybersecurity that have just created more technical debt in that space.

Security operational processes are intrinsically inefficient because they have been—almost always—reversely engineered around the capabilities of specific tools selected on a whim, under pressure, just to close down audit observations, or because the CISO "used them elsewhere."

Nothing is ever joined up because there was never any overarching vision beyond the immediate need (to close an audit point, to react to an incident). So operational tasks mushroom in all directions and become overlapping, repetitive, and poorly managed.

Meanwhile, analysts are burning out at the receiving end of those excessively manual processes and ending up leaving the cybersecurity industry to get out of boring jobs where they spend their day cutting and pasting data into Excel spreadsheets to produce useless reports designed to put ticks in compliance boxes. The whole thing becomes attritive and simply alienates talent at all levels.

At the heart of the problem lies—conveniently put there by the tech industry—the constant confusion between tool and process.

Just to take a few examples, the acronyms DLP (data loss prevention) or IAM (identity and access management) by themselves do not refer to tools or sets of tools; they refer literally to the description of processes.

For example, any DLP implementation must start with an identification of key stakeholders, the sensitive data to protect, the way it is currently exchanged, the way it is currently tagged or labelled (or not), the objectives and constraints of the stakeholders around the protection of the data, the internal or external threats susceptible to steal or leak the data, and finally leading to building up a way to engineer DLP (as a process) to make it work across the firm. (It should include process elements such as the handling of anomalies and alerts and the granting of temporary or permanent exceptions, themselves probably subject to some form of approval workflow (or the interfacing of the DLP process with pre-existing processes in that space).

It's only once you have gone through that phase of analysis and process design that you should start looking for tools to enable your DLP initiative to succeed.

Starting the other way round (i.e., starting with tool selection and defining the process around the capabilities of the selected tool) is bound to create friction with pre-existing practices and the expectations or capabilities of stakeholders, leading to poor deployment, poor acceptance, or both.

As CISOs, I am sure we have all done it under pressure at some stage of our careers (I know I have). But it remains a mistake—and probably one of the costliest for a CISO to make—because it creates distrust with stakeholders and, over time, with senior management, who can't help but see the escalating financial demands from CISOs in return for poor execution and continuing breaches.

The solution to the broader security operations problem lies in decluttering the cybersecurity estates, through reengineering and smart automation of operational processes.

I like the suggestion from Greg Day (VP and CSO, EMEA, Palo Alto Networks):

"For every one new solution, remove two legacy solutions."

But once again, to achieve this, you have to start from the process end of your practice. The "one new solution" you add has to be added from a perspective of process realignment and simplification, and the two you remove have to be removed from the same perspective. Do not forget that processes are enacted by people who are creatures of habit and have to be trained and led on the path of change, not just expected to go with the flow.

In all cases, process has to come first, then people, then technology. The cybersecurity industry–listening to the sirens of tech vendors–has been doing it the other way around for the best part of the last twenty years. Now the accumulated burden becomes too much to carry in the face of unrelenting threats.

Things need to change, but buying more tools won't help unless they truly have estate decluttering and smart process automation at their heart.

92

Towards Clearer Governance for OT Security

(25 November 2021)

It Is Not Rare for OT Security to End Up in Some Form of Organisational No-Man's-Land

This interesting interview with Andy Norton puts things in perspective around IT and OT security: "The Top 5 Cybersecurity Threats to OT Security."[49]

Historically, IT and OT belong to different worlds—or at least different parts of the enterprise.

If we look back, operational technology has always been typically air-gapped in the manufacturing sector, often running on proprietary hardware and software platforms. It belonged to the realm of plant and operations managers and was managed by them and their suppliers. It used to evolve on the same time frames as plants and machinery.

Security and safety were always key components with OT, but exploiting a vulnerability to cause harm was never that straightforward (although the air gap didn't stop the Stuxnet attack ten years ago). Patching vulnerabilities was often in the hands of the suppliers, and stopping the plant or altering operations to apply a patch to prevent a low-probability attack was never high on the list of priorities for operations managers. Historically, there was never an OT security concept as such; it was just part of designing manufacturing systems and running the plant.

Information technology always evolved on different (shorter) cycles. Historically, it belonged to the realm of head office and the admin world in the manufacturing sector. But with the advent of the internet and then the cloud (and now remote working at scale since the COVID pandemic), the IT environment—and the supply chains it supports—have become more and more interconnected, and with hyperconnectivity came a significant increase in attack surfaces and associated cyber threats. IT security had to become more and more reactive in response, even if proactive, defence-in-depth principles have continued to provide solid levels of security if properly applied across the depth and breadth of the enterprise.

That's where the problems started with OT, because as Andy Norton points out, gradually the air gap between OT and IT was bridged, and it was bridged opportunistically—across industries—often to introduce point solutions without any appreciation of the risks involved (potentially) and certainly without any kind of overarching picture or strategy. And now the technological acceleration coming with industrial IoT sensors and 5G connectivity is in the process of taking this to a new level.

Overall, the IT/OT overlap was never structured, designed, and secured as any kind of "interconnection." For many, it just happened.

In the emergence of an OT security strategy, it did not result that there might have been an IT security strategy in the way, or that in establishing an OT security department there was an IT security department in the way

In addition, OT devices and sensors rarely fit in any predefined IT box. Many are still proprietary. They're not designed to run software agents in the way IT devices do, as Norton points out. They are often limited by their own architecture or the technological capacity of the legacy strata to which they belong.

As a result, they are not easy to integrate into a pre-existing IT security operations framework. They can be difficult to map out with precision, and many end up ignored—but still connected to the wider IT network and potentially exposed to any threats it may carry.

Fundamentally, ownership around OT security was rarely clarified in spite of its evolutions over the past decades and its growing dependency on IT. It is not rare for OT security to end up in some form of organisational no-man's-land, having become too hybrid and too complex for plant managers to, as well as too alien for IT security managers to integrate properly into their practices.

The **2021** Colonial Pipeline hack might have acted as an eye-opener for many manufacturing and energy firms, even if, in essence, it was not an attack on its OT systems.

But before jumping to tech solutions, clarifying ownership and governance around OT security has to be the place to start for organisations finding themselves in that type of conundrum.

OT security needs to be structured as a practice in itself, as part of a broader set of cybersecurity practices and assigned roles, responsibilities, and resources. It also has to be embedded across the business structure of the firm—and its operational silos—in order to develop acceptance and trust with plant and operations managers.

Once the field is mapped out and the extent of the problem is assessed, ameliorative road maps can be drawn to build up OT security levels, together with an effective and efficient interface with IT security operations. But as always, it will involve action at process, people, and technology levels—preferably in that order.

93

Zero Trust Is Not About "Zero": It's about "Trust"

(20 October 2022)

Putting Technology First Is the Biggest Mistake You Can Make with Zero Trust

Many vendors and cybersecurity professionals are relaying the view that zero-trust technology is now essential for organisations, large and small, to defend against against current cyber threats in the context of the hybrid enterprise.

At high level, systematically verifying credentials every time an asset or a function is accessed by a user sounds like an over-engineered paradigm which flies in the face of defence-in-depth good practices, which have prevailed for two decades, i.e., the effective protection of the enterprise resulting from the layered application of controls at people (e.g., awareness training), process (e.g., monitoring and incident handling) and technology levels (e.g., logical access controls).

Having said that, given the size and complexity large enterprises have reached, their inherent dependency on digital interconnectivity across cloud-based ecosystems and supply chains, and their (also inherent) endemic inability to deliver across corporate silos on the most essential aspects of cybersecurity, a heightened degree of network security could make sense for some, at least for those that feel they have the capability to execute in that space.

But implementing any form of "zero-trust" platform remains a complex endeavour, and those focusing only on its technical dimension are missing the point in my opinion.

Fundamentally, mandating a degree of least privilege is as old as cybersecurity good practice, and in that context, "zero-trust" could be seen as a valid default position in theory, but taken at face value, it remains an unworkable one: For employees to do their jobs, they have to be trusted somehow to access the digital assets they need to perform their duties.

The direct consequence of that paradigm is that you will need to grant trust to your staff, and that it will have to be done against some form of authoritative source. Someone in your organisation will have to be accountable for deciding which employee is authorised ("trusted") to access which asset (and to do what), and more importantly, which employee is no longer entitled to such access.

This is key: Any least privilege principle only makes sense coupled with a least retention privilege. Simply because people leave or change jobs, and sometimes those moves happen in good spirit, and sometimes, they don't.

What we start to see emerging here is the basis of a process, which is mostly technology- agnostic, and could well be in place and functioning in some ways in many organisations around existing logical access controls. But the more granular you make it, the more complex (and costly) it becomes to operate and maintain.

Behind this process lies the concept of an operating model because such process can only function rooted in a clear and accepted definition of accountabilities and responsibilities for all its players.

That's where all "zero-trust" projects should start: by engaging with all stakeholders with the view of building the framework of an operating model acceptable to all.

That's also where most of them fail when they put technology first, like many logical access controls or data loss prevention initiatives before them.

Putting technology first in those contexts is the biggest mistake you can make.

Those projects have to start process-first, identify all process stakeholders from the start, engage with them, explain to them the need for control, listen to their priorities and constraints, and build acceptance around their expectations of what is going to work for them, and what isn't.

Cybersecurity leaders, pushing those types of initiatives and facing stakeholders unwilling to accept or to understand the need for such level of control, have to ask themselves where this reluctance is coming from, and address without complacency those concerns which may be rooted in the failure of past projects in that space.

Success will come from asking stakeholders what will work for them and delivering on that basis; not telling them afterwards what they need to do, pushing down on them another layer of unwanted technology.

That type of technology-first approach only generates friction with stakeholders; it leads to frustration, rejection, and over time, a mountain of technical debt made of half-deployed solutions.

Zero-trust initiatives structured in that way, like all their predecessors, are simply heading for that pile.

All this also contributes to building the sentiment amongst business communities that cybersecurity is costly, complex, and in the end, useless in the face of endless cyber-attacks.

This is perhaps the most dangerous aspect of it all.

94

The Key Ingredients of a Successful GRC Programme

(16 March 2023)

It Has to Start with a Degree of Integration between Threats, Risks, Controls, and Protective Measures

The GRC acronym (governance, risk, and compliance) has been around for over ten years, but still, many organizations struggle with the successful delivery of GRC programmes across their IT function.

Many of those programmes fail because they are designed in silos, around the functional capabilities of specific tools, often selected without a proper assessment of their fit within the firm's IT and risk environments. It results in overly complex and expensive integration projects, or the under-utilization of the tools due to data unavailability or inconsistency.

In my experience, for IT GRC programmes to deliver meaningful value, it is key to start from a process perspective and to ensure that business threats, technology risk scenarios, protective measures, and control activities are properly aligned.

The level of risk a firm carries in relation to a particular risk scenario can only be determined through a structured and independent assessment of the measures in place (or not) to protect the firm from that scenario; if sufficient measures are in place, senior executives can then be given the assurance that the associated risk is low, or at least controlled; if the protective measures in place are not deemed sufficient or cannot be verified, flags must be raised and actions taken.

For this to work, it has to start with a degree of integration between threats, risks, controls, and protective measures.

Technology risk scenarios cannot be arbitrary. They have to be derived from—and linked to—a structured analysis of the threats the business is facing.

They cannot just be placed in a risk register, next to a mitigation, transfer, or acceptance statement "hoping for the best."

They have to permeate through and drive the firm's technology policy framework.

In other words, technology policies, procedures and standards have to be designed and architected not simply with the view of adhering to good practice or addressing specific issues, but with the view of protecting the business from those technology risk scenarios (while ensuring that the firm also meets its regulatory obligations).

As such, it should be possible to map each content element of those policies, procedures and standards to one or several technology risk scenarios (those they are designed to protect against).

Collectively, they should be underpinned by an operating and governance model documenting the roles and responsibilities of all parties involved in their execution to protect the firm.

The "compliance" part of the technology GRC framework should be driven by a controls plan, validated with all stakeholders and defining the set of tasks, automated or not, by which the execution of the technology policies, procedures and standards is continuously or periodically verified by an independent function.

Because the content of the technology policies, procedures and standards would have been mapped to the technology risk scenarios, the reporting resulting from the execution of the controls plan should inform on the actual level of protection of the business from those risk scenarios and allow the translation of those results into technology risk—results which could, in turn, be integrated within the enterprise risk, governance, and regulatory reporting frameworks.

I am not saying this would be simple to put in place, in particular in large firms where a significant legacy of policy material may exist, but only such degree of integration—in my view—can bring meaningful results to senior executives and enable them to understand and manage the level of risk the firm carries.

Even in large organizations where a degree of automation will be required for this to work, it is key to start with the operational architecture of such integration and its validation with all stakeholders, before looking for a toolkit solution.

Once again, this is the typical area where "Process and People first, THEN Technology" is key to success.

95

Around 26.7% of UK Security Budgets Unspent in 2022, according to a Recent Survey

(27 April 2023)

What's Really Going On with the CISOs and Their Budgets?

The 2023 UK Cybersecurity Landscape report from Expel makes interesting reading[50].

Based on the feedback of five hundred IT decision makers, it paints the usual picture around security operations of constant attacks, tools proliferation, analysts burnout, and high attrition rates.

There is nothing really new in all this, and we have been commenting on those matters at least since 2021.

While the bulk of the emphasis in the report – and in the commentaries it has attracted – seems to be on staff wellbeing and turnover, it is a statistic hidden on page 5 that has drawn my attention.

The survey found that "on average, 26.7% of allocated security budgets went unspent" in 2022, leaving, on average, an excess of £50,000 of available cybersecurity budget going to waste last year in each responding organisation.

In the context of the constant cacophony of CISOs complaining about their lack of resources and their difficulties in getting funding, the statistic is plainly staggering.

Or is it really?

In fact, it echoes some of our field experience, and needs to be seen in the context of the "when-not-if" paradigm around cyber-attacks, and the change in top-level dynamics it is inducing around cybersecurity.

Frankly, CISOs struggling with budgetary issues in the current context genuinely have to look in the mirror and ask themselves what underlying issue the situation might be hiding.

CIOs often don't have any problem in justifying the cybersecurity lines in their budgets, in the face of constant cyber-attacks: You truly have to be a brave CFO to cut down on those. Actually, cybersecurity is probably the best protected and most resilient part of the CIO's budget, in particular in the context of the current post-covid downturn.

The problems are elsewhere.

The "when-not-if" paradigm puts the focus strongly on the execution and delivery of security measures: This is no longer strictly about finding a balance between risk appetite, compliance requirements and costs, but about protecting the business from real threats that can strike at any time with real impact.

The commentary in the Expel reports rightly points to "organisational stress" in its explanation of the statistic ("problems abound, with no clear path on how best to tackle them"), then moves on to address alert fatigue, burnout, staff well-being, and high turnover as if it was directly and obviously related.

I think the issue runs deeper than that. The underspending cannot be simply put down to the difficulty in finding or keeping resources to execute.

Cybersecurity is fundamentally a cross-functional discipline and has always been. You cannot be successful with large scale initiatives around identity and access management, data loss prevention or privacy compliance for example, without the effective involvement of business units, HR and other support functions—and all geographies where relevant.

CISOs are poorly equipped in dealing with those matters because they have been trapped for the last decade in the firefighting of technical incidents and have failed to develop the type of management and political acumen they now require to meet the expectations of senior stakeholders.

So I think the problem around underspending does not lie so much in there being "no clear path" about what to do, but with the CISOs being reluctant to face the rest of the business with real transformative initiatives that would consume the allocated budgets, but also would require them to step out of their firefighting technical comfort zone.

Putting it differently, it is, in my view, their fear of failure, linked to their discomfort around management and politics, that leads to considerable underspending by the CISOs.

The way forward to break that logic will invariably involve looking at the role of the CISO differently, possibly splitting roles and responsibilities to allow the emergence of an elevated CSO role able to steer cross-functional initiatives, maybe by linking them to others in fields such as resilience, privacy or compliance.

It will not remove all tensions around staffing and skills over the short-term, but it could create different dynamics and possibly open the field to different—non-technical—profiles, which would allow for a different narrative to build up around cybersecurity to continue attracting more talent.

One thing is certain: complaining about stress and burnout will never solve the underlying problems faced by cybersecurity functions.

The cybersecurity industry needs to confront the roadblocks that have led to those situations and engage in some self-examination.

It cannot be simply reduced to the business refusing to commit enough resources, as the statistic we have been commenting on appears to show.

96

Cybersecurity: The Secret Sauce for Small Businesses

(11 May 2023)

Dispelling Five Myths around Cybersecurity for Small Businesses

Data and technology have become central to the business in most companies including small firms, and in particular since the Covid pandemic which has forced many towards an accelerated digital transformation or a complete reinvention.

Cyber threats are more active than ever, with firms—large and small—falling victims to indiscriminate cyber-attacks on a continuous basis: This is increasingly being seen as a matter of *when*, not *if* for most industry sectors.

In addition, regulations have been tightening worldwide around personal data (GDPR, CCPA and many others), fines are growing, and regulators have been targeting all firms irrespective of size.

All this is changing the context in which small businesses need to approach cybersecurity.

Still, in small and mid-size businesses, the main roadblock is often a lack of understanding of what needs to be done around security and privacy to ensure sufficient protection and how priorities must be set in the current climate in support of the digital, remote, and cloud-based enterprise.

At best, it leads to putting in place isolated and disjointed protective measures.

At worst, senior stakeholders simply don't know where to start and some technical illiteracy gives way to misconceptions, which—in turn—deprioritise action around security in spite of legitimate and growing concerns.

Time to dispel a few of those myths to help small businesses move forward.

Myth #1 - Security measures are an annoyance; they create friction and turn customers away.

> *This is less and less the case, as people get hacked and learn the hard way the need for stronger security.*
>
> *Ruthless data monetization, personalization or aggressive data surveillance, on the other hand, are increasingly a source of ethical concerns with customers and staff, in particular amongst younger generations.*

Myth #2 - We have other priorities; it will divert resources away from essential activities.

In fact, security issues are most likely to turn customers away in the current climate.

Maintaining good security levels is an essential activity and may generate sales if you turn it into a competitive advantage and weave it into your USP.

Myth #3 – We can't afford it; it's too expensive for us.

Basic measures don't have to be very complicated or expensive and will go a long way to provide a degree of protection.

Incidents, on the other hand, are expensive to deal with and retrofitting security and privacy measures under duress after something has happened will be painful.

Cyber insurance is also getting more and more expensive, and less and less reliable due to the accumulation of exclusions.

Myth #4 – It won't happen to us because we are too small.

This is now practically baseless. Cyber-attacks and data breaches are constantly in the news. Cyber threats are more virulent than ever and evidence abound that they target all firms irrespective of size.

Myth #5 – It's not really our problem because we are "in the cloud."

You remain responsible for the security of your data and liable to your clients in case of a data breach, and in addition, make sure you have read the "small print." The contract with your cloud provider is likely to be shamelessly one-sided (in their favour).

The key for small businesses, their owners, and their leaders is to move away from those ready-made excuses and own the topic as an integral part of the environment in which they trade, not something alien to it.

Beyond loss avoidance and business stability, good security and privacy practices build digital trust.

They support valuations, reduce risk and regulatory or legal friction.

As the reflection of good business ethics, they can be turned into a competitive advantage to attract talent, retain customers and become a key ingredient to your mid to long-term "secret sauce."

97

Going the Right Way about Cybersecurity Transformation

(1 June 2023)

Cybersecurity Transformation Cannot Be Seen as a Straightforward Change

This interesting piece in the *Harvard Business Review* should be a must-read for all transformational CISOs.[51]

Its focus on the true dynamics of change and the fact that change leaders focus too much on the "what" of change and not the "how" bring out obvious parallels with situations we are seeing all too often in the field around cybersecurity transformation.

Irrespective of their original level of cyber maturity, most organisations have the tendency to treat cybersecurity transformation as a controllable, straightforward type of change, warranting directive approaches.

In keeping with the purely technical and operational focus that has been plaguing cybersecurity approaches for decades, transformation is often architected around projects and the deployment of tools. Stakehokders are broadly told what to do and are expected to follow rules; if and when they don't, this is pinned down to lack of "training" or "awareness"; two other projects and low hanging fruits many CISOs are keen to regard as the alpha and omega of cybersecurity.

This culture of "blaming the user" is regressive, and in the end, all this is rarely transformative in itself: Projects are vulnerable to adverse prioritisation and are often reshaped as business priorities evolve. More often than not, they do not deliver on their primary objectives in a way that would match initial expectations.

Engineering true dynamics of change around cybersecurity has to start with two essential steps:

First of all, *the proper examination of past failed approaches or initiatives in that space.*

Although cybersecurity has been making significant gains in visibility at top level over the past few years, it did not appear on the board's agenda out of thin air and has been evolving for over two decades. Examining without complacency what might have gone wrong in the past and confronting the true roadblocks that would have prevented change to stick is a fundamental prerequisite.

This is likely to lead cybersecurity transformation leaders towards cultural and governance issues, as well as possible under investments.

Often, the latter (under investments) is simply a symptom of the former (cultural and governance issues) and is easily illustrated by situations where money, which was previously denied <, appears out of nowhere at the first sight of an incident, a near-miss, a regulatory visit, or simply a bad audit report.

Confronting those types of cognitive biases, or at least acknowledging them, is essential in understanding the dynamics of change around cybersecurity.

This is where many training and awareness programs go wrong: They frame the argument as a rational argument—something that has to be explained or taught—instead of focusing on the deeper cultural issues at the heart of the matter.

This is taking us to our second essential step: *the need to acknowledge cybersecurity as a cross-functional discipline and to build trust with all stakeholders.*

Nothing lasting can happen in that space without listening first to all the parties that have a role to play in protecting the business from cyber threats, understanding their constraints, their fears, their priorities, and where they might see conflicts around the objectives of the cybersecurity transformation programme.

There cannot be any more fundamental aspect in engineering true dynamics of change around cybersecurity.

Imposing new measures or practices onto stakeholders without prior engagement and a true exchange of views simply creates friction, and over time, rejection or cynicism in the face of endless rules. Overall, it breeds frustration and incomprehension around what cybersecurity is about.

Going back to the language of the authors in our starting article, the combination of "emergent" and "masterful" change driven top-down by senior execs is likely to be the best blend for cybersecurity transformation ("creating the conditions for change" and "trusting people to deliver"), as is often the case for any type of complex change.

That's the main point: cybersecurity transformation cannot be seen as a straightforward change; cybersecurity transformation is complex and transversal and needs to be treated as such in all its dimensions.

98

The Cybersecurity Numbers Game Is a Dangerous One for CISOs

(3 August 2023)

The Real Long-term Currency Here Is Trust

Which vendor cybersecurity survey are we meant to believe?

- This one—from Panaseer—arguing that CISOs would require a 40% increase in their budgets to be confident to mitigate security risks?[52]
- Or this one—from Expel—stating that 26.7% of security budgets were left unspent in 2022 in the UK? [53]

Let's start by repeating the obvious: This is vendor-led content, more than "proper" research. Those surveys claim to analyse results from hundreds of respondents—and those numbers are probably true—but little analytics is generally applied to the data beyond the calculation of percentages and the commentaries alongside the data are always tainted by the views of the sponsors and the potential use cases of their products.

They should be seen as indicators, nothing else; but they often match an amount of anecdotal evidence we collect in the field regularly.

In fact, those two surveys don't really contradict each other, but they certainly paint a contrasted picture, and it feels strange that the CISOs asking for more money could be the same who actually struggle to spend it.

It might sound counter-intuitive, but I think that the CISOs struggling to spend it are more likely to be the *rare* ones who did get that large budgetary increase in their last round.

There is no doubt in my opinion that a vast proportion of security budgets in large firms is used to prop-up legacy processes, and the monumental technical debt of security estates built around countless tools. Toolkit consolidation is a necessity in large firms: They simply cannot continue to operate the bloated security estates and manual processes of the past, given the current constraints on skills, the mounting regulatory pressure and the constant escalation of threats.

It is a mistake to think that this can be solved quickly and simply by throwing more money at the situation.

Transformative efforts need resources of course, but they also need time, vision, and drive. And support from above in manners that exceed budgetary commitments because cybersecurity is, by essence, cross-functional.

This is where many CISOs go wrong in building up their case towards decision makers: they think this is a rational argument, to be won with facts, data, and numbers.

This is the school of thought that has led to the creation of countless security ROI and cost-cutting models, and some of those models might have served their purpose in some situations: after all, they offer the appearance of science and being visible at spending around cybersecurity protects top executives; it puts ticks in the right boxes with auditors and regulators—at a time where personal liability is becoming a top concern for many—and if breaches keep happening, execution failures can be blamed on the CISO who becomes the natural scapegoat.

Without realising it, CISOs playing that sort of numbers game often end up weakened and exposed.

In fact, even when taking up a new job and finding a clear legacy of underspending and underbudgeting, CISOs must not start by asking themselves "how do I justify spending more?" but "where does that situation come from?"

Long-term battles with top execs are not fought and won in the field of numbers. They belong to a different terrain.

The real long-term currency here is the trust between the CISO and the rest of the leadership team.

And it has to start by the CISO listening to all stakeholders, their constraints, their problems and their priorities instead of telling them upfront what they're doing wrong and what needs fixing, always pushing a technical agenda.

With trust as its foundation, the dialogue between the CISO and stakeholders acquires a different dimension.

Top executives run the firm: they know its strengths and weaknesses, its culture, its governance intricacies, its difficult personalities, and its territorial wars.

They will also have an appreciation of cyber risk—at their level—because it's constantly in the news and many would have been exposed to it, in their current job or elsewhere.

This appreciation will be rooted in the broader risk context the firm is facing, and in its general risk management practices. This is well illustrated by this great piece from McKinsey.[54]

That's the context CISOs need to grasp and in which their approach needs to be rooted before jumping to ready-made technical assumptions and asking for millions.

If they achieve it and connect their demands and their delivery to the expectations of senior executives, they stand a chance of entering a virtuous circle where trust breeds success and success breeds trust, and start to break up the endemic spiral of failure that has been plaguing cybersecurity practices for the last two decades.

99

Hiring Managers: Be Realistic Around Cybersecurity Profiles

(7 September 2023)

Looking for Hybrid Profiles That Cannot Exist Is Just Fuelling the Perception of a Cybersecurity Skills Gap

Commenting on one of my Linkedin posts, one of my readers mentioned "absurdly dissonant requirements" in CISOs role descriptions, mentioning as an example "serve as the point person for contact with regulators; proficiency in Python, Golang, or similar dynamic programming language."

Sadly, this is all too common, and I am sure most cybersecurity recruiters would concur. It is a situation that goes a long way beyond the anecdotal and reflects in my opinion a real dimension of the cybersecurity skills gap problem.

It is often the sign of a lack of understanding or an overly simplistic view of the transversal challenges around cybersecurity and how it is actually delivered across an organisation.

Many hiring managers end up complaining of an acute cybersecurity skills gap after several months of search and countless hours of interviews without realising that they are simply looking for hybrid profiles that never existed and simply cannot be engineered, irrespective of the current market conditions.

In fact, it is not new, and as early as in 2018, as we were working on our "First 100 Days of the New CISO" series, we were already commenting on the fact that many hiring managers "*may not be sufficiently cybersecurity-savvy to frame and express precisely what they are looking for in a CISO,*" leading to a sense of disconnect between expectations and reality for incoming CISOs, which in turn was fuelling their short tenure.

Since then, the continued acceleration of the digital transformation pressures and the COVID pandemic have exacerbated the demand for cyber talent: now that every firm in every industry must be responsive to cyber threats, finding candidates with relevant cybersecurity skills is difficult enough, and looking for an impossible skills blend is doomed to fail.

Another problem quite common with cybersecurity role descriptions is the level of experience demanded.

The cybersecurity profession, as we know it today, has no more than twenty-five years of existence in some industries (finance, pharma, energy), and considerably less in many others.

It has evolved constantly over the past two decades, and continues to evolve, as we have put in evidence with the Security Transformation Research Foundation in 2019[55], but it remains a young field.

Insisting on ten years of experience in middle-management or senior analyst positions ignores the history of the industry and the way people develop; it simply creates unnecessary barriers, fuels tensions on the recruitment market, and aggravates the perception of a skills gap, which is, in fact, an expectations gap.

Hiring managers have to be more realistic about not just the cybersecurity skills market but also the state of the cybersecurity industry at large. They need to give opportunities to younger profiles, simply because this is a young industry, and understand that they may have to offer packages to train, develop and retain cyber staff.

And finally, there is also a role to play for recruiters, in my opinion, in pushing back on unrealistic search specifications, or at least in educating the hiring managers in relation to the reality of market conditions and the skills structure across the cyber industry.

100

A Reality Check around Cybersecurity Benchmarking

(21 September 2023)

The Benchmarking Question Is Often a Symptom of Trust Erosion Between CISOs and Senior Execs

For as long as I have been involved in cybersecurity, I have heard top executives asking for benchmarking data around their cybersecurity practice.

It might have been in terms of maturity, security spending, or frequency of breaches, but "how are the others doing" has always been a fairly common question.

I think this goes way beyond "herd mentality," and context is key to position the right answer, so before going any further, CISOs facing that type of situation must ask themselves where the concern is coming from.

If the question is coming up in a context of budgetary or strategic orientations discussions, it often reflects a need for reassurance, if not plain discomfort, with regards to what is being proposed.

Top executives should know that each organisation is different, even across the same industry (many would have built their careers moving from one firm to another across that spectrum).

They should also understand that differences in cyber maturity and risk appetite can drive different approaches, and that organisations don't easily share sufficient quantitative data at that level to allow meaningful comparisons: they themselves may not be comfortable seeing disclosed to competitors how much they are budgeting for cybersecurity for example.

The objective could be to drive the CISO's ambitions up or down, but in most cases, the benchmarking question is politically loaded, and it has never been a simple one to answer quantitatively with any degree of accuracy.

Most CISOs have historically tried to address it in a qualitative manner based on anecdotal evidence gathered at conferences or through industry forums, but window-dressing a few anecdotal data points to make them look bigger than they are can be a dangerous and misleading game.

Only a small number of very large management consulting firms might have the necessary elements of data or the reach to collect it; but even that reach is likely to be limited to the large firms able to afford their services, and they will have to anonymise or aggregate the findings to respect the confidentiality of their clients.

CISOs might be better off in many cases by sidestepping the question: For most firms, there is simply no defendable, sufficiently accurate, quantitative answer to the cybersecurity benchmarking question.

CISOs should focus instead on the underlying motivation of the senior executives behind the question.

Trust between them is of paramount importance to any transformative initiative around cybersecurity, and the benchmarking question could be symptom of trust erosion.

That's a far more serious matter to address than the collection of illusory comparative data.

Trust, at this level, will have its foundations in mutual respect and that has to start for the CISO by listening to the real priorities and constraints of the leadership team, and understanding the implications these may have on cybersecurity orientations, for good or for bad.

They will have to elevate their game to look convincingly beyond the tech horizon and showcase their understanding of the key governance and management matters at the heart of the cross-functional nature of cybersecurity in large firms.

As the "when-not-if" paradigm around cyber-attacks becomes prevalent across the boardroom, CISOs must also focus their attention on demonstrating their long-term ability to execute on transformative measures and stop relying only on their short-term firefighting skills to build up their case.

It is likely that benchmarking will cease to be concern for senior executives if they have the sense cybersecurity is in firm hands and driven in a direction that matches their expectations and the needs of the firm.

101

Back to Basics around OT Security

(23 November 2023)

Data May Be "the New Oil" for the Manufacturing World, but It Cannot Be Taken for Granted

This interesting piece in the Journal of Petroleum Technology[56] made me think, not least because it does not mention in any way the data security imperative that needs to be at the heart of any data-driven digital transformation process.

I have not written much around OT security, but it keeps coming across my desk, and it is undoubtedly one of the hot topics of the moment, with countless tech vendors jumping on a band wagon they assume will be lucrative.

If we were to play the prediction game, I would argue this will be a hot topic for the years to come, given the level at which security maturity levels appear to be in some industries.

Back in 2021, I was concerned with the IT/OT convergence and the threat level this was introducing to previously isolated OT environments, that were otherwise more difficult to secure given their specificities. I was also concerned about the lack of integrated governance across IT and OT worlds, preventing a coordinated response to increasingly common threat agents and attack vectors.

I think those concerns are still relevant, but they seem to be underpinned on the OT side by a worrying lack of understanding around those threats.

Data is a vulnerable asset, whether collected by industrial sensors, payment systems, or any type of business platform.

The minute you start basing business decision on data-driven analytics, of course, data quality becomes paramount, but you need to go beyond a generic concept of "quality" and understand what its constituent parts are, in particular in terms of availability, timeliness and accuracy.

These concepts underpin the I and the A of the well-known CIA triad in the IT world (confidentiality, integrity, availability), and they need to be recognised and accepted as security concepts in the OT world as well.

The need to protect the integrity and availability of data should not be seen as alien to a data-driven digital transformation programme.

It should be seen as an integral part of it, requiring the adequate deployment of protective measures in relation to the threats the industry might be facing.

There will be, of course, variations from one sector to another, but in particular when it comes to critical national infrastructure protection, those aspects are essential and cannot be just an afterthought.

To be successful, all this requires a sound appreciation of the threats involved, and the way they have been developing over the past decade—and continue to develop.

Industrial sensors and devices collect more data than ever; they are connected to communications networks that are faster and more reliable than ever; the ability to process this data at speed and at scale is greater than ever and is being augmented even further by the development of machine learning and artificial intelligence models—this is the reality of the current OT world.

But networks can be slowed down or made to fail by DDOS attacks; machine learning models can be rendered inaccurate by poisoned data, maliciously or inadvertently: this is also the reality of the current OT world.

Senior executives in that space need to wake up to this new reality and accept it.

Going back to the industrial example we started from, data may be "the new oil" for the manufacturing world but it cannot be taken for granted.

It needs to be protected as a valued and valuable asset, and this will probably require a shift in mindset for some.[57]

102

Don't Expect Cybersecurity to Work in Firms Where Nothing Does

(19 January 2024)

You Cannot Expect the CISO on Their Own, Bottom Up, to Reverse Widespread Business Dynamics, Where Short-Termism Prevails Everywhere Across the Business

I have written at length about the difficulties many large organizations encounter with cybersecurity and their endemic execution problems when it comes to protecting themselves from cyber threats.

While the diagnostic is relatively clear in my view, there is one aspect that needs repeating and frames the entirety of the problem in many firms.

You cannot expect cybersecurity projects to deliver in firms where projects, in general, don't deliver, where there is no accountability against original objectives, and where no one looks beyond alleged quick wins in *any* project.

With business projects, in the end, it all boils down to well-established business concepts: return on investment, customer acquisition costs, time to market, etc. You kill or stop (or reframe) a project when it costs too much, goes too slow, or because business priorities have shifted. You simply cut your losses and everyone moves on. It happens all the time, and those decisions may involve multimillion-dollar investments—amounts many CISOs would like to have at their disposal in those firms and which dwarf the costs of most cybersecurity initiatives.

Some firms are in constant upheaval, constantly churning out new initiatives in spite of whatever may be already underway, constantly killing or repositioning ongoing projects.

For some, it's simply their way of working, taking to an extreme the Zuckerberg "go-fast-and-break-things" principle. This is often seen as a sign of good business health and a strong market; as long as there is growth and profits are good, the guys upstairs won't really care.

At the other end of the spectrum, some firms exhibit similar symptoms for the opposite reasons: because they are struggling to keep the lights on and are constantly juggling with existential threats.

Don't expect cybersecurity projects to do well, where what I have highlighted here is the dominant business mindset.

Why? Because very often there is no real quick win for those projects, after two decades of adverse prioritisation and constant arbitration between costs, regulatory compliance and some form of—often simplistic or misguided—appreciation of risk appetite ("we'll accept the risk" becoming the ultimate bullet that brings all discussions to an end).

Where cybersecurity maturity is low and has been low for ages, transformative initiatives cannot be driven simply by the deployment of some technical solutions. They need to reach into business and support practices, and preferably in that order: process, people, then technology.

Focusing on technology first and stopping at alleged quick wins before the initiative is killed or deprioritised, simply achieves nothing around cybersecurity.

Over time, technical debt piles up; operational complexity breeds manual processes; manual processes breed attrition in an already tough skills market; security analysts burn out and breaches keep happening.

Only putting things in the right perspective in terms of timeframes, looking over the mid to long-term and thinking in terms of process and people first (then technology), can be transformative on a subject as complex and cross-functional as cybersecurity.

It's much harder for CISOs than buying the next shiny tool, leaving after two years with the whole thing half-finished, and blaming "the business" in the process.

But it's the only way forward around security transformation. To succeed, it requires management experience, personal gravitas, and political acumen on behalf of the CISO—leadership skills more than raw technical skills.

But you cannot expect the CISO on their own, bottom up, to reverse widespread business dynamics, where short-termism prevails everywhere across the business.

It requires unambiguous, visible, credible and constant support from a cybersecurity champion at the top of the organisation.

That combination of an experienced CISO who is a real business leader more than a technologist and a respected top exec ready to throw their weight into the battle is the real and ultimate secret sauce around cybersecurity transformation.

The First 100 Days of the New CISO

103

The First 100 Days of the New CISO

(15 March 2018)[58]

There is some form of management reality beyond the "**100** days" journalistic cliché. How does an incoming executive make an impact in a new role? What are the real time frames to look at, and what can be expected and over what horizon? What are the key issues that should raise a red flag during the first few months in a new senior position? And which can be ignored?

These are the themes we have been exploring on the Corix Partners blog since November **2017** around the specific role of the incoming CISO.

Of course, each and everyone's own path to success will ultimately depend on the specific context of their arrival—from their own previous experience at this level of responsibility to the firm's security management maturity. However, we believe that this series of articles will prove helpful in guiding most CISOs through their first steps in a new organisation and provide them with a useful road map for making an impact in their new job.

Our experience drives us to split the new CISO's road map into three different time horizons that can be roughly encapsulated into a six-day, six-week, or six-month paradigm. These three milestones represent good opportunities for the incoming CISO to focus on what truly matters at each step and to highlight what they should not yet be concerned about.

In our opinion, it is key for any new CISO to hit the ground running, so your first six days should be dedicated to engaging actively with your direct management and staff. As much as possible, you must meet with them face to face to start building a stronger personal bond. Make use of those first interactions to understand how reporting lines work in your new organisation (upwards, downwards, and sideways across matrix models) to position the challenge ahead and identify key preexisting roadblocks. The only thing that should worry you at this point should be the inability to properly schedule those key first meetings because stakeholders don't have time for you. Now would also be a good time to get the finance questions straight:

Do you have a budget allocated, and how is it managed?

Without appropriate resources, you won't be able to achieve much.

Your first six weeks should be the natural continuity of the first six days. Only by meeting as many relevant stakeholders as possible will you be able to accurately assess the situation you are inheriting as a CISO. The key at this stage is to *listen, listen,* and *listen* instead of coming up with ready-made solutions or focusing only on the burning fires. Travel if you must, and take time to gather your thoughts, then start drafting a strategic framework (ameliorative directions, time frames, and high-level costs) to address your findings in relation to the objectives and challenges identified during your first week.

Your main objective around this time should be to get your strategic framework validated with your boss, but you should be fully prepared if your plan is properly costed. It should be rooted in tangible field observations and the expectations of key stakeholders. Lack of engagement from your management beyond merely tactical and technical topics and a general lack of interest from stakeholders for a truly transformative agenda should raise red flags.

Once validated, the next step must consist of executing your strategic framework, and it will start with the formal setting up of an appropriate governance and operating model, as well as getting as many senior team members and stakeholders on board as you can. You should now be getting ready to implement what is very likely to be a medium- to long-term plan, and you must resist being pushed or drawn into tactical firefighting. Focus on infusing a sense of clarity among all stakeholders, both about timing and objectives.

As it turns out, your sixth month in the job should correspond approximately to your first one hundred (working) days, and it is a good time to start looking back on your journey while recognising that you are really only getting started.

While a hundred-day framework is a useful model to think about getting up to speed in your new role, you must keep in mind that any lasting change in an organisation's InfoSec practices is likely to require steady work over a period of several years.

So while this series of articles should help you hit the ground running, always keep in mind that if your objectives are rooted in delivering lasting change around cybersecurity, you are in for a marathon, not a sprint.

104
The Person, the Role, and the Culture of the Firm

(2 November 2017)

There is some form of management reality beyond the "**100** days" journalistic cliché. How does an incoming executive make an impact in a new role? What are the real time frames to look at? What can be expected, and over what horizon? What are the key issues that should raise a red flag during the first few months in a new senior position? Which can be ignored? Those are the themes we will be exploring in this new series around the specific role of the CISO.

The Person, the Role, and the Culture of the Firm

It is, alas, necessary to start this series with a long list of caveats and questions. Every person is different, every organisation is different, and to a large extent, every CISO role is also different.

Although we will be identifying common trends in the coming articles—looking in turn at the first six days, six weeks, and six months of the incoming CISO—they must be understood and placed by the reader in their specific personal context and in the specific context of their organisation. In particular, the heterogeneity in maturity levels among firms in terms of security management must be acknowledged.

The following guiding questions are key for each reader to relate the series to their personal frame of mind:

- Is this your first CISO job? What were you doing before? Are you coming into this from an IT background or not?
- Is this your second CISO job? What happened in the first one? Why did you leave? How long did you stay?
- Is this your third CISO job (or more)? (Then why are you reading this?)
- Is this an internal move? Upwards? Sideways? Or are you joining a new firm?
- What are your expectations with the new job? Was it a real positive decision to move into security or just a holding pattern waiting for better things to emerge? Was the decision made for you? (Were you pushed into this? Did you have a choice?) Was it a political calculation (i.e., "security people don't get sacked")?
- What motivates you? Building teams? Managing people? Doing stuff?
- What are your time frames with regard to the new position? How long do you see yourself staying in the job? What would be your next job after this one? Is your career something you care about and actively build? Or do you take a more passive approach to career-building?

The above is not just an endless HR checklist but the real context in which each reader should place this series.

The CISO role is not just another senior management role. It can be an extremely complex and transversal position, where you may be expected to articulate security concepts from the board down across all layers of the enterprise, juggling between technical and business terms while always remaining credible.

You will have to deal with data breaches one day and compliance problems the next, while battling cognitive or emotional biases at the managerial level above you and beside you. You may feel exposed or vulnerable.

Your reporting line, the personality of your boss, and the skills and structure of the team you inherit—if any—will only be pieces of a much bigger jigsaw. In large firms, you will be immersed in a complex political game across the GRC galaxy, in a context where the "three lines of defence" model is rarely applied in its purest form and sometimes poorly understood. And there may be international or multicultural aspects to contend with as well.

All that in the specific security maturity context of each organisation—a context that will vary from firm to firm and will be the sum, for better or worse, of all your predecessors' actions as well as countless management decisions around the security space spanning the best part of the last twenty years.

Those decisions and attitudes will have created a culture around security that the incoming CISO needs to grasp quickly, because everything they do or say during their first few months will be seen internally through that prism.

Unsurprisingly, listening will be key throughout that phase, until all challenges are clearly positioned and the new CISO can start articulating a strategic framework to address those challenges and then a model for its execution.

These are the topics we will be exploring in the next articles in this series.

The CISO role is not just another senior management role. It can be an extremely complex and transversal position, whose role may be extended [illegible] [illegible] [illegible]

[illegible]

[illegible] reporting line [illegible] [illegible] of [illegible] [illegible] [illegible] which [illegible] [illegible] and [illegible] [illegible] internal [illegible] aspects [illegible] with [illegible]

All [illegible] the specific [illegible] [illegible] that [illegible] [illegible] [illegible] management [illegible] [illegible] best [illegible]

These lessons and [illegible] [illegible] the [illegible] [illegible] do [illegible] their [illegible] [illegible]

[illegible] all [illegible] [illegible] model [illegible]

These are the topics we will [illegible] [illegible]

105

The First Week: The Firm and Its People: Positioning the Challenge

(16 November 2017)

Many of the management tips we will be building up in this series could apply to any executive taking up a senior job in a new organisation. But the role of the CISO is particularly sensitive in many aspects and has its own dynamics. It is often poorly understood by management and still seen by some as a necessary evil, or as an imposition by auditors or regulators. Even where threats are understood and the need to protect the firm against cybercrime is on the board's agenda, what the role exactly entails is not always clear for all stakeholders (as may be the case for a CFO or Head of HR position). So the need to effectively engage all parties from the start is key for the new CISO.

The Month Before

Your first week in the new job starts a long time before you arrive. You'll need to understand the true nature of the new business you're getting into—its culture, its geographical footprint, and all the aspects that will help you "hit the ground running."

It should involve true and solid homework, but more importantly, you must try to network with ex-colleagues and contacts who work or have worked there and get as much insider information as you can.

Expect the first few months to be hard work. Not all firms are well managed, and you cannot expect security to be well managed in a firm that isn't. Likewise, you cannot expect good security governance where corporate governance is poor. You might have been hired to "sort security out." Do not expect this to be easy.

Six Days (the First Week): The Firm and Its People: Positioning the Challenge

Bosses

You need to have a clear understanding of your reporting line and meet with your direct boss face-to-face (not remotely) straight away. Personal interactions are key in senior roles, and you'll have to develop a direct and strong relationship and personal bond with your line management. Those things are rarely built up over conference calls.

In large firms, where you may have to contend with a matrix organisation and a functional manager, you need to meet with them too and understand how the matrix model really works. You'll need to gauge the relative strength of each matrixial direction and whether they complement or antagonise each other. If your functional boss is not based where you are, you should at least speak to them during your first week and then immediately schedule a trip to visit them.

You must hear from your management directly, in their own words, what the true dominant challenge of your role is. Build a security practice? Rebuild it? Run it? Optimise it? Transfer it to another part of the organisation? What happened to the person previously occupying your role? What amount of legacy do you have to deal with, and what is the perception your management has of it?

Those first meetings must be clear, open, and unencumbered on all sides. Crucially, they must happen straight away.

You should schedule periodic meetings with your management at the same time. A monthly frequency is probably best to start with. It will give you an immediate target to work against (i.e., your next meeting with them). These meetings do not need a fixed agenda to start with as it is obvious that you will be in a discovery and planning phase for a while.

Of course, you would have been told all sorts of things throughout your hiring process, and you would have gathered your own "intelligence" about your new organisation as part of your own preparation phase, but now you will start to see it from the inside. You will need to assess the politics and the rules of internal power and understand your bosses' reporting line, the overall structure of the team you a part of, and the key players around you, as well as the current structure of your own team (if you have one).

Staff

If you have a team structured under you, you should, of course, meet with all your team members in due course (size-permitting), starting immediately with your own direct reports. You should meet face-to-face with all those who are based where you are and speak to all the others. More than mere introductory opportunities, those meetings are the ideal vehicle to gauge personalities and hear grievances. It obviously goes both ways, and your staff will forge their "first impression" of you through those meetings. Don't talk too much. Simply ask them what they expect from you and listen to them.

There will be a fine line not to cross, as you must not give them the sense that you are committing to fix all their problems (which may or may not be well-founded, and you're unlikely to have all the facts to be the judge of that). Expect politics may be played, and some may try to test you. Worry not—you will get a lot more of that in the weeks to come.

Money

During this first week, you also need to identify the budget you have (if any) and how it is managed. You should meet with your departmental finance team and understand straight away where you stand with regard to the current and next budget cycles. How much was your department allocated in the last budget? How much has been consumed? What are the rules to authorise spending? What is your signing limit (if any)? When does the next budgetary cycle start, and when are the next budgetary submissions due?

Without autonomous resources, you'll be dependent on others. This is a key aspect to address upfront.

That's quite a lot to cram into a few days, but should you achieve it, you'll be off to a good start.

The Key Things to Worry about in the First Week (Which Should Raise a Red Flag Because They Concern the Real Profile of Your New Role and Management Priorities)

- Your direct boss hasn't got time to meet with you.
- You are not allowed to schedule travel to meet your functional boss on grounds of costs.
- You haven't got a proper budget or cannot identify the right finance team to talk to.

The Things Not to Worry about in the First Week (Which Are Just Management Opportunities for You to Address)

- Your direct boss cannot clearly articulate his priorities with regard to your role.
- Your functional boss is okay to meet you but didn't know you had been hired.
- Your own direct reports do not open up, and you do not learn much from meeting them.

106

The Six-Week Horizon: The Firm and Its Management—Defining and Validating a Strategic Framework

(30 November 2017)

This is really the time-horizon over which the new CISO must start assessing their new position. Once again, many of the management tips we will be building up in this series could apply to any executive taking up a senior job in a new organisation. But the CISO role is often a complex transversal role; it is easy to get disheartened—particularly in large organisations—and indeed, it becomes relevant to start paying attention if red flags start accumulating two months into the job.

At this stage, you should have started to get a feel for the organisation you have entered, and you would have established first contacts with key team members and your direct management.

You need to continue to meet with your team members, preferably face-to-face whenever possible. You should meet each team member—if the size and geographical dispersion of your team allow—even if it's just for a very short introduction. Do not hint at any possible organisational changes, even if you start to sense that some will have to eventually take place.

If you identify personal or HR issues, consult with your direct line management and take guidance before jumping into action. Many of those issues are often rooted in a past that might have been more complex than what was disclosed to you by the employee. If necessary, you should meet with the HR department, but only when in possession of all the relevant facts.

Expect that your team members (and others as you continue to meet people) will start bringing "problems" to you and will "test" you. That's a good and natural reaction, and you must play along. It is key for them to get to know you and gauge your management style. At the same time, you have only been on the job for a few weeks and cannot make miracles (they must understand that too).

Expect as well that many people will tell you what needs fixing, how to do it, and why it hasn't been done in the past. That is also unavoidable and a good sign. It will invariably bring a mix of real value and political noise, but you must listen to it.

Overall, this is an opportunity for you to get to know the people around you, but you must not allow the short-term firefighting dynamics to take over. You need to continue discovering the true extent of your environment, and meeting with key stakeholders around you outside your team should be the real backbone of those first six weeks.

Primarily, you should identify who your key stakeholders are across the firm and who the key external third parties and suppliers in your environment are from the meetings with your staff.

Apply the same approach you used for the meetings you held during your first week. Ask people what they expect from you, how you can help them, and more importantly, listen to them.

Do not hesitate to travel during that phase, particularly if your organisation has a large multinational footprint. Travelling will introduce a different rhythm of work and may help you gather your thoughts.

In all cases, start organising the notes and observations you would have accumulated throughout your first few weeks and building your own assessment of the situation you have inherited. The focus of that first assessment will depend to a large extent on the key challenge of your role, as defined by your management and positioned during your first week:

Fig. 13. Focus of the New CISO First Assessment

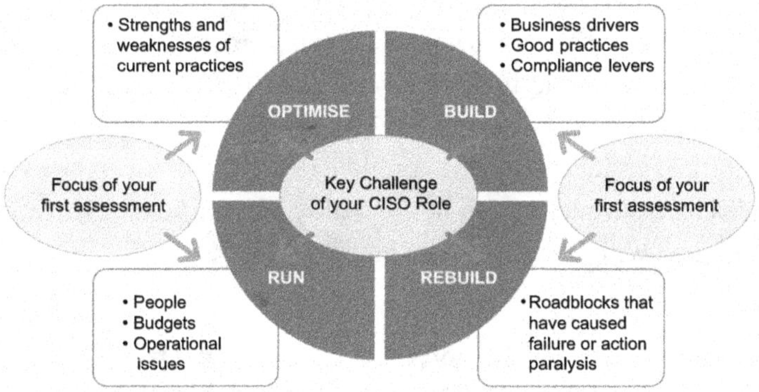

Your strategic framework should express in simple terms what you want to do to address the challenge given to you. It should reflect the key findings of your assessment and set directions, time frames, and high-level cost estimates for what you are proposing to achieve in response to your findings.

Make all necessary caveats around unknown aspects, and if necessary, offer multiple ameliorative options or action paths.

Trust your instincts, look over the right time frames in terms of execution, and do not focus only on alleged “quick wins.” There are things that can be done in six months and some that may take a year or two to be completed, depending on the complexity of your environment.

Most importantly, do not hint at organisational changes at this stage, even if your meetings so far have made it clear to you that some will have to take place. That should come next as a matter of execution of the strategic framework once agreed.

Share your strategic framework with your direct reports once advanced enough. Collect their feedback, and make the necessary amendments, then take it to your boss for validation.

That validation meeting with your boss is really the objective you should have been working towards across the whole period. You should not fear it, and if you have followed the approach highlighted here, you should have all the facts and the confidence to sail through it. Your case should be as strong as it can be as long as it is clear, simple, rooted in the reality of your field observations, and aligned with the challenges given to you.

The Key Things to Worry about in the First Six Weeks (Which Should Raise a Red Flag Because They Concern the Real Profile of Your New Role and Management Priorities)

- You are struggling to meet stakeholders; they say they haven’t got time to meet you.
- Stakeholders openly reject any form of value proposition from you that steps beyond tactical firefighting.

- You still haven't got any form of clarity around budgets, and nobody wants to talk to you about it. You have missed key budgetary deadlines, and you will have to wait until the next round.

The Things Not to Worry about in the First Six Weeks (Which Are Just Management Opportunities for You to Address)

- Stakeholders don't seem to understand what you say.
- Your team members don't seem to understand what you say.
- You come across serious operational issues or acute immaturity problems that go way beyond what you were told or what you were expecting.

107

The Six-Month Horizon: The Firm and Its Culture—Defining and Validating an Execution Framework

(18 January 2018)

This is the point when you really get stuck in. By now, you would have been in the new CISO job for about two months, and it should start to feel less and less like a new job. Of course, this is not really about **100** days, and you should also start to realise it.

Over the past six weeks, you would have met with your management and your team. You would have met with key stakeholders around you and developed a sense of the challenges ahead, including the cultural and geographical diversity of your new organisation. You would have built a sense of what needs to be done, where you are in terms of budgetary cycle and the resources you have or could claim to deliver. You would have consolidated all that into a strategic framework that you would have presented back to your management, taking into account their objectives for your role, and the expectations of all stakeholders. It would have been hard work, and it probably feels like you have already been there for a long time. You are ready to go.

At this point, we have to assume that your management has broadly accepted your assessment of the situation and the approach you proposed to move forward. If that's not the case, you need to examine the points of divergence and decide the best course of action. If those are too salient, you should leave. Period. Everybody can make a mistake, and this is probably best for all parties if those issues are highlighted early on. If you believe there is still room for manoeuvre and the adjustments are positive, you should play on. This is for you to judge and no one else.

If you stay on, the first thing you need to put in place at this stage is the governance model that will carry you through the execution of your strategic framework.

It needs to fit within the organisation around you, and you must start by understanding the structure of existing management committees, their membership, and terms of reference. You will need a senior security management committee to supervise your strategic delivery and arbitrate on conflicts, but you must avoid excessive and useless committee duplication. It needs to be chaired by the most senior stakeholder you can convince, ideally a board member and your boss's boss. This is key to showcasing the importance and value of security for the firm. You should draw on the contacts with stakeholders built up during your first weeks to identify the people who are the most likely to help you move forward, and you must not compromise on the seniority of the membership. Schedule the first committee meeting as soon as possible. This is your true starting point. An overview of your strategic framework and high-level time frames should offer a natural agenda. Their formal endorsement of your objectives and their ongoing oversight will be the backbone against which all your actions will rest.

In parallel, you need to build the target operating model that will support your strategic delivery. This is entirely dependent on your strategic objectives in terms of content and structure, but it needs to be clear and simple. This is, to some extent, related to your reporting line and very likely to be influenced by your relationship—personal and functional—with the CIO.

You will need to validate the target operating model with your management, senior team members, and key stakeholders. Depending on your corporate employment culture and the extent of the changes you are proposing, you may need to consult with the HR department. In turn, you may need to involve employee representatives or worker councils. It will take time, which is why you need to get this started as soon as possible and keep it as clear and simple as possible. This is also why you need the backing of the most senior executives you can gather around your project.

It needs to be a medium- to long-term move rooted in your strategic assessment of the situation you found and aligned with your transformation objectives over the same time horizons.

Once all is agreed upon, align the structure of your own team and update job descriptions, performance metrics, and where necessary salaries and compensation levels at the first opportunity. You may need to hire (and maybe fire), which will also take time and effort—another reason to get to this point as quickly as you can.

It should now be clear that this period of several months following the conclusion of your assessment phase should be about installing the execution framework that will carry your strategic delivery plan.

During that phase, you must stay focused on your medium- to long-term management objectives and resist being drawn or pushed into tactical delivery. There may be urgent issues requiring your time and attention or incidents to deal with, but they are just that—tactical diversions. They are not what you are here for. You are here to deliver the strategic framework agreed upon with your management and the senior security committee.

At the same time, set expectations at the right level. True and lasting change takes "the time it takes," and it is irremediably killed by short-termist flip-flopping. If you need to deviate tactically from your long-term goals, make it clear this is only tactical and temporary and in due course will get back on track. Make it clear to all stakeholders that you will stay in the job for the time it takes. That's the true "secret sauce" to real and lasting transformation.

And now, get things underway. Clarity should be there over what needs to be done, by whom, and over what time frames. Keep things simple, break them down into small chunks as much as you can, and get them done one after another. That's the only way to "eat an elephant," as the old joke goes.

The Key Things to Worry about in the First Six Months (Which Should Raise a Red Flag Because They Concern the Real Profile of Your New Role and Management Priorities)

- You cannot attract or retain the right senior stakeholders at the security management committee, particularly as the chairperson.

- Organisational rigidity and HR constraints prevent you from making the necessary adjustments to your team.

- Tactical firefighting is still the only thing stakeholders around you associate with security (instead of the structured and proactive protection of the business from real threats).

The Things Not to Worry about in the First Six Months (Which Are Just Management Opportunities for You to Address)

- Progress is slow.
- You lose more team members than expected (or some you didn't want to lose).
- Fundamental business changes (mergers, acquisitions) seem to disrupt everything around you (these are often the best times to drive real transformation).

108

The Transformational CISO: Making an Impact and Driving Change, and What Happens Beyond the Six-Month Horizon

(1 February 2018)

Through this series, we have examined how an incoming CISO can create the conditions to truly make a difference in their new job.

Of course, as we stated in the introductory article, all companies are different from one another, and so are most individuals. Each will be at its particular stage in terms of security or managerial maturity.

But beyond the journalistic "**100** days" cliché, there is real and strong management common sense in having the objective of making a real impact over a six-month horizon (which is not so far from **120** business days after all!).

The CISO role, irrespective of its actual exact content and reporting line, will always be peculiar. It is not a true C-suite role, and security topics can have the tendency to scare senior executives who associate them with problems and costs.

So creating a strong bond of trust with all stakeholders will be key to the success of the new CISO. This will come through patient listening; development of a clear vision; achievable transformation objectives over realistic time frames; and a sense of leadership that puts clarity, simplicity, and consistency at the core of your daily work.

We have said it repeatedly in earlier articles. This is a complex role that requires extensive management experience, personal gravitas, political acumen, and a solid grasp of the internal workings of an organisation (particularly in large firms). It requires the real field experience of a battle-hardened professional. This is not a job for an ex-auditor or a lifelong consultant.

Staying the course will also be paramount. In essence, what gets mapped out and put underway at the end of the first six months is the first cycle of work.

It will now have to be delivered, and it is likely to be a multiyear effort. Management acumen, staff focus, and budgetary resources will have to be sustained. Tactical disruptions will have to be handled. The whole show will have to stay on the road, and success will have to be sold.

To achieve real and lasting change, the CISO must not leave at the end of this first cycle but stay through the transition period that will follow, map out, and drive—or at least supervise—the following cycle. True and lasting transformation will come out of that second cycle of change, as the impact of the first one gets accepted and stakeholders start getting used to working differently with a security practice that is coherent and brings value.

Once the initial vision has been established and stabilised, it will have to be optimised. Each of these cycles—creation, stabilisation, optimisation—could last two to three years in any complex organisation. So the real tenure of the transformational CISO has to be considered on a six- to nine-year horizon, and certainly nothing much shorter if the change objectives are to be lasting and fundamental.

It is a very significant commitment for the CISO, who will have to be rewarded and incentivised to stay the course. It will also be very significant for its management. Many organisations are simply incapable of thinking over such a long-term horizon, but those that can will reap the rewards and build for themselves a true security culture that can only be a competitive advantage in today's world.

So six days, six weeks, six months, six years—beyond one hundred days, here is probably the real timeline to consider for the transformational CISO.

109

First 100 Days of the New CISO: How to Avoid the "Curse of Firefighting"

(2 August 2018)[59]

Constant Firefighting Downgrades the Role, and the CISO Must Fight to Avoid Its Gravitational Pull

With regard to many other C-level roles, the chief information security officer (CISO) position is a fairly recent creation for many organisations. Although it started to emerge over fifteen years ago, it has been spurred further recently by growing concerns over cybersecurity and highly publicised data breaches. Figuring out its right place within organisations is still quite a hot debate between management and security experts.

How an incoming executive needs to approach such a complex role is also a hot debate. Many experts—including us—have written about this and have framed the topic using the "first one hundred days" journalistic cliché. In our own series, we took issue with the fact that most consultants' analyses and suggestions fail to consider the incoming CISO within the broader context and organisational complexity of the firm.

In large organisations, no function exists in a vacuum, and getting anything done requires aligning your strategy with other stakeholders' priorities, business cycles, and budget cycles. It will always take time, as well as political and managerial acumen—but nothing, in our opinion, that could not be set in motion to an extent with the first six months in office.

In practice, the real challenge always lies in balancing strategic, longer-term views with the tactical aspects of the day-to-day function. It is unavoidable that an amount of time during the CISO's first months in the job will be spent dealing with tactical firefighting and that it will impact their ability to elevate to the level required to start weighing in on key strategic issues.

As one of our contributors pointed out (a CISO at a large services organisation), "The hundred days often end around day three."

There is no way around this. If you want to stay in place in this kind of role for more than one hundred days, you must deal with the day-to-day emergencies. You must meet expectations before you can transcend them.

This is especially true when the CISO reports directly to the CIO, which often results in concentrating the role on its most technical dimensions and is accentuated further by the short-termist culture of many IT executives.

It is a context where it is easy for the CISO to be tempted to give up and think that tactical issues will always win and prevent the role from ever elevating beyond mere firefighting. Even worse for organisations, this situation is often self-perpetuating. A tactical mindset breeds tactical attitudes, and short-termism is hard to escape once you start indulging in it.

Taking this somewhat fatalistic view to its logical conclusion, it becomes the type of situation where the positioning of the CISO within the organisation is bound to evolve and move under a CSO type of position whose responsibility would be to elevate the transversal topic of cybersecurity to address the more and more pressing questions from the board and senior stakeholders on these matters.

This would leave the CISO with the downscaled but unambiguous task of dealing with the day-to-day firefighting aspects of the function while it becomes the role of the CSO to push strategic cybersecurity initiatives throughout the organisation.

While in our opinion the emergence of CSO roles is unavoidable in many large organisations due to the increasing pressure on boards around cybersecurity matters—and the emergence of broader transversal topics, such as resilience or privacy—it is achievable for the CISO to elevate their position to a highly strategic and respected level. But it will require strong managerial acumen and personal gravitas to know how to deal with the tactical while aiming for strategic goals. It comes down to the personal profile of the individual involved and their experience. This is certainly not a junior role anymore in any way.

It will be a bumpy ride, especially at first, as day-to-day issues will inevitably arise. They will distract and could “nudge you off course,” as another of our contributors (a CISO in a large airline organisation) put it, but the challenge is to get back on course and carry on.

Meaningful change will happen over time, through hard work, full commitment to a transformative agenda, and maybe bottom-up approaches, but also by always looking for top-down drivers and leveraging on them when they appear. Once achieved, the long-term rewards, both tangible and reputational, of the transformation delivered will be for the CISO to grab.

110

The First 100 Days of the New CISO: From Tactical Firefighter to Change Agent (and Why It Matters to Get Your Hands Dirty)

(13 September 2018)[60]

Dealing with the Tactical Aspects of the Function during Your First Weeks in the Job Doesn't Have to Be Detrimental to the Success of a Longer-Term, Transformative Agenda

Much has been written about the chief information security officer and how to best transition into the role for an incoming executive. A somewhat-recurring theme in many pieces on the topic revolves around the balance to be found between short-term firefighting and the need to build a strategic, elevated vision.

Spending your first weeks in the role dealing with ever-arising tactical issues could, indeed, steer you away from the longer-term, transformational agenda that is often the reason you're in the job in the first place.

Based on my interviews with several CISOs about their first months in the role, I would like to propose a slightly less dramatic attitude towards tactical firefighting. It turns out that dealing with the day-to-day tactical aspects of the function during your first weeks in the job doesn't have to be detrimental to the success of your longer-term, strategic agenda and your elevation to the status of change agent.

In fact, it may be quite the opposite. You should see getting your hands dirty, handling day-to-day emergencies, as a way towards becoming a successful CISO.

First of all, being able to observe the current reaction and appetite of your organisation to tolerate risks and crises will help you tremendously in your assessment work.

Tactical firefighting is arguably the best way to learn about how cybersecurity is actually implemented, pinpoint what doesn't currently work, and help shape your transformation to deliver better outcomes—pretty much like a real-life fire safety drill. This can complement (and possibly prove much more informative than) any stakeholder interviews and meetings you will be conducting.

A healthy amount of tactical firefighting will also help you determine the appropriate levels of acceptable and tolerated risk and come up with a more value-added and focused transformation plan—which is what you're looking for, after all. Taking into account how various stakeholders within the organisation approach the topic of cybersecurity allows the design of a strategy that's both easier to implement and more efficient.

A particular occurrence of firefighting could serve as a springboard for constructive discussions and some amount of useful storytelling to help design a plan that fits perfectly with the organisation's aspirations and needs.

Similarly, this could dramatically help you get your message across to key stakeholders and gather support around your transformation agenda. Indeed, if everything were all rosy and good in the organisation, people would likely not put security on top of their priorities. Instead, people will know you, and you in turn will know people. An ambitious transformation plan will also be an easier sell as your usefulness and your reason for being in the role becomes clear to key decision-makers within the organisation.

At least one of my interviewees attributes her lack of success to the fact that she was not able to gather the stakeholder support needed to get the job done, so that's something you should not overlook.

Balancing between tactical firefighting and a strategic agenda remains as important as ever, especially once you realise how the former may help the latter. You will need to win the hearts and minds of your stakeholders and understand the culture of the organisation to then be able to drive change and make it stick.

Use it to your advantage to build a security transformation vision that drives value, achieves quick wins, and speaks the business language.

111

The First Hundred Days of the New CISO: Expectations versus Reality

(11 October 2018)[61]

The Situation the New CISO Finds on Arrival Is Often Different from What They Were Expecting, but Who's to Blame?

A painfully recurrent complaint among chief information security officers is the disconnect between what they were promised during the recruitment process, and the actual situation they find upon starting the job.

Indeed, it is quite common to hear freshly hired CISOs blame their less-than-smooth transition into the role on "broken promises" (some explicit and some simply assumed), such as inadequate resources or insufficient attention dedicated to cybersecurity by key stakeholders.

This is a real issue, as it often results in CISOs not staying long enough in the job to drive any real or lasting change and leads to the long-term stagnation of the cybersecurity posture of many large firms and the InfoSec industry at large.

There are several possible reasons for this disconnect between what a new CISO is told and what they find on arrival:

It may be that the very stakeholders who supported the recruitment of the new CISO into the role are gone by the time the CISO starts. This is not uncommon within large organisations where people—and the priorities they push for—tend to come and go. Little can be done about this, except trying to gather support from new allies within the firm, but it can be very unsettling for the CISO.

Another issue is that hiring managers may not be sufficiently cyber-security-savvy to frame and express precisely what they are looking for in a CISO. It may result in a misalignment between what the CISO thinks they are in for and what is actually expected of them. This is often used as an easy excuse by recruiters for an inadequate hire and begs the question of whose fault it actually is.

Beyond those reasonably common issues that can affect any senior position, there are more fundamental problems around cybersecurity senior roles:

Plaguing the whole security industry is the issue of semantics. In cybersecurity, the same term is often used to mean drastically different things—sometimes leading to profound misunderstandings between parties.

Challengingly for the CISO, for example, the concepts of risk or threat can mean different things to different people, and quite a lot can end up "lost in translation." For an excessively tech-oriented CISO with little managerial experience, "threats and vulnerabilities" could mean "hackers, ransomware, and missing patches." For their management, it could mean "fraud, insiders, and lack of managerial supervision."

More generally, it could also be that the CISOs are part of the problem in that they do not listen enough to key stakeholders to understand what is actually expected of them, often merely focusing on the technology front because it's their comfort zone or their pet subject.

If what's expected of them is to step up as a transversal change agent, it could become a significant drawback for the CISO and a major source of disappointment for the people who hired them.

This is the typical type of situation where distrust sets in and the promised resources or budgets do not materialise, leading to more frustration for the CISO.

Conversely, there are still some organisations only looking for a CISO with a highly technical profile to deal with the daily tactical firefighting. In such a context, trying to push for an ambitious cybersecurity transformation plan that the organisation is not ready to accept or even understand could be quite complicated.

An agenda of governance and cultural change could be what the organisation needs, but the CISO should not be surprised to be met with reluctance, incomprehension, and politics. They should instead roll up their sleeves and start working relentlessly on convincing, engaging, and finding allies while addressing tactical quick wins. This is the type of situation wherein proving your worth by getting your hands dirty could break deadlocks.

Both the CISO and those who hire and manage them must therefore engage in some healthy self-criticism around "broken promises" and, most importantly, clarify any misunderstanding between them as early as possible.

Leaving after a couple of years, or less, because the CISO doesn't feel empowered or think they've been mis-sold the role does not seem like the right managerial attitude, and the situation has the potential to become self-perpetuating.

Trying to identify and address the underlying misunderstandings and roadblocks would be more beneficial, both to the organisation and the individual.

Only then will the CISO be able to feel—and, in fact, *be*—successful in the role (and those to come).

112

Changing Jobs in a Global Pandemic: The New First Hundred Days of the CISO

(13 May 2021)

Focusing Only on Tactical Firefighting Is a Major Mistake, Even in a Global Pandemic

The last twelve months have changed things considerably for the CISO. Cybersecurity has been centre stage, and even more now after the SolarWinds and Colonial hacks. Still, this could be a blessing or a curse.

The pandemic keeps evolving on a global scale, and while some countries may be reaching the end of the tunnel, others are still in the midst of the most dramatic phases.

Global business is still significantly impacted, and there is no sign of a "new normal" in sight for many industries.

Still, people are changing jobs (and CISOs in particular) as many firms wake up to the need to ramp up cybersecurity measures in the face of the accelerated digitisation of their business or their large-scale move to remote working.

But in the face of the new situation created by the pandemic, the approach we highlighted back in **2018** around the "First **100** Days of the CISO" needs adjusting.

It still makes sense for any incoming executive to approach their first period in a new job in a structured way: meet with business stakeholders and listen to their expectations first in relation to the role, then build a strategic framework addressing those and an execution framework to deliver it.

But two aspects have changed fundamentally:

While stakeholders are more likely to recognise cybersecurity as an important agenda item, they are still likely to be focused on short-term objectives, either in terms of crisis response or in terms of bounce-back strategy. They may not be receptive to long-term views. As a matter of fact, they may not have any form of long-term visibility for the moment, as the global pandemic continues to unfold worldwide.

That's the second main issue. One hundred days is probably an irrelevant time frame here, irrespective of how you frame it. (Back in **2018**, we articulated it into six days, six weeks, and six months, encompassing around one hundred business days.) Nobody can be sure what the world will be like in one hundred days, let alone in six months.

So how should an incoming CISO approach their new role?

Meeting with key stakeholders and team members as soon as realistically possible and listening to their objectives, concerns, and priorities is still key as a starting point.

Back in **2018**, we strongly advocated in favour of travelling and meeting face-to-face—where required—to develop a stronger personal bond. This is not likely to be possible for the short term, so most of those discussions will have to take place remotely.

Let's face it. This is a problem, and the absence of direct personal interaction could distort the perception the new CISO develops of the firm and its culture—for good or for bad. The most important for the CISO at this stage is to remain aware of that. But establishing direct communication channels with the business—as solid as they can be at the moment—is more essential than ever.

Second, it is likely—as we have already highlighted—that a short-termist agenda will emerge from those discussions. The temptation will be extremely high for the CISO to focus only on alleged low-hanging fruits and on firefighting, at least until the worst of the crisis is over. To be honest, this is the way many CISOs have traditionally approached their first one hundred days anyway, so more than a "temptation," it will be a line of least resistance—or even a well-trodden path for some.

As a matter of fact, we highlighted back in **2018** that it was a dangerous path to follow and a "curse," unlikely to lead to the development of truly transformational dynamics around cyber-security. That is still the case, but realistically, it will be a trend difficult to oppose for the new CISO.

In fact, this is the very element that makes the new first one hundred days of the CISO far more complex than ever before.

It is no longer just a matter of balancing tactical and strategic objectives while validating strategy and execution frameworks. It could be about doing this in the absence of clear, strategic visibility from the business, as the path out of the COVID crisis emerges, and in a context where those directions may evolve or change, depending on the turns the crisis may still take.

The new CISO must talk constantly with business stakeholders to understand how this context is moving and build their own cybersecurity strategic options—possibly, scenario-based and ready to be embedded into the post-crisis business strategy as it aggregates. And all this should be in parallel to short-term tactical work to keep the lights on.

Make no mistakes. This is now becoming a matter of survival for the CISO role at any form of senior leadership level.

"Constant firefighting downgrades the role, and the CISO must fight to avoid its gravitational pull," we wrote back in **2018**.

Focusing *only* on low-hanging fruits and alleged quick wins fails to leverage on the opportunities presented by the pandemic to cement cybersecurity as a true dimension of business strategy, and the new CISO could find their role relegated forever to middle management layers, alongside other technical operational matters.

Conclusion

113

Cybersecurity Is Not Working: Time to Try Something Else

(4 January 2024)

The Bottom-Up Approaches Most Have Been Pushing for Twenty Years around Cybersecurity Have Simply Failed

I think it is time to accept that the role of the CISO, in its historical construction, was never born out of a positive and proactive management decision.

It was very rarely created, at first, in response to the true realization by senior management of the need to protect the business from real and active threats.

The original iteration of the role, in the late nineties for the early adopters, belongs to that first decade of InfoSec, which was entirely dominated by risk and compliance considerations. The Security Transformation Research Foundation established this quite clearly through its 2019 semantic analysis of the content of seventeen annual Global Security Reports from EY.[62]

Information security was simply seen by senior execs as a constant balancing act between regulatory compliance, risk appetite, and, above all, costs.

The role of the CISO appeared in that context at best in response to audit or regulatory observations, at worst, at their imposition, and almost as a necessary evil in some cases.

Of course, the role has evolved since then, but an entire generation of security practitioners has been trapped in a bottom-up mindset, always in search of ways to justify its legitimacy towards the business.

This is amply demonstrated by the endless debate around the CISO's reporting line, and in particular the obsession of some with a board-level reporting, or the evolution of the role in some firms towards IT risk or information risk constructions, attached to a broader enterprise or operational risk function.

Generally, those moves, all well-intentioned and aimed at broadening the acceptance of necessary security measures across the firm, have rarely worked to a full extent.

Over two decades, those bottom-up approaches have collided with endemic corporate short-termism and dysfunctional corporate governance practices and have failed to deliver essential levels of good practice and to protect against constantly evolving threats, as demonstrated by the endless string of cyber-attacks we are witnessing today.

All this has left many CISOs frustrated and is fuelling their short tenure—short tenure which, by itself, has become the root cause of the long-term stagnation of cybersecurity maturity in many firms.

But now, in addition, the agenda is shifting at board level. Cyber-attacks are increasingly seen as a matter of "when," not "if," weakening all lines of discussions that have tried over the years – bottom-up – to talk about cybersecurity in terms of risk and bringing it closer to corporate risk practices in a quest for legitimacy.

Risk is about things that may or may not happen; it can be accepted, transferred, mitigated.

The "when-not-if" paradigm around cyber-attacks pushes the debate into a different dimension.

And many CISOs are not really prepared when the dialogue with top execs shifts overnight from "why do we need to do this?" to "how much do we need to spend?"

This is no longer about "convincing" them about an alleged "return-on-security-investment," but about getting things done, and getting them done now.

But many CISOs, changing jobs every two years or so, have not learnt to get things done in large firms; they have not developed the political acumen and the management experience they would need.

Many have simply remained technologists and firefighters, trapped in an increasingly obsolete mindset, pushing bottom-up a tools-based, risk-based, tech-driven narrative, disconnected from what the board wants to hear which has now shifted towards resilience and execution.

This is why we may have to come to the point where we have to accept that the construction around the role of the CISO, as it was initiated in the late '90s, has served its purpose and needs to evolve.

The first step in this evolution, in my opinion, is for the board to own cybersecurity as a business problem, not as a technology problem.

It needs to be owned at board level in business terms, in line with the way other topics are owned at board level. This is about thinking the protection of the business in business terms, not in technology terms.

Cybersecurity is not a purely technological matter; it has never been and cannot be. The successful protection of the business from cyber threats requires to reach across corporate silos, including IT of course, but also business and support functions and geographies.

There may be a need to amalgamate it with other matters such as corporate resilience, business continuity, or data privacy to build up a suitable board-level portfolio, but for me, this is the way forward in reversing the long-term dynamics, away from the failed historical bottom-up constructions, towards a progressive top-down approach.

I refute the idea that board members would not have the necessary skills to drive a meaningful top-down engagement around a subject as specific as cybersecurity.

To me, this is just a remnant and the last line of defence of the tech-focused bottom-up spirit that has been dominating for over two decades.

Board members may not have the skills to drive a top-down engagement in the way bottom-up engagements have been framed for the past twenty years, but that doesn't mean that they would not be able to comprehend the matter, owning it and driving it at their level and in their own terms, possibly with some external assistance.

The hard reality is that the technology-focused bottom-up approaches most have been pushing for twenty years around cybersecurity have not worked.

It is simply time to try something else.

About Jean-Christophe Gaillard

JC Gaillard is the Founder and CEO of Corix Partners, a London-based Boutique Management Consultancy Firm and Thought-Leadership Platform, focused on assisting CIOs and other C-level executives in resolving Cyber Security Strategy, Organisation and Governance challenges.

He is a leading strategic advisor and a globally-recognised cyber security thought-leader with over 25 years of experience developed in several financial institutions in the UK and continental Europe, and a track-record at driving fundamental change in the Security field across global organisations, looking beyond the technical horizon into strategy, governance, culture, and the real dynamics of transformation.

French and British national permanently established in the UK since 1993, he holds an Engineering Degree from Telecom Paris and has been co-president of the Cyber Security group of the Telecom Paris alumni association since May 2016.

He runs the Corix Partners blog and the "Security Transformation Leadership" publication on Medium.

He is a Fellow of the Chartered Institute of Information Security (FCIIS), a member of the Forbes Business Council and contributes regularly to the London Tech Leaders website; he has also posted regularly in the past on the Business Transformation Network, The Digital Transformation People, IoTforAll, Business 2 Community, TechNative and Experfy platforms.

He is an expert contributor on the CIO Water Cooler, and has previously published articles on InfoSecurity Magazine, Computing, the C-Suite.co.uk, Info Sec Buzz, Disruption Hub, and the IoD Director websites.

He was involved with techUK as part of their Cyber People Series, which explores how CISOs should engage at C-Suite and Board level, with two reports on the theme released in December 2020 and December 2021.

He has also collaborated with leading analysts firm Kuppinger Cole in Germany, with the Association for Data and Cyber Governance in the US and with the Edutec Alliance in Brazil.

He was listed in the top 10 of UK 30 most influential thought leaders on Risk, RegTech and Compliance by Thomson Reuters in April 2017, and in the top 100 global social media influencers for financial services by Refinitiv in July 2019.

He is a 2022 Onalytica Cyber Security Influencer, and was also identified by them as "Social Media Amplifier" on Risk Management in April 2021, and as a "Key Opinion Leader" on Data Management, IoT Connectivity and RPA in December 2020 and January 2021, as well as an influential voice and sub-topic expert on hybrid work and the future of work in January 2022.

He has been ranking consistently in the top 5 of global influencers with Thinkers360 on Cyber Security, and in the top 10 on

Leadership and Management. He was listed as one of their Top Voices for 2023 in October 2023.

He is the author of "***Cyber Security: The Lost Decade – A Security Governance Handbook for the CISO and the CIO***" first published in September 2017 with updated annual editions released every year up to 2021, "***The CyberSecurity Leadership Handbook for the CISO and the CEO***" released on Amazon in February 2023 and "***The Cybersecurity Spiral of Failure***" released on Amazon in January 2024.

He produces the Cybersecurity Transformation Podcast on Spotify, an independent podcast with a different take on what's happening in the cybersecurity industry, which entered its 5th series in 2024.

He founded and animates the Security Transformation Research Foundation, a dedicated think-tank and research body affiliated to Corix Partners, aimed at approaching Security problems differently and producing innovative and challenging research ideas in the Security, Business Protection, Risk and Controls space.

He has held Board Advisory and Non-Executive Director positions with IAM Experts and Strata Security Solutions and has been a member of the NextWorld Capital European Advisors Network.

Connect with JC Gaillard and Partners

Website: https://www.corixpartners.com/contact
Linkedin: https://www.linkedin.com/in/jcgaillard/
Twitter: @Corix_JC

Neil Cordell: https://www.linkedin.com/in/neilcordell/

Natasha McCabe: https://www.linkedin.com/in/natasha-mccabe/

Vincent Viers: https://www.linkedin.com/in/vincent-viers/

Endnotes

1. The date after each article indicates when it was first posted either on the Corix Partners blog (https://corixpartners.com/blog) or on LinkedIn Pulse. Multiple dates indicate that the article was first posted on LinkedIn Pulse then on the Corix Partners blog, or that it was originally published on the Corix Partners blog in multiple parts. Most of the articles in the book were also syndicated at later dates on other blogs such as Medium, The Digital Transformation People, CIO WaterCooler, Business 2 Community, or The Innovation Enterprise.

2. RSA Cybersecurity Poverty Index, June 2015.

3. "How to Achieve Effective Cybersecurity in a Hyperconnected World," February 2015, https://www.computing.co.uk/opinion/2396800/how-to-achieve-effective-cyber-security-in-a-hyperconnected-world

4. "Repelling the Cyberattackers," McKinsey & Co., 2015, https:// www.mckinsey.com/business-functions/mckinsey-digital/our- insights/repelling-the-cyberattackers.

5. "Risk and Responsibility in a Hyper-Connected World," World Economic Forum with McKinsey & Company, January 2014.

6. https://corixpartners.com/cyber-security-in-a-hyperconnected- world-blog/.

7. "Organising InfoSec for Success," Corix Partners blog, April 2015, http://www.corixpartners.com/organising-InfoSec-for-success-blog/. Moving towards the type of model highlighted here could imply splitting legacy CISO roles and developing a different and more structured target operating model around information security.

8 "Cybersecurity: When True Innovation Consists of Doing Now What You Should Have Done Ten Years Ago" Corix Partners, December 2016, https://corixpartners.com/cyber-security-true-innovation-consists-now-done-ten-years-ago/.

9 Peter Berlich, "For Security, Organizational Structure May be Overrated," February 2015, https://www.InfoSecurity-magazine.com/blogs/organizational-structure-overrated/.

10 Ernst and Young, "Life Sciences," Global Information Security Survey, 2014.

11 "Information Security: Three Governance Challenges for the CIO This Year," http://www.thecsuite.co.uk/CIO/index.php/security/210-governance-challenges-for-cio-4435435.

12 Daniel Kahneman, "Thinking, Fast and Slow," 2011.

13 JC Gaillard and Vincent Viers.

14 "The CISO Merry-Go-Round," The Digital Transformation People, 2017, www.thedigitaltransformationpeople.com/channels/people-and-change/the-ciso-merry-go-round/.

15 JC Gaillard and Vincent Viers. Originally published as an abbreviated version on the Kuppinger Cole blog, "The Digital

Transformation and the Role of the CISO," July 2018 (https://www.kuppingercole.com/blog/guest/the-digital-transformation-and-the-role-of-the-ciso).

[16] WEF, October 2019, https://www.weforum.org/reports/the-cybersecurity-guide-for-leaders-in-today-s-digital-world.

[17] "Repelling the Cyber Attackers, McKinsey & Company, July 2015.

[18] "Risk and Responsibility in a Hyperconnected World," January 2014.

[19] "CISO churn – Why it's happening and how to stop it", Raconteur, August 2021 - https://www.raconteur.net/technology/ciso-churn-why-its-happening-and-how-to-stop-it.

[20] "Organizational cyber maturity: A survey of industries", McKinsey, 2021 - https://www.mckinsey.com/capabilities/risk-and-resilience/our-insights/organizational-cyber-maturity-a-survey-of-industries.

[21] "Cybersecurity: A Look Across Two Decades", The Security Transformation Research Foundation, September 2019 - https://securitytransformation.com/wp-content/uploads/2017/07/CyberSecurity-A-Look-Across-2-Decades-FINAL1-19SEP2019.pdf.

[22] "A technology survival guide for resilience", McKinsey, March 2023 - https://www.mckinsey.com/capabilities/risk-and-resilience/our-insights/a-technology-survival-guide-for-resilience?cid=soc-web.

[23] Boyden, "Cybersecurity: Is your Board on board?" 2016.

[24] https://www.clubciso.org/downloads/.

[25] "Why Do Chief Security Officers Leave Jobs So Often?," February 28, 2021, https://www.govtech.com/blogs/lohrmann-on-cybersecurity/why-do-chief-security-officers-leave-jobs-so-often.html.

[26] "Cybersecurity: A Look Across Two Decades", The Security Transformation Research Foundation, September 2019 - https://securitytransformation.com/wp-content/uploads/2017/07/CyberSecurity-A-Look-Across-2-Decades-FINAL1-19SEP2019.pdf.

[27] RSA, Cyber Poverty Index, 2016.

[28] RSA Cybersecurity Poverty Index, 2015.

[29] "Repelling the Cyberattackers," McKinsey & Company, 2015, https://www.mckinsey.com/business-functions/mckinsey-digital/our-insights/repelling-the-cyberattackers.

[30] "A New Posture for Cybersecurity in a Networked World," McKinsey & Company, March 2018, https://www.mckinsey.com/business-functions/risk/our-insights/a-new-posture-for-cybersecurity-in-a-networked-world.

[31] Jason Choi, Harrison Lung, and James Kaplan, "A Framework for Improving Cybersecurity Discussions within Organizations," McKinsey & Company, November 2017, https://www.mckinsey.com/business-functions/digital-mckinsey/our-insights/a-framework-for-improving-cybersecurity-discussions-within-organizations.

[32] "Risk and Responsibility in a Hyperconnected World: Implications for Enterprises," McKinsey and Company, 2014, http://www.mckinsey.com/business-functions/digital-mckinsey/our-insights/risk-and-responsibility-in-a-hyperconnected-world-implications-for-enterprises.

[33] "CISOs under the Spotlight," https://www.globalservices.bt.com/en/insights/whitepapers/cisos-under-the-spotlight and https://www.helpnetsecurity.com/2021/02/04/ciso-responsibilities/.

[34] Dr Keri Pearlson and Nelson Novaes Neto, March 4, 2022.

[35] "IANS Research", June 2023 - https://www.iansresearch.com/resources/press-releases/detail/with-sec-rule-changes-on-the-horizon-new-research-reveals-only-14-of-cisos-have-traits-desired-for-cyber-expert-board-positions.

[36] "7 Pressing Cybersecurity Questions Boards Need to Ask (Keri Pearlson, Nelson Novaes Neto)", Harvard Business Review, March 2022 - https://hbr.org/2022/03/7-pressing-cybersecurity-questions-boards-need-to-ask.

[37] "Risk and Responsibility in a Hyper-Connected World," World Economic Forum with McKinsey & Company, 2014.

[38] "Risk and Responsibility in a Hyper-Connected World," World Economic Forum with McKinsey & Company, 2014.

[39] "How to Achieve Effective Cybersecurity in a Hyperconnected World," February 2015, https://www.computing.co.uk/opinion/2396800/how-to-achieve-effective-cyber-security-in-a-hyperconnected-world

[40] "Big Picture, Countering Cyber Threats to Business," Institute of Directors, spring 2013.

[41] JC Gaillard and Neil Cordell.

[42] JC Gaillard and Neil Cordell.

[43] JC Gaillard and Neil Cordell.

[44] JC Gaillard and Vincent Viers.

[45] JC Gaillard and Vincent Viers.

[46] Jim Boehm, Nick Curcio, Peter Merrath, Lucy Shenton, and Tobias Stähle, "The Risk-Based Approach to Cybersecurity", October 2019, https://www.mckinsey.com/capabilities/risk-and-resilience/our-insights/the-risk-based-approach-to-cybersecurity.

[47] "Je ne porte pas de sweat à capuche, pourtant je travaille dans la cybersécurité."

[48] "Security Operations on the Backfoot: How Poor Tooling Is Taking Its Toll on Security Analysts," October 2021.

[49] IT Security Guru, November 11, 2021. https://www.itsecurityguru.org/2021/11/11/the-top-5-cybersecurity-threats-to-ot-security/

[50] "The UK cybersecurity landscape: Challenges and opportunities", Expel, 2023 - https://expel.com/uk-cybersecurity-landscape/.

[51] "The Most Successful Approaches to Leading Organizational Change (Deborah Rowland, Michael Thorley, and Nicole Brauckmann)", Harvard Business Review, April 2023 - https://hbr.org/2023/04/the-most-successful-approaches-to-leading-organizational-change.

[52] "Increased spending doesn't translate to improved cybersecurity posture", HelpNetSecurity, June 2023 - https://www.helpnetsecurity.com/2023/06/22/average-cybersecurity-budget-increase/.

[53] "Expel Publishes New Research on the Cybersecurity Challenges Facing British Organisations", BusinessWire, April 2023 - https://www.businesswire.com/news/home/20230419005237/en/Expel-Publishes-New-Research-on-the-Cybersecurity-Challenges-Facing-British-Organisations.

[54] "Actions the best CEOs are taking in 2023", McKinsey, 2023 - https://www.mckinsey.com/capabilities/strategy-and-corporate-finance/our-insights/actions-the-best-ceos-are-taking-in-2023.

[55] "Cybersecurity: A Look Across Two Decades", The Security Transformation Research Foundation, 2019 - https://securitytransformation.com/wp-content/uploads/2017/07/CyberSecurity-A-Look-Across-2-Decades-FINAL1-19SEP2019.pdf.

[56] "Navigating the Digital Transformation", Journal of Petroleum Technology, November 2023 - https://jpt.spe.org/navigating-the-digital-transformation.

[57] "Tapping into dormant data can boost industrial SMEs' competitive edge", McKinsey, November 2023 - https://www.mckinsey.com/industries/industrials-and-electronics/our-insights/tapping-into-dormant-data-can-boost-industrial-smes-competitive-edge.

[58] JC Gaillard and Vincent Viers.

[59] JC Gaillard and Vincent Viers.

[60] Natasha McCabe, JC Gaillard, and Vincent Viers.

[61] JC Gaillard and Vincent Viers.

[62] "Cybersecurity: A Look Across Two Decades", The Security Transformation Research Foundation, 2019 - https://securitytransformation.com/wp-content/uploads/2017/07/CyberSecurity-A-Look-Across-2-Decades-FINAL1-19SEP2019.pdf.

www.ingramcontent.com/pod-product-compliance
Lightning Source LLC
Chambersburg PA
CBHW071230050326
40690CB00011B/2060